American Political
Ideologies

American Political Ideologies

Ideologies

An Introduction to the Major Systems of Thought in the 21st Century

Brian R. Farmer

McFarland & Company, Inc., Publishers

Jefferson, North Carolina, and London

Preface

The final decades of the twentieth century represented perhaps a watershed in terms of global ideological conflict, with the collapse of the Soviet Union, the marketization of the economy of the People's Republic of China, and the accompanying diminished importance of the ideological discord between democratic capitalism and Leninist socialism in global politics. Coterminous with the disintegration of the Cold War, there was hope in both academic and political circles that ideology would therefore also diminish as a force driving political conflict. It was hoped that pragmatism, cooperation, and rational analysis would emerge to become the driving forces behind politics in the new millennium.

Unfortunately, much like Mark Twain, who once wired the Associated Press to inform them that reports of his death had been greatly exaggerated, the voice of ideology has announced to the world repeatedly in the post–Cold War era that any suggestions of its demise are premature. From the disaster at Waco, Texas, in 1993, to the Oklahoma City bombing of 1995, to the impeachment of President Clinton, to the terror attacks of September 11, 2001, to the polarization of American politics in the George W. Bush era, to the American invasion of Iraq, to the Russian school tragedy in Beslan in 2004, to the London terrorist bombings of 2005, ideology has repeatedly played a major role in both national and international politics and proven its resiliency and relevance in the contemporary world.

It is the position of this author that ideology has played not only a significant role, but perhaps the *most* significant role, in both domestic and international politics in recent years. Consequently, the continued preeminence of ideology in the post–Cold War era has prompted the compilation of this book.

Perhaps all individuals are both ideologically driven to a degree and empirically driven to a degree, but the masses throughout the world that

1

exert great influence on politics (whether under democratic or authoritarian regimes) tend to be ideological in their thinking to a much larger degree since they typically lack detailed political knowledge. Consequently, people require ideology to fill the void created by the absence of in-depth political knowledge and thus provide rationale and explanation for the complex political world around them. The result is that the normative, ideological approach, rather than the scientific approach, is the standard of the masses in politics, both in the U.S. and on a global scale. Given that critical thinking and rational analysis based on facts are typically not the driving forces behind politics, and ideology is instead the driving force, it should not be surprising that politics has continued to be so polarized, contentious, and deadly in the post–Cold War age.

The specific ideological development that prompted the writing of this text on ideologies is the polarization of American and international politics in the post–Cold War era into uncompromising and ideologically driven camps. In American politics, for instance, religiosity, rather than income, was the better predictor of presidential voting preference in the election of 2004. What this trend suggests is that American politics is apparently now driven less by class and monetary interests than by values and beliefs. This development represents a shift in American politics away from the class-based political party system that had dominated American politics since the Great Depression and toward politics based on value conflicts. The predictable result of the emerging ideologically driven politics in the United States has been sharp political polarization and difficulty in reaching political compromises, developments that hardly appear beneficial. The impasse over the budget and subsequent government shutdown during Newt Gingrich's "Republican revolution" is a case in point.

Similarly, in international politics, the most important center of conflict since the 9/11 terror attacks appears to be ideological in character. It has taken the form of violent culture clash between radical Islam in the tradition-oriented developing nations, and democratic capitalism in the United States and its Western allies. The results of this clash thus far have been uncompromising, deadly, and intense, with little hope of reconciliation in the near future. Thus, it seems appropriate that more attention should be given to understanding the ideological underpinnings driving political conflict in the post–Cold War era.

It should also be noted, however, that the collapse of the Soviet Union does not mean that Marxism is dead or completely irrelevant in the new millennium. Relations remain strained between the United States and communist Cuba under Fidel Castro, and American relations with communist China remain somewhat tense in spite of China's conversion to a market economy. Similarly, communist North Korea was one of the three countries in President George W. Bush's "axis of evil" that Bush viewed as hostile to the U.S. and other capitalist democracies. The mere selection of the word "evil" suggests that ideology once again is playing a major role.

In addition to these conflicts, the Latin American spin-off from Leninism, known as dependency theory, continues to have influence in the developing world, with the result that conflict between free market ideology and the ideology of anti-colonialism remains a source of political conflict between lesser-developed countries and the advanced capitalist democracies of the industrialized West. Consequently, in spite of the end of the Cold War and the shift to conflict between democratic capitalism and Islamism, any survey of major ideologies in the post–Cold War era should necessarily revisit Marxism-Leninism and dependency theory.

It should be mentioned, however, that perhaps no selection of major ideologies would be satisfactory to everyone, and that the selection of the ideologies presented here is not exhaustive, but was chosen somewhat subjectively at the discretion of the author. Others may argue for a greater emphasis on other ideologies besides those that receive extensive coverage here as more important major ideologies of the post–Cold War era. Similarly, the categorization of ideologies is by nature somewhat imprecise, and scholars are not always in complete agreement. The academic literature, for instance, on what exactly is true Marxism or true "Islamism" fills entire libraries with an unending barrage of conflicting arguments.

The primary selection criterion for the ideologies presented in this volume was essentially the relevance of the ideology to the major political conflicts of the contemporary era in the subjective estimation of the author. While one may argue that libertarianism is not a major ideology and therefore should not be included, it was included because it is so difficult to determine where classic liberalism ends and where libertarianism begins; hence, which ideology is the more important force in driving the free-market wing of the American Republican Party is difficult to determine. Similarly, one may argue that conservative extremism is no longer a major political ideology in the contemporary era (if one is referring to Nazism or fascism); however, radical Islamists certainly display numerous elements of conservative extremist ideology in addition to significant elements of traditional conservatism.

Again, clear lines between the ideologies often are not easily drawn. For example, in August 2005, evangelist Pat Robertson, who is generally thought of as a traditional conservative, publicly called for the assassination of Venezuelan president Hugo Chavez during a program on his CBN television network. Having made such a statement, should Robertson therefore be categorized as a conservative extremist? A survey of scholars of ideology might produce a variety of answers. I hope that the selection and categorization of ideologies for this volume will be acceptable to most.

The ideas for this book were not born in a vacuum, but have been borrowed from the cumulative knowledge of literally hundreds of scholars. In academia, there is an ideal that one should demonstrate independent or autonomous ideas separate from those that have gone before. A second ideal is that academicians should be concerned with preserving the cumulative knowledge of those who have labored before and must assign credit where credit is due. The two ideals are somewhat in conflict with one another; it appears impossible to demonstrate independent or autonomous ideas while simultaneously crediting the previous cumulative knowledge. That being the case, it is most likely that no ideas contained in this book are completely original. I only hope that I have been fair to the people whose writings and ideas I have borrowed from so heavily in order to construct my own survey of the relevant major contemporary ideologies.

At this juncture, I want to take a small amount of space to express my appreciation and gratitude to Denise for her love and support through this project, and to all those at Amarillo College who put up with my generally boorish behavior daily. I especially wish to thank my division chair, Jerry Moller, and my esteemed colleagues Dr. Jim Powell and Dr. Alan Kee, who provide intellectual stimulation and sanity in the insane world. I also want to express thanks to Professors Aie-Rie Lee, Lawrence C. Mayer, and Neale Pearson at Texas Tech University for introducing me to the study of ideology some years ago in graduate school, and for directing me to the writings of Seymour Lipset that sparked my original interest in the subject. I should also express my appreciation to the Texas Tech University Library for continuing to provide a world-class research facility, and to Nan Kemp in interlibrary loan at Amarillo College for her indispensable assistance.

Introduction: The Continued Preeminence of Ideology

At mid–twentieth century, noted scholars Henry Aiken (1956), Daniel Bell (1960), and Morton White (1956) were arguing that ideology was no longer as important as it once was. What these scholars and others essentially argued was that rational analysis was taking the place of ideology in politics and that an exhaustion of political ideas in advanced industrial democracies had culminated in acceptance of welfare-state capitalism. There would still be political conflict, to be sure, but the basic ideas that government intervention into the free market was necessary for steady and more even economic growth, and that social action was a proper realm for government at least to some degree, had been accepted by all mainstream political parties. For example, in 1936, Democrat Franklin Roosevelt campaigned on continuation of the New Deal; his opponent, Republican Alfred Landon, essentially campaigned on the same platform, but with the claim that he could carry out the New Deal's programs more efficiently and without deficits (Nash et al., 1987). Whether Landon could have done so is beside the point. The fact is that both parties were essentially accepting the New Deal programs as within the proper scope of government responsibility, and major ideological divisions over the proper role of government had been minimized.

These ideological differences, however, were perhaps never quite as minimized as Aiken, Bell, and White inferred; rather, the public had so greatly accepted the New Deal during the Great Depression that all the conservatives could do was go along. The ideological underpinnings of conservatism would continue unreformed among a core minority through the Depression and World War II years to be released with a vengeance later. Indeed, it is evident that Aiken, Bell, and White were somehow overlooking the McCarthyism and right-wing anti-communist hysteria of the 1950s that immediately preceded their writings. At any rate, it is difficult to look at the Cold War and McCarthyism and conclude that the nation was experiencing an end of ideology in any real sense of the word. Instead, conservatives had acquiesced to the New Deal only due to its popular support, and liberals had jumped onto the anticommunist Cold War bandwagon for similar reasons. The outward appearance of ideological congruence thus arose, when in reality the old conservative/liberal divide was still raging underneath.

The superficially closer ideological congruence of the two major parties at mid–twentieth century appears to have greatly eroded by the early 21st century. The policies of the Republican Party and conservatives in general in the United States since World War II have been driven more by ideologies than by pragmatism and sound analysis, thus destroying the apparent ideological congruence that had developed from the Great Depression until the Vietnam War era. Furthermore, the ideologies that have driven America's more recent conservative revolution, whether it be the Reagan Revolution, Newt Gingrich's Contract with America, or the "compassionate conservatism" of the George W. Bush administration, are ideologies that have been pursued repeatedly throughout American history. Thus, the new conservatism apparently lacks little in real qualitative ideological difference from the conservatism of old. In other words, the ideology that recent conservatives have poured forth is merely old wine in new bottles.

For example, the economic doctrine of laissez-faire, preached so frequently in conservative circles, was the dominant conservative view in the era following the Civil War almost a century and a half ago. Liberals argue that the laissez-faire approach led only to worker exploitation, income inequality, monopoly capitalism, unsafe products, and environmental degradation during the Gilded Age of late 19th century America. Liberals claim that laissez-faire capitalism is the world of company stores and company scrip, of Upton Sinclair, of Charles Dickens—a world of great suffering for the masses. Consequently, conservative efforts to eliminate or at least greatly reduce the role of government in the free marketplace are said to be essentially efforts to return America to the 19th century, when ⅓ of the meat packed in Chicago was unfit to eat, when the standard water supply for American factory workers was an open barrel, and when 50 percent of children died before the age of five (Farmer, 2003). Hence, liberals argue that a return to laissez-faire is not a return to policy by sound analysis as the scholars of the 1950s argued, but instead is a return to a very old and historically discredited ideology.

Similarly, liberals argue that the church-state blend espoused by the Christian Coalition wing of American conservatism has proven itself to be flawed repeatedly throughout human history. To illustrate this view, liberals claim to see parallels between the Taliban in Afghanistan, the Roman Catholic Church's Inquisition in medieval Europe, and the views of the Southern Baptist Convention. Liberals argue that to blend church with state is to return to the time before the American Revolution when colonists in Virginia were whipped for heresy and Puritans in Massachusetts were executed for witchcraft. They see it as a return to the days when scientists were threatened with death if their discoveries conflicted with the teachings of the leaders of religion, and citizens were condemned to death for heresy, or simply for thinking differently. Essentially, a return to a church-state blend is a return to the eighteenth-century system that the authors of the Constitution abandoned. Liberals contend that those who espouse and preach these ideologies are essentially ignoring these lessons of history as well as empirical data and theoretical flaws in the ideologies themselves, thus prompting the United States to drift toward ideologically-driven catastrophe.

In the presidential election of 2004, religiosity, or how often an individual attends church, was a more important predictor of one's voting preference than income, suggesting that ideology, rather than class, is now the most important factor in determining partisanship in American politics. In short, the higher the religiosity, the more conservative one is likely to be, and the lower the religiosity, the more likely it is that one will associate with the Democratic Party (Msnbc.msn.com/id/6409042/). An investigation into the nature of these ideological perspectives, including their problems, contradictions, and conflicts with competing ideologies, is the subject matter of this book, but it will be left to the reader to determine whether one ideology is superior to another.

Ideology as a Political Guide

Few American government textbooks contain a chapter dedicated exclusively to ideology. This omission is somewhat befuddling since Americans are guided politically more by ideology than by facts and knowledge, because in order to be guided by facts and knowledge, one must first actually know something. One need go no further than the "Jaywalking" segments on *The Tonight Show with Jay Leno* to come to the conclusion that many Americans are generally ignorant on political issues and know very little about historical and political facts. Night after night, Leno asks some of the most basic questions such as: Who wrote the Declaration of Independence? or Who wrote the Gettysburg Address?—only to get responses such as Britney Spears or Puff Daddy. While it is true that Leno's comedy is unscientific, empirical studies of public political and historical knowledge tend to support the same conclusion one might reach from watching Leno's antics.

These studies indicate that Americans in general are seriously deficient even in some of the most basic aspects of political and historical knowledge. For example, in a national assessment test in the late 1980s, only a third of American 17-year-olds could correctly locate the Civil War in the period 1850–1900; more than a quarter placed it in the 18th century. Furthermore, 14 percent credited Abraham Lincoln with writing the Bill of Rights, and 10 percent credited him with the Missouri Compromise (which would have been quite an accomplishment for someone who was 11 years old at the time). Finally, 9 percent named Lincoln to be the author of *Uncle Tom's Cabin*. While this knowledge of history is abysmal, performance on questions concerning current affairs yield equally poor results. In a 1996 public opinion poll, only 10 percent of Americans could identify William Rehnquist as the chief justice of the United States. During the 1980s, the majority of Americans could not correctly answer whether the Reagan Administration supported the Sandinistas or the Contras in Nicaragua, and only a third could place Nicaragua in Central America (Schudson, 2000, 16).

These results do not mean, however, that the American public necessarily knows less than their leaders. In 1956, President Eisenhower's nominee for ambassador to Ceylon was unable to identify either the country's prime minister or its capital during his confirmation hearing. In 1981, President Reagan's nominee for deputy secretary of state, William Clark, admitted in his confirmation hearings that he had no idea how America's allies in Western Europe felt about having American nuclear missiles based there (Moore, 2001, 88). For his part, George W. Bush once referred to the Kosovars as "Kosovians" and thought a Slovenian foreign minister was from Slovakia (Miller, 2000, 198). Perhaps most revealing, however, was Bush's statement in *Glamour* magazine during the 2000 presidential campaign where he confused the Taliban in Afghanistan with "some band" (*Glamour*, 2000). Similarly, during the Super Bowl at the White House a month before his invasion of Iraq, Bush asked his invitee Kanan Makiya of the Iraqi National Congress, an exile group that Bush hoped to place in power in Iraq, what were the differences between Shiites, Sunnis, and Kurds (Phillips, 2005, 101).

This is not to say, however, that American schools have gotten worse, or that Americans and their leaders are more ignorant than they have been in the past. In 1945, for example, 43 percent Americans polled could name neither of their U.S. Senators. In 1952, only 67 percent could name the vice president (Schudson, 2000, 16). With this type of ignorance, it is perhaps surprising that democracy in America has worked as well as it has. If there are so many Americans who are evidently lacking even the most basic historical and political knowledge, as the surveys suggest, then they must be making their political decisions based on something other than knowledge. That something is ideology.

Ideology Defined

Ideologies are belief systems through which people view and interpret reality. In the words of Milton Rokeach (1972), "Ideology refers to more or less institutionalized sets of beliefs—the views someone picks up." Ideologies are not reality, but instead produce simplified versions of reality for those who view the world through ideological frameworks. Ideology interprets and explains what is wrong with society in simplistic terms and provides simplistic prescriptions purported to solve all societal ills. In general, people are very good at identifying someone else's ideology and noting the flaws in their precepts, but people may not even recognize that they themselves are normally just as ideological. In the United States at present, there are scores of differing ideologies, some mainstream, and some on the political fringe. The fringe ideologies, such as Nazism, are easily recognizable as ideologies by the public and generally scorned for their blatant deviations from social mores and accepted norms.

Consider, for example, the character Lilith (the wife of Frasier) on the TV situation comedy *Cheers*. Lilith is a satirical portrayal of radical feminist liberation ideology, an ideology that exists as a political fringe ideology in the U.S. The character is humorous to many because the majority of viewers can readily discern the flaws and fallacies of an ideology that is not their own. Similarly, another fringe ideology that the majority of Americans readily recognize as such is the radical black liberation ideology. Pop culture has parodied this ideology in innumerable ways: from Damon Wayans' "Homey the Clown" character on *In Living Color*, to Chris Rock's "NAT X" character on *Saturday Night Live*, the comedians have viciously lampooned an ideology that essentially holds, in the words of Rock, that "the white man did it to me." The routines are humorous to many because the majority of Americans recognize the ideological flaws and they may have recognized approximations of those flaws in the ideologies of a real person with whom they are acquainted.

Not all ideology, however, is so easily laughed off. If we consider racist Nazi ideology, for example, we will find that it simplistically teaches that all of the world's problems are created by subversive Jews and other minorities. The "final solution" of the Nazis in Germany in World War II therefore included the genocide of Jews and others whom the Nazis considered societal problems, with the result that ten million people died in the Nazi death camps. Nazism, of course, is only a fringe ideology in the United States and therefore does not appear to be a dangerous force in American politics at the moment. It should be remembered, however, that Nazism was only a fringe ideology in Germany as late as 1928. The fact that the Nazis came from political nowhere to assume power in Germany five years later, and then overran Europe within a dozen years, is a testimony to the mobilizing power of ideology. If American politics has become more ideological in recent years rather than more practical, then it arguably has also become more dangerous.

There are three dominant ideologies in the United States: classic liberalism, traditional conservatism, and contemporary liberalism. These three ideologies form the core of the two major political parties and are generally reflected in the major parties' platforms and prescriptions. Classic liberals and traditional conservatives tend to be conservative Republicans, while contemporary liberalism is the dominant ideology in the Democratic Party. Conservatism is also home to a pair of important fringe ideologies, libertarianism and conservative extremism, that have become worthy of discussion as well in the post–Oklahoma City bombing era. Islamism is essentially the equivalent of traditional conservatism and conservative extremism in Islamic societies and a major ideology with which America is currently in conflict. Communism and dependency theory are two major far-left ideologies with which the major American ideologies were in conflict for much of the latter half of the twentieth century. These ideologies and their contradictions will be discussed in greater detail in the following chapters.

1

American Political Socialization, Theory, Values, and Beliefs

Political Socialization

Political scientists assume that political attitudes, values, and beliefs are learned. This, however, is only an assumption. It is certainly within the realm of possibility that there is a gene that determines whether individuals are liberal or conservative. If that is the case, then the conservatives are perhaps in trouble, because those liberal scholars in charge of genetic research will surely find and eradicate the gene that turns people into Republicans. Until then, however, we will continue with our perhaps flawed assumption that political attitudes and beliefs are learned, rather than innate.

If we assume that political attitudes are learned, then the process of forming those political attitudes becomes a major focus. This process is termed political socialization, and there is an immense body of scholarly research that deals with this subject. In these studies, scholars have determined, through the analysis of the political attitudes of adolescents, that these attitudes essentially develop during the formative years between ages 11 and 15 (Hyman, 1959; Lane, 1959; Adelson and O'Neil, 1970). Survey research conducted on children at the beginning of the formative years (age 9–10) reveals that children normally do not have a coherent political perspective prior to age eleven. Children may know whether they like a particular president, for example, but they are generally unable to respond with any coherent ideological pattern when they are posed with more veiled and in-depth questions that cause one to think about policy without familiar labels.

Similar survey research on persons at age 16, however, reveals that by that age people normally have developed coherent political attitudes and that the core ideology around which those attitudes revolve may not change substantially throughout the rest of their lives. In other words, whatever political perspective people have adopted by age 16 may be the basic political perspective that they hold for the rest of their lives. This being the case, it becomes very important to understand the elements that work to shape political attitudes during those formative years between the ages of 11 and 15.

Socialization Agents

PARENTS AND FAMILY

Parents and family are widely considered by scholars to be the most important political socialization agents in society. This conclusion is supported through empirical research that has revealed a strong correlation between the political attitudes of parents and those of their children (Hyman, 1959). When both parents are strongly leaning conservative, research suggests that there is approximately a 90 percent chance that their children will have similar political views. The same thing can be said for those who are strongly leaning liberal. In cases where the parents are of opposing political persuasions, there appears to be a weak tendency (56 percent) for the political attitudes of the children to be consistent with the political attitudes of the father rather than the mother. There is some dispute among scholars as to why this is the case, with some scholars arguing that people purposefully socialize their daughters differently from their sons and thus make their daughters less political. Consequently, children are more likely to adopt the politics of their father, who is the more political of the two parents. If this is not the case, and the different political path of daughters and mothers is not a genetic gender difference, then the difference must be explained through other socialization agents.

PEERS

Scholars have identified numerous psycho-social characteristics that are inherent among youth. Endemic to the politically formative stage in the life cycle (ages 11 through 15) is the need to have, and a preference for, a high affiliation with peers to that of family and adults (Csikszentmihalyi and Larson, 1984). As such, peers are most certainly important socialization agents during the formative years; however, the research suggests that peers are less important as a *political* socialization agent than parents and family due to the low place of politics in the hierarchy of priorities among adolescents during the formative years. During adolescence, individuals tend to focus their conversation more on relationships and youth activities such as sports, music, and academic pursuits. Hence, the impact of peers as a political socialization agent during the formative years is somewhat muted.

SCHOOL

School, of course, is also an important socialization agent, since it is at school where people interact for about seven hours per day during the formative years. During these years, however, schools normally must reinforce attitudes learned in the family and community and are not therefore generally radical socialization agents.

The reasons that schools tend to reinforce conservative family and community values can be traced to the traditional public school structure. Typically, local school boards (the official policy-making bodies for the schools) are elected. Persons who are not residents of the school district are normally ineligible to run for the school board, meaning that the members of the school policy-making body are drawn from within the community itself. Since these board members are drawn from within the community, it follows that their values are likely to reflect those of the community from which they were drawn—especially when they are democratically elected. In general, democratically elected officials at any level must reflect the values of the electorate or their electability becomes questionable. Democracy and the government it creates will generally reflect the character of its people, and school boards are certainly no exception to this rule. It is difficult to conceive of a democratic system where voters routinely elect school board members who espouse radically different value systems from those of the voters. It also follows that if these school board members stray too far from family and community norms, they are simply unlikely to be elected. Secondly, if radical individuals do somehow win an election and then attempt to implement ideas that are outside of societal norms, they will most likely find themselves at odds with the community and voted out during the next election. Teachers within the school district operate under similar constraints since their livelihood is controlled by elected school board officials and indirectly by the electorate itself. As a consequence, most teachers at the primary and secondary level dare not stray too far from the norms of the surrounding community.

For example, in New York City (a city that Bill Clinton carried twice in presidential elections, in a state where Hillary Clinton is a senator), a teacher was fired in the 1990s for his association with the North American Man/Boy Love Association, or NAMBLA, a group that advocates sex between adult men and young boys. The slogan for the group is "sex after eight is too late" (Etzioni, 1994, 11). It turns out, evidently, that the liberals in New York City did not want a potential pedophile teaching in their schools any more than do the conservatives in rural America. Evidently, opposition to pedophile teachers is both nonpartisan and nonregional in character.

So who are those liberal teachers in public schools indoctrinating children with radical ideas, anyway? In most communities, the majority of teachers will be from within that community or from another community within a hundred-mile radius. For example, in Amarillo, Texas, the school with the largest representation of graduates in the Amarillo Independent School District is West Texas A&M, the closest four-year school to Amarillo, located in the town of Canyon, about 15 minutes from Amarillo. Similarly, the city with the largest representation of students at West Texas A&M University is Amarillo. Finally, the majority of teachers in the Amarillo Independent School district live in Amarillo. In other words, a typical teacher in the Amarillo Independent School District is likely to be someone who went to school in Amarillo or somewhere nearby, attended a university near Amarillo, and now teaches and resides in Amarillo. Such a person is unlikely to have values that are far from the norms of the community since he or she is a product of that community. Consequently, his or her norms and values typically reflect those of the community of which he or she is a part. This is not to say that there are not some teachers that do not reflect the norms of their community; however, such individuals will face pressure to keep radical deviations from the norms of the community to themselves under threat of reprisals.

For example, in very socially conservative towns in the "Bible belt," regardless of one's personal position on gay rights and the 14th Amendment, it might be wise for any public school teacher to refrain from enthusiastically pushing a gay rights agenda in the public school system unless that teacher enjoys parental confrontation. If, for example, a public middle-school government teacher were to argue that under the 14th Amendment, "equal protection under the law" and equal "privileges and immunities" cannot be denied to all persons "born or naturalized in the U.S.," that teacher would certainly be correct. If that same teacher followed that statement by pointing out that the 14th Amendment protections apply to gays because they, like heterosexuals, may be "born or naturalized in the U.S.," that teacher is still correct, but also could possibly expect mild parental confrontations. If, however, that teacher made the decision to take the argument a step further and say that the 14th Amendment requires that the government recognize gay marriage—marriage being a "privilege" extended to heterosexuals, but not homosexuals, and thus arguably a 14th Amendment equal privileges violation—one might expect that teacher to be on the receiving end of some more serious parental confrontations. Discussions of the matter between the parents and school administrators, as well as between school administrators and the teacher, are perhaps likely to follow. Most teachers prefer to avoid this type of unpleasant confrontation and thus keep their discussions closer to societal norms.

If, however, this hypothetical teacher took the argument even one step further and argued that the 14th Amendment requires that gays must be able to adopt children (after all, heterosexual couples enjoy this privilege), one might envision that not only would all parental hell break loose, but there may be lawsuits, vandalism, a terminated contract, a media event, and a prayer vigil of elders from the local church outside that teacher's door. Even the most radical teachers normally want to avoid this type of confrontation with community, not to mention the unemployment that may follow. What this illustrates is that public school teachers are very much constrained by the values of the community in which they teach, and teachers may vary seriously from the norm only at their own peril. As a consequence, radical political ideas are more likely to be learned somewhere besides the public schools.

MEDIA

Another group of major socialization agents that have been accused from time to time of imparting radical ideas on America's youth are the mass media. Survey data reveals that the vast majority of conservatives believe that the mass media in the U.S. are pushing a radical left agenda. Furthermore, most Americans believe that the media are very influential in shaping political attitudes (Janda et al., 1992).

This view has been supported somewhat by empirical research. For instance, much attention was given to a study of the impact of television on kindergarten children in the 1980s (Singer and Singer, 1981), where two groups of children watched two different television programs. In this study, children who watched adventure shows such as *Batman* began to exhibit more aggressive behavior in an apparent imitation of what they had viewed on television. Conversely, the children who watched *Mr. Rogers' Neighborhood* did not exhibit similar aggression, suggesting that the media have the power to influence social behavior.

If, however, the media are incredibly effective as an ideological socialization agent, and if the media are overwhelmingly liberal as some have charged, then why are all Americans not liberals? One can only conclude that the media are either ineffective as an ideological socialization agent or the media are not in fact pushing a liberal agenda. Instead, scholars tend to argue that the media are more important in setting the political agenda, but less important in the formation of ideology or partisanship (Janda et al., 1992). In other words, the media are effective at determining what Americans will be debating, but they are not so effective at shaping individual opinions one way or the other surrounding that debate. John Steinbruner (1974) argues that the human mind is programmed with decision mechanisms that screen out information that the established set of responses in the brain are not programmed to accept. In other words, people tend to psychologically tune out messages that conflict with preconceived notions or things that they believe to be true. For example, in the 1990s, a story hit the media concerning logging in the Pacific Northwest that was threatening the habitat of the spotted owl. Liberals, typically more in favor of environmental protection, protested the logging that threatened the habitat of this endangered species, while conservatives protested the protection of the owl at the expense of business and human needs. In either case, the media presentation of the story placed the spotted owl on the political agenda, but individual reactions to the story were pre-programmed based on ideological predispositions, and arguments conflicting with individuals' pre-programmed responses were generally tossed aside.

Proliferation also hinders the media as a political socialization agent since those in the formative years may simply delete political information from their personal media spectrum. Young persons in their formative years (11 to 15) are in many cases less likely to be watching CNN or C-SPAN than MTV and VH-1. This is a phenomenon that has developed within the last 30 years, however. Many of those who came of age prior to the 1970s had only three television channel options, and during the State of the Union address, those options were reduced to one as all three networks carried the president's speech. In contrast, the adolescents of the 21st century may have scores of TV channels and can stay tuned to the mass media 24 hours a day and still tune out political information in its entirety if they so desire. There is perhaps little that one can gain in the way of political information from an evening of Ozzy Ozzbourne and Anna Nicole Smith.

WORKPLACE

The workplace often has been cited as a political socialization agent, and its impact on the formation of political labor movements is of obvious importance since individuals may spend more waking hours in the workplace than with friends or family. The impact of the workplace, however, is hindered because the workplace experience is generally post-formative in character. In other words, if the formative years for political attitudes are ages 11 through 15, the impact of the workplace is seriously lessened since most individuals do not enter the work force until about age 16. As a consequence, by the time that an adolescent becomes employed for the first time, that person's political attitudes may already be largely set.

This is not to say, however, that the workplace cannot be politically influential. In general, the political socialization power of the workplace increases when there is little diversity of function in the workplace and workers work in proximity with one another. Labor unions have exploited such situations for purposes of political socialization for over a century, but the socialization power of the workplace even under these conditions is difficult to separate from other socioeconomic factors that influence political attitudes.

RELIGION

Religion has become increasingly political in orientation since the late 1970s, especially Protestant fundamentalist churches, under the influence of individuals like Jerry Falwell and Pat Robertson, who tend to mix religious beliefs with political concerns. Additionally, there appears to be a strong correlation between Protestant fundamentalist beliefs and political conservatism (Kellstedt and Green, 1993). For a number of reasons, however, empirical research has been somewhat less conclusive than one might think.

First, effectiveness of religion as a political socialization agent is difficult to determine because its impact is so difficult to separate from family influence during the formative years. In other words, most adolescents in the formative years between ages 11 and 15 generally attend church (if they attend at all) with their parents. As a consequence, it is difficult to determine if the impact on their political attitudes that one may attribute to church is primarily attributable to church or to parents. Obviously, one might expect the church to have some impact among those who attend regularly, but how much? Where can the line be drawn between church influence and parental influence? To compound the problem further, conservative parents typically take their children to a conservative church that teaches the same conservative politics that the parents teach at home. In such situations, it is difficult to determine where church influence begins and parental influence ends (Kellstedt and Smidt, 1993).

Another factor that makes the impact of religion difficult to determine is the uncertainty of the causal order. While empirical research shows that fundamentalist Protestants are much more likely to be conservative than Catholics and non-fundamentalist Protestants, whether or not it is their religions that have shaped their political views is unclear. In other words, do people become Republicans because of what is taught in fundamentalist churches, or do people choose conservative-leaning churches because they are already conservative themselves (Kellstedt and Green, 1993)?

Another factor that hinders the impact of religion as a socialization agent is the degree to which people pay attention and understand the political messages. In the words of Welch et al. (1993), "In view of the many mechanisms that intervene between communicator and target audience—inattention, selective perception, distortion—it is unwise to assume that church members perceive clearly the messages intended by the clergy." In other words, it is difficult for the preacher to politically influence the congregation if no one is listening. It is perhaps worth mentioning again, that political attitudes are generally formed between the ages of 11 and 15. Is this the age where people pay attention to the preacher in church?

American Values and Beliefs

The United States is a very pluralistic society with many diverse groups and beliefs. As such, there is perhaps no political issue where Americans display unanimity, and there is no coherent set of beliefs that one could indisputably call American political theory. However, there are a number of areas where Americans exhibit general trends in opinion surveys, and some of those trends are rooted in a long history of relatively consistent American political behavior. Among those consistencies during the period following World War II has been a penchant for conservatism in comparison to the world's other developed democracies. In general, this tendency is often referred to in Europe as "American exceptionalism."

ROOTS OF AMERICAN EXCEPTIONALISM

The roots of this American exceptionalism can be found not only in the conservatism of the seventeenth-century Puritans of Massachusetts Bay, but in the traditional conservative principles of Edmund Burke, the eighteenth-century British conservative who recoiled at the disorder of the French Revolution and called for the continuation of the traditions and institutions of the past. Burke's English conservatism, which migrated across the waters with the emigrants to the New World, was founded on six basic principles: a deep suspicion of the power of the state; a preference for individual liberties over equality; a strong sense of patriotism; a belief in established institutions, traditions, and hierarchies; skepticism concerning the ideas of progress; and a preference for rule by elites. Americans in general tend to view all six of Burke's principles more favorably than their European counterparts do, thus resulting in Americans generally being more conservative than Europeans and therefore accounting for their exceptionalism (Micklethwait and Wooldridge, 2004, 13–14).

FEAR OF STATE POWER AND TOLERANCE FOR INEQUALITY

Examples of American exceptionalism that conforms to Burke's six tenets of conservatism are abundant. For starters, Americans are far more fearful of a strong central government and of socialism than are Europeans, with lower taxes and lower central government expenditures (in spite of greater military spending) than their European counterparts. Reflecting the Burkeian conservative preference for individual liberties, the American Constitution contains a Bill of Rights, designed to protect individual liberties, that is absent from some European constitutions, including the "uncodified" constitution of the United Kingdom. The purpose of many of the rights recognized in the Bill of Rights, such as the Third Amendment ban on the quartering of soldiers in the home and the Fourth Amendment protections against unreasonable search and seizure, is to limit the arbitrary use of government power. This fear of central government power in the United States that was exhibited by the authors of the Bill of Rights reflects an American tradition that has continued through the present in a manner that is truly exceptional by world standards. For instance, although his statement was most likely hyperbole, "Mr. Conservative," Barry Goldwater, once spoke for millions of Americans when he stated, "I fear Washington and centralized government more than I do Moscow" (quoted in Weisberg, 1996, 42). The European revulsion at the reelection of George W. Bush suggests that Goldwater's perspective, which resonated with American conservatives, is inconsistent with the political views of most Europeans. Meanwhile, in the United States, even Democratic Party politicians, such as Bill Clinton, who once proclaimed that "the era of big government is over," must run against state power in order to get elected.

Reflecting their fear of state power, love for the free market, and disdain for collectivism beyond that of their European counterparts, the American government spends less as a percentage of GDP than the rest of the world's developed democracies. Americans also tolerate higher levels of income inequality, thus conforming to Burke's suspicion of the powers of the state and preference for liberty over economic equality. The result of the American penchant for Burke's conservatism is that the United States is the only developed democracy that does not have a system of fully socialized health care, and it is the only Western developed democracy that does not have government-provided child support to all families. Japan and every European advanced democracy also provide paid maternity leave while the U.S. does not (Micklethwait and Wooldridge, 2004, 11–20). Perhaps American president Grover Cleveland best summed up the American attitudes in the 1890s when he stated, "I do not believe that the power and duty of the General Government ought to be extended to the relief of individual suffering" (quoted in Roark et al., 2005, 630).

President George W. Bush's attitudes toward international institutions have tended to reflect a degree of similar skepticism. For example, as president, Bush has opposed American participation in the International Criminal Court, rejected parts of the Biological Weapons Convention, and opposed the Comprehensive Nuclear Test-Ban Treaty and the Ottawa Land Mine Convention. Bush also has made no effort to steer the United States toward ratifying the Kyoto Protocol on global warming and withdrew the country from the 1972 Anti-Ballistic Missile Treaty with the former Soviet Union. Finally, when Bush was confronted with resistance in the UN to his plan to oust Saddam Hussein from Iraq militarily in 2003, he made it clear that the United States would do the job unilaterally if necessary (Micklethwait and Wooldridge, 2004, 296–298).

PRO-BUSINESS AND ANTI-UNION

The United States is exceptional in comparison to Europe in the extent of its decidedly pro-business and anti-union culture. Perhaps President Calvin Coolidge said it best in the 1920s when he declared that "the business of America is business." Unions in the United States historically have been connected in the minds of the public with bomb-throwing radicalism (e.g., the Chicago Haymarket riots of 1886), communist infiltration (the series of strikes that accompanied the Red Scare of 1919), and organized crime and violence (the celebrated disappearance of union leader Jimmy Hoffa in 1968). As a consequence of the anti-union culture (along with other economic shifts, such as the decline of American manufacturing), union membership in the U.S. was only 12.5 percent of the work force in 2004, much lower than in most European countries. Also, days lost to strikes in the U.S. are much lower than the European average (U.S. Department of Labor, 2005).

INDIVIDUALISM

Perhaps as important and salient as any other American trend is that the U.S. is a very individualistic society. Essentially, the role of the individual in American society tends to take precedence over the state. This perspective grew out of the writings of not only of Burke, but of John Locke, from whom the Founding Fathers borrowed heavily in writing both the Declaration of Independence and the Bill of Rights. The Lockean individualist perspective grew out of the Age of Enlightenment and the struggle of the American colonists in the 18th century to release themselves from monarchical rule. Lockean individualism can be seen in countless facets of American society, from lax laws of incorporation, to expansive criminal rights, to the icons of pop culture (Bellah et al., 1985).

In general, Americans want to be able to conduct their business and their private lives without governmental interference. In this, Americans are not unusual; however, it is the degree to which Americans will go to ensure that they are let alone that is indeed exceptional. Robert Bellah et al. (1985, 17) summed up the American individualist perspective by stating that Americans believe that "[A]nything that would violate our right to think for ourselves, judge for ourselves, make our own decisions, live our lives as we see fit, is not only morally wrong, it is sacrilegious." As a consequence, murderers walk free on the streets in America because policemen violated their due process rights. Similarly, the air in Houston, Texas, is reputedly among the dirtiest in the country because state environmental laws are lax compared to those of other states. Since such laws are viewed as government interference that violates the rights of people to do business, many of the industrial plants along the Houston Ship Channel operate under the grandfather clause.

Also in Texas, laws requiring individuals to wear motorcycle helmets were repealed because such restrictions are viewed as violations of the right to personal choice. This repeal came about in spite of the fact that few would argue that motorcyclist are safer without a helmet. Instead, it is obvious that the prospect of millions of Texans riding around on motorcycles without helmets has a negative impact on society as a whole. After all, society as a whole will eventually pay indirectly for the medical bills for thousands of motorcycle riders who were injured while riding without helmets. Society will do so through increased insurance premiums, and through the higher taxes needed to compensate for the increase in bad debts at county hospitals because of the increase in serious head injuries that necessarily follows the repeal of a motorcycle helmet law.

Texas, however, is not alone in its staunch individualism. Individualism is so pervasive in America that many popular heroes, both real and fictional, have strong individualist streaks. Movie and television police dramas, for instance, for decades have been dominated by individualistic police characters that must do things their own way. From Clint Eastwood's *Dirty Harry*, to Peter Falk's *Columbo*, to the ever-changing cast of *NYPD Blue*, the fictional police hero typically must work outside of standard operating procedures, if not from outside of society as a whole, in order to produce the results necessary for positive reform of society. The celluloid police hero is perpetually in trouble with the well-intentioned and intelligent but "by-the-book" lieutenant for gross violations of department rules, and it is common for the hero to be suspended or voluntarily go into temporary retirement so that he can continue to chase villains unrestrained by anti-individualistic rules.

As it is in American fiction, so it also is with American non-fiction heroes. Non-fictional individualists in America often enter politics and become senators (ex–Vietnam POW John McCain), governors (ex–Navy Seal and professional wrestler Jesse Ventura, and actor and body builder Arnold Schwarzenegger), and even presidents (ex-mercenaries and war heroes Theodore Roosevelt and Andrew Jackson). All of the above fit the mold of Rambo or Dirty Harry in that they tended to march to the beat of a different drummer and retained their individualistic attitudes after they moved into the public arena to attempt societal reform.

The American preference for individual liberties has also come to mean that the U.S. has a much more expansive right to bear arms than most other advanced industrial democracies, many of which outlaw handguns. In contrast, the Second Amendment to the American Constitution proclaims that "[a] well regulated Militia, being necessary to the security of a free State, the right of the people to keep and bear Arms, shall not be infringed." Handguns are therefore legal to one extent or another in all fifty American states, and the United States has a significant gun lobby that simply does not exist in many other developed democracies (Micklethwait and Wooldridge, 2004, 176–178).

At any rate, this elevation of the individual in the midst of the common good is certainly more common in the U.S. than in Eastern societies. In Eastern cultures, such as in Japan and the Middle East, greater emphasis is placed on society as a whole rather than on the rights of individuals. These societies are known in political science terms as "holistic" societies, where the common good tends to take precedent over the rights of individuals (Nakane, 1986, 1–22). Extreme examples of holistic behavior include the Japanese kamikaze pilots in World War II and the suicide bombers of al Qaeda. In both cases, it is certainly not the good of the individual suicide bomber that is elevated; but theoretically, the death of the suicide bomber benefits the societal common good. In the case of Japan in World War II, the sacrifices of the kamikazes were intended to prevent an American invasion and thus preserve the whole of Japanese society. In the case of al Qaeda's suicide bombers, the purpose is to please Allah and therefore benefit the common good through Allah's blessings (White, 2001, 47–54). In either case, the suicide bomber is analogous to a honeybee that stings someone who threatens the hive. The bee dies shortly after the sting, but the death of that bee may save the entire hive if the threat is driven away. Americans, in contrast, tend not to have such a honeybee mentality. Consequently, the kamikaze attacks of World War II and the suicide bombers of al Qaeda are very difficult for individualistic-thinking Americans to understand, and these bombers' self-destructive actions in World War II, on 9/11/01, and in Iraq, have left Americans bewildered.

SELF-RELIANCE

An important facet of American individualism is self-reliance. Alexis de Toqueville in his classic work, *Democracy in America (1835–1840)*, noted that Americans insist on always relying on their own judgment rather than on "received authority" in forming their own opinions, and that Americans tend to stand by their own opinions regardless of the positions of authority figures. This reliance on self and aversion to "received authority" helps create a situation where common persons can rise to high positions in America; however, it can also create a climate where common Americans distrust their political leaders and refuse to follow those who may, in fact, have greater knowledge.

Individualism has another side effect as well. Since Americans generally believe that individuals should rely on themselves rather than on society as a whole, among many Americans there is a lack of empathy for societal "losers" and a tendency to view the societal underclass as those who have failed to take the necessary initiative to take care of themselves. As a consequence, there is a social stigma associated with welfare or other forms of government aid to the poor. For example, during the Great Depression of the 1930s, an estimated 50 percent of Americans who qualified for government relief programs did not apply for relief in order to avoid the social stigma of being "on the dole" (Freidel, 1964, 15–16).

A further problem with American individualism is that it often conflicts with traditional societal structures, such as church, which also have broad support in American society. For example, some American individualists choose to engage in sex outside of marriage, abuse alcohol, engage in homosexual relationships, join nudist colonies, smoke marijuana, or pierce their bodies and get tattoos. Almost all of these activities run counter to the teachings of traditional churches. Which of these activities are legitimate government interests and which are matters that should be left to individual discretion and choice are matters of debate, and exactly where such lines between government interests and individual choice should be drawn, there is no complete consensus.

Another common American political belief related to individualism is that politics and government are justifiable and honorable only to the extent that they improve the human condition. In this perspective, governmental institutions may be disobeyed or abolished if they overstep their bounds and disparage people's rights without a clear and present gain in the public good. These principles can be found in the Declaration of Independence, where Thomas Jefferson and the Founding Fathers claimed that the purpose of government is the preservation of rights and that any government that destroys such rights should be abolished. As such, individual liberties are only limited when they threaten to conflict with the public good and the rights of others. For example, the Second Amendment guarantees the right to bear arms; however, in the wake of airliner highjackings that began in the 1960s, and in consideration of the current concerns about terrorism, the right has been forfeited at airports. Similarly, students may not exercise their right to bear arms by pointing guns at the professor because such activity violates the professor's (individual) rights to "Life, Liberty, and pursuit of Happiness." In other words, the right of one person to keep and bear arms is curtailed where the rights of another begin.

CRIME AND PUNISHMENT

The U.S. is exceptional from other developed democracies in that it still implements the death penalty while advanced European democracies and even many developing nations do not. In fact, the only other advanced industrialized democracy to sanction the death penalty is Japan. The death penalty is banned (except in extreme cases such as treason) in 110 countries, and the only countries that execute people on the same scale as the United States are China, Iran, Saudi Arabia, and the Congo, none of which is generally considered a world leader in the protection of human rights. American exceptionalism in crime and punishment, however, is not limited to capital punishment, but extends to other forms of punishment as well. The American incarceration rate is much higher than that in Europe, including five times the incarceration rate in the United Kingdom (Micklethwait and Wooldridge, 300–302).

"VALUES" POLITICS

Reflecting Burkeian conservatism's belief in established institutions, traditions, and hierarchies, as well as skepticism concerning the ideas of progress, the U.S. is unique among industrialized democracies in that "values" politics, a manifestation of American religiosity, has supplanted the politics of income distribution and class as the greatest political divide. The U.S. is decidedly the most religious of advanced industrialized democracies; there simply is no European parallel with the American Christian right that played such a pivotal role in the election of the Protestant Texan, George W. Bush, to the highest office in the United States (Micklethwait and Wooldridge, 2004, 11–12). What Bush's election and the role of religious conservatives in the 2004 election demonstrate is that American conservatism is decidedly more concerned with Burkeian traditional societal structures such as church and family than its European counterparts.

President George W. Bush in particular is known for intermingling his faith with his politics in a way that causes Europeans and secular Americans to shiver, but which evangelical Protestant Americans find appealing. For example, in a 1999 debate leading up to Iowa's Republican presidential caucuses, Texas governor and presidential candidate Bush named Jesus Christ as the political philosopher or thinker with whom he most identified, adding, "because he changed my heart" (quoted in Micklethwait and Wooldridge, 2004, 144). While secular Europeans are bewildered at such a statement and secular American liberals may scoff, conservative Americans generally reacted favorably and supported Bush for the presidency over Democrat Al Gore, who was connected in the minds of many of America's evangelical Christians with the sexual indiscretions of President Clinton. The election was so close nationally that it took 36 days and a U.S. Supreme Court decision for Bush to emerge as the winner, but among Protestant fundamentalists, he won in a landslide.

PATRIOTISM

The U.S. is also exceptional in comparison to other advanced industrialized democracies for its patriotism. Europeans tend to be less patriotic than Americans, not because they do not love their homelands, but because patriotism in Europe has been associated with numerous wars, including two world wars in the last century, that ravaged the continent. Compounding the difference in patriotic fervor between Europe and the U.S. is the fact that it was the United States, not Europe, that suffered a devastating attack from outsiders in 2001. As a consequence, patriotism in the U.S. soared to abnormally high levels after the terror attacks. Polls after the attacks revealed that 90 percent of Americans were "proud to be Americans" and conservative Republicans were even prouder than liberal Democrats (Micklethwait and Wooldridge, 2004, 299–300).

While it is true that the polls after the terror attacks may reflect only a short-term spike in patriotic attitudes among Americans, it is unquestionable that patriotism runs deep in America over the long term, and is especially acute among conservatives. For example, hyperpatriotism has developed even in traditional bastions of liberalism in the United States, such as the University of California at Berkeley. In 2003, conservative students at Berkeley established a newspaper titled *The California Patriot*; they celebrated the 34th anniversary of the hippie-associated People's Park riots of the 1960s by descending on the park in a noisy display of patriotism, where they waved flags, chanted "U.S.A.," and sang "The Star-Spangled Banner" and other patriotic songs. These conservative students do not, however, represent an extreme deviation from the norm in the United States. Even under normal circumstances (without the effects of terror attacks), eighty percent of Americans respond in surveys that they are "very proud" of their country. In no other developed democracy is the flag displayed more obsessively or the national anthem sung more frequently. Furthermore, sixty percent of Americans believe their culture superior to those in other countries, as opposed to 30 percent in France and 40 percent in Germany and the U.K. (Micklethwait and Wooldridge, 2004, 279, 299–300).

MILITARISM

The United States is also exceptional among developed democracies for its militarism, reflecting Burkeian conservatism's strong sense of patriotism and a conservative distrust of human nature. As a consequence, American military spending is more than all of the other countries of NATO combined, and amounts to some 45 percent of the military spending for the entire world. The European Union's total spending on military equipment is approximately half that of the United States, and spending on military research and development in Europe is approximately a fourth that of the United States. China's entire military budget has been less than the annual increase in military spending under the conservative President George W. Bush. Americans overwhelmingly supported George W. Bush's military invasion of Afghanistan and, at the outset, displayed similar support for Bush's invasion of Iraq, while Europeans were generally much more apprehensive and more favorable toward diplomatic solutions (Micklethwait and Wooldridge, 2004, 211, 245).

WIDE-OPEN SPACES

Finally, the United States differs from its European and Japanese counterparts in its wide-open–spaces geography and the impact that that geography has had on American politics. The great expanse of the United States allowed a certain degree of isolation during the early years of the Republic that could not be enjoyed by the Europeans, and thus shaped American politics differently. The vast American wilderness also allowed escape from the bonds of society into the individualistic frontier where authority was much less imposing. The frontier experience therefore nourished the spirit of conservative individualism and allowed that individualism to grow in the U.S. in a way that it could not in Europe and Japan.

AMERICAN CONCEPTION OF EQUALITY

"Equality" is another political area where Americans are exceptional in comparison to other advanced democracies, in that Americans are willing to tolerate much greater economic inequality as long as they believe they have provided equality of opportunity. Nevertheless, equality is a multifaceted concept that is among the most important in American political thought.

The roots of the American views of equality arose out of the Age of Enlightenment that influenced American founders such as Thomas Jefferson. The American view of equality is reflected and shaped by Jefferson in the Declaration of Independence where he asserted that "all men are created equal." Although Jefferson's intention may have been merely to assert that the American people were equal to the English people at the time and therefore entitled to the same status under law, the concept has grown as the nation has developed in its democratic journey. Obviously, Jefferson's "all men are created equal" was not as inclusive as it might sound, since it did not elevate the status of black slaves; Jefferson himself was a slave owner. But later generations of Americans would take Jefferson's words at face value rather than limiting them to Jefferson's intentions and actions.

Alexis de Toqueville pointed out in *Democracy in America* that equality has a long tradition in America, beginning with a great sense of equality that existed among the immigrants who settled the shores of the original American colonies. In the words of Toqueville (speaking of New England), "the germs of aristocracy were never planted in that part of the union." Toqueville goes on to explain how the American laws of inheritance abolished the English tradition of primogeniture and installed a system where all children shared equally in inheritance, thus eliminating the English economic system based on landed gentry and inheritance and replacing it with a more merit-oriented system. Add the experience of settling the American frontier, another great equalizer, and what emerged is a culture that is in some ways greatly egalitarian. One might argue that the very first successful English colony in America—Jamestown, Virginia—began the trend toward egalitarianism in an environment where everyone was equally starving, and only 60 of 2000 colonists survived from 1607 to 1609 (Brinkley, 2003, 35). The experience obviously obliterated some class barriers at Jamestown, since 97 percent of the colonists were equally dead by 1609, and the threat of starvation clearly transcended any other class barriers.

Among the ways that Americans conceive of equality is in terms of equality of opportunity (Fowler and Orenstein, 1993, 98). Americans generally believe that everyone should have an equal opportunity to succeed, especially in economic life. The concept of equal opportunity takes for granted that results will vary greatly depending on talent, drive, health, inheritance, and, of course, just plain luck. The important thing is not that some will achieve more than others, but that all have the opportunity to achieve. It should be stressed that this equality of opportunity is only an ideal and will never be completely achieved in reality. Clearly some have a better chance at becoming a millionaire or a president than others, given that they might have a father who was a millionaire or a president himself.

Another facet of equality stressed by Americans is political equality (Fowler and Orenstein, 1993, 98). The concept of political equality includes the rights of all people to participate in government and the political process. Political equality also includes equal treatment under law. Like equality of opportunity, political equality is an ideal that Americans strive toward; however, complete political equality remains elusive. For example, aggregate statistics reveal that black men typically receive harsher sentences for the same crimes as compared to other groups in society (Siegel, 1989, 488). Some of this inequity is undoubtedly tied to economics: African-Americans as a group still earn significantly less income per capita than the general population. A lack of income translates into poorer quality lawyers, which evidently translates into jail terms.

A third major facet of equality in American political thought is the concept of the equal value of each individual human life. This concept is embodied in Jefferson's "all men are created equal," but it also has a basis in the Christian value system that is so pervasive in American society that stresses the concept of equality before God. For instance, the Apostle Paul, in Galatians 3:28, argued that "there is neither Jew nor Greek, slave nor free, male nor female, for you are all one in Christ Jesus." The point Paul was trying to make is that everyone is equal in the Lord's eyes, regardless of sex, ethnicity, or economic status. Americans essentially adopted this Pauline view, as evidenced, for example, by the current system for the rationing of human organs for transplants: organs are theoretically not awarded to the highest bidder, or to one sex or ethnic group over another, but instead allocated based on who needs them the most. In other words, the heart patient who is closest to death is the one who goes to the top of the list for a transplant, regardless or ethnicity, sex, or economic status.

One aspect of equality that Americans in general clearly do not embrace is the concept of equality of condition. This is the essentially Marxist idea that all human beings, regardless of intellect, education, etc., should be equal in terms of their income and material possessions. Americans reject such an idea as communist, but the idea itself did not necessarily originate with Marx. Plato, for instance, explained to his pupil Aristotle that within any organization, no one should earn more than five times as much as the lowliest worker. Similarly, early Christians in Jerusalem evidently adhered to equality of condition, according to the book of Acts (2:44–45), where it is stated that they "had everything in common, selling their possessions and goods, they gave to anyone as he had need." The parallel with Marx's "from each according to his abilities, to each according to his need" is almost uncanny. For emphasis, the writer of Acts even includes the story of Ananias and Sapphira (5:1–11), who deceitfully kept back a part of their property for themselves rather than donating it to the entire church community. The deceitful couple are then immediately struck dead by the Almighty for their selfish and anti-egalitarian actions.

Americans, in contrast, generally reject such "share the wealth" plans, believe that life is what you make it, and do not see any problem with CEOs making hundreds of millions of dollars while others make minimum wage, as long as each supposedly had the equal opportunity to be wealthy. According to a poll published in *American Enterprise* magazine in 1990, only 29 percent of Americans thought it was the government's job to reduce income differentials. In contrast, 60 to 70 percent of Britons and Germans and 80 percent of Italians and Austrians indicated that reducing inequalities was part of the government's job (*Economist*, 1994). As a consequence, American society has been measured by the Brookings Institution, Rand Corporation, Lynn Karoly, and World Bank, as the most unequal (in terms of income) of all developed industrialized democracies (*Economist*, 1994).

Americans tolerate these gross inequalities in spite of economic studies, such as that of Torsten Persson and Guido Tabellini in the June 1994 issue of *American Economic Review*, suggesting that income inequality may be harmful to economic growth. In this study of 56 countries, the analysis revealed a strong negative relationship between income inequality and growth in GDP per capita. Similar results have been produced by the Institute for Public Policy Research (*Economist*, 1994).

AMERICAN CONCEPTION OF JUSTICE

Justice has been a subject of politics and government from the earliest codifications of law and political science. Plato uttered this "first question" of political science as a simple interrogative—"What is justice?"—offered in *The Republic*. Similarly, if we turn again to the Bible, we find that the cry of the prophets (Jeremiah, Micah, and Ezekiel) in the ancient Jewish scriptures was often for God's justice. The prophets sought justice for the poor, the suffering, the widows and orphans, and the enemies of the Jews. Americans, of course, have their own conception of the answer to Plato's original question and their own versions of justice that they cry for. The American versions, however, again reflect their exceptional conservatism in comparison to other advanced democracies.

The American conception of justice includes the multifaceted American conception of equality discussed in the section above. In other words, if people are denied equal opportunity, Americans generally perceive it to be unjust. Similarly, most Americans now tend to view the denial of equal treatment under law or the denial of equal political rights to be unjust by definition. Additionally, if organs needed for human transplants were allocated to the highest bidder rather than based on needs, or were reserved for whites only, most Americans would view the situation as unjust. Justice, however, is not synonymous with equality in American thought even though American conceptions of equality play major roles. Instead, the American conception of justice includes the concept of "just deserts."

The idea behind the concept of "just deserts" is that each individual receives his or her rewards based on merit. In other words, if an individual works very hard to finish at the top of the class, and scores in the 98th percentile on the MCAT, then there is a very good chance that person may be accepted to medical school somewhere prestigious, such as Harvard. If that same individual continues to work hard and finishes at the top of the class at Harvard Medical School, then perhaps that person can continue to study and become a top specialist. In American society, the medical specialist in our example is likely to become very wealthy, far wealthier than most fellow citizens. Americans in general, however, do not object to our hypothetical medical specialist's wealth. After all, our specialist worked and studied very hard to achieve success, and wealth is merely the "just desert" or proper reward for this hard work. The basic idea of just deserts in this case is that as long as the opportunity existed for all Americans, it is fine if those who achieved it become extremely wealthy.

In contrast to our medical specialist example, and examples that could be given of Bill Gates–style meritorious success, there are millions of others in America who achieve very little monetary or material success. Consider, for instance, the case of the homeless person who lives in a refrigerator box, does not work, and spends most of every day consuming alcohol. There is a large group of Americans (conservatives in general) who would consider the homeless state of this person to be his "just desert." Since he doesn't work and drinks too much, he therefore doesn't deserve any condition better than his homeless state. His activity in life (or lack of it) merits no better condition in this perspective.

One major impact of the American view of justice as "just deserts" is that it tends to hinder liberals in their efforts to reduce income inequalities. For instance, when the federal government filed anti-trust suits against Standard Oil at the beginning of the 20th century and against Microsoft at the end of that same century, most conservative Americans opposed the government action because John D. Rockefeller and Bill Gates had earned their wealth. Conversely, the idea of justice as "just deserts" tends to erode support for welfare programs because American individualists tend to believe that the "lazy" poor people are responsible for their own poverty and therefore do not merit the government assistance.

AMERICAN CONCEPT OF FREEDOM

Freedom, like justice and equality in the American conception, is another multifaceted concept; in fact, there is not complete unanimity in American politics on exactly what are the meanings of freedom. According to Fowler and Orenstein (1993, 81–86), the American conception of freedom generally includes political freedom, civil liberties, economic freedom, and other particular freedoms listed in the U.S. Constitution. Each of these aspects of freedom will be discussed below.

The concept of political freedom essentially entails the liberty to participate in government and politics. Unfortunately, universal political freedom was not originally guaranteed in the U.S. Constitution; the matter was left for the States to determine. The next 180 years of American history following the writing of the Constitution included a protracted struggle of the disenfranchised to gain full participation rights. Landless Americans, women, minorities, and young persons aged 18 to 21 would eventually all gain full participation rights by 1971, but it certainly was not without a struggle. Whether one is discussing participation rights for women, or for minorities, or for non-property owners, those with full participation rights tended only grudgingly to give up their exclusive possession of rights to those who demanded full participation. Once the struggle was won, however, there were typically few sentiments for repeal (the case of blacks in the American South following the Civil War being a notable exception). Since 1971, when the 26th Amendment extended participation rights to age 18, for instance, there has not been a concerted movement on the American political scene to return to the disenfranchisement of persons aged 18 to 20, or for any other particular group. Thus, at least for now, the struggle for political freedom in the U.S. appears to be settled on the side of universal participation rights. If American low voter turnout is any indication, the struggle to get people to exercise that freedom is another matter.

A second facet of the American concept of freedom is the concept of civil liberties (Fowler and Orenstein, 1993, 82). Civil liberties include the right to be treated with respect as a citizen with equal privileges and equal treatment under the laws. The idea is that there should not be one law in America for the poor and another for the rich, nor one for the men and another for the women, nor one for whites and another for blacks, but all are to be treated equally under law regardless of class, sex, ethnicity, etc. Like political freedom, the struggle for civil liberties has permeated American history. Unlike political freedom, however, the struggle over civil liberties is permanent and ongoing. For instance, courts and legislative bodies have been struggling with affirmative action for over three decades, and the entire concept remains both unevenly applied and controversial. Gay rights activists argue that gays "born or naturalized" in the U.S. must therefore receive equal rights or "privileges" under the 14th Amendment. Thus, gay rights groups push for the "privilege" or "right" of marriage between same-sex couples. Simultaneously, the Christian Coalition maneuvers to counter the expansion of rights and privileges for gay Americans claiming that gays may be born in the U.S., but homosexual activities conflict with the teachings of the Bible and therefore their rights and privileges should be limited on the basis of morality.

Civil liberties, however, like the concepts of equality and justice, are only ideals and have not been fully realized in American society. American society is replete with groups and individuals who argue, rightly or wrongly, that they have been denied equal privileges. Furthermore, recent developments in the War on Terror that have led to the incarceration of hundreds of enemy combatants at Guantanamo Bay have led to new questions and disputes concerning American conceptions of civil liberties, including whether or not these liberties apply to such captives, and the balance between those liberties and security.

A third facet of freedom as it exists in the American conception are the particular freedoms listed in the Constitution, such as right to remain silent, right to a speedy and public trial, freedom from unreasonable search, prohibition against excessive bail, etc. Particular freedoms also include liberties that have been constructed by the Supreme Court, such as the right to privacy, that are not specifically enumerated in the Constitution. Most of the disputes over such freedoms, such as when speech may be abridged or what constitutes "due process," are eventually settled by those very same courts, although the public also pushes for legislation to either protect or limit particular freedoms under certain circumstances. In other words, the list of particular freedoms in the U.S., like other freedoms, is not finite, but in a state of constant change.

The final piece of the American conception of freedom is economic freedom, or the freedom to choose one's own economic course in terms of occupation, and control over one's own assets. In other words, Americans generally believe that individuals should be able to choose their own occupation, as opposed to being born into it as in the Indian caste system. Furthermore, Americans believe generally that there should be no limits hindering occupational choice based on sex, ethnicity, or religion. For example, laws limiting blacks to employment only in agriculture or domestic servitude (such laws did once exist in the American South) are viewed as limits on freedom and therefore antithetical to the American way. Parents may encourage their children to choose one occupation over another, but the final decision remains with the individual rather than the parent.

Similarly, there are no legal restrictions on how Americans may spend (or misspend) their assets (although, once again, there were once laws in the U.S. that penalized blacks for "misspending" their income). Complete control over one's own assets may mean that one may live in a poor neighborhood, yet own a luxury car, a television satellite dish, and expensive jewelry, and remain completely within the law. While such spending patterns may be condemned by some as inappropriate allocations of one's assets, they are certainly legal economic choices.

POLITICAL OBLIGATION

The concept of political obligation refers to duties and responsibilities that one has in society regardless of one's personal preference. For instance, in Texas, individuals are obligated to stop and render aid at the scene of an accident if they are the first on the scene, regardless of whether they want to do so. Americans are also obligated to pay taxes, serve on juries, and generally obey the laws of the land. In spite of these requirements, political obligation in general is lightly regarded in the U.S. (as compared to some other developed democracies such as Germany, Japan, and the United Kingdom), and obligation is typically only required upon the consent of the individual. For example, Americans may opt out of obligations to serve their country in combat by claiming conscientious objector status, or by asserting that their religion precludes such behavior. The world champion boxer, Muhammad Ali, is perhaps America's most famous conscientious objector. Ali opted out of combat duty in Vietnam in the 1960s because he claimed that his peaceful religion, Islam, prevented him from combat duty.

Ali, however, is not alone in his low view of political obligation. For instance, only about 40 percent of Americans typically show up for jury duty when summoned, even though Americans say they believe in trial by jury of one's peers in opinion surveys. Similarly, during the Vietnam War, thousands of Americans shirked their obligation to serve the military by fleeing to Canada. The list of leading American political figures who did not serve in Vietnam is long and includes Presidents Bill Clinton and George W. Bush, former House Speaker Newt Gingrich, frequent Presidential candidate Pat Buchanan, and radio talk show host Rush Limbaugh. According to Ivins and Dubose (2002, 6) and others, George W. Bush did not even fulfill his obligations in the Air National Guard, yet defeated heavily decorated Vietnam veteran John Kerry. Pat Buchanan, who is evidently now an avid jogger, reportedly did not go to Vietnam because of his bad knee (Franken, 2003, 228), and Rush Limbaugh was reportedly exempt from service due to his periodontal cyst (Franken, 2003, 228). One can surmise from this that Americans are evidently not overly rigid concerning political obligations. Perhaps this is why President Carter responded a few years after the Vietnam War by pardoning the draft dodgers. Obviously, this means that failure to seek military service, or to even shirk it, does not mean future political failure for American politicians, and any attempts by politicians to reinstate a military draft are bound to encounter resistance.

Nature v. Nurture Debate

REALISM

Thus far in this chapter, basic areas where Americans are in some sort of general agreement have been the subjects of discussion. When it comes to the character of human nature, however, there is nothing approximating a consensus; instead, there is a deep divide among Americans related to ideology and partisanship. The great schism is essentially over the basic good or bad character of human nature. There are two dominant views that will be discussed below.

The first of these two views is the realist or "nature" view. Realists believe that nature or genetics play a dominant role in determining human behavior and argue that humans as a group are naturally bad and uncooperative. As such, humans require coercion in order to ensure proper behavior. For example, the posted speed limit on most Texas highways is 70 mph. Many individuals drive near the speed limit, but perhaps most tend to drive their vehicles a few miles per hour over the speed limit. Obviously, these individuals know that 72 mph is over the speed limit because there are "SPEED LIMIT 70" signs in Texas every few miles.

The realist perspective can easily explain this deviant behavior. In this perspective, drivers know the speed limit, but being "bad" by nature, they intentionally break the rules and go over the speed limit anyway. However, they do so by minuscule increments because the officers of the Texas Department of Public Safety will generally not issue citations for two to three miles per hour over the speed limit, but can be expected to do so for violations in excess of five miles per hour over the posted limit. That being the case, in the realist conception, people can be expected to cheat a little on the speed limit because they are naturally bad, but may avoid cheating enough to invoke coercion (fines). In other words, in the realist conception, people engage in criminal behavior (speeding) because they are essentially bad by nature. As such, education, rehabilitation, counseling and the like are useless. The only thing such bad people will react to is coercion; therefore, criminals should be fined, incarcerated, flogged, or executed, depending on the severity of the crime. Realists tend to be politically conservative and their prescriptions tend to be coercive in character, including incarceration, corporal punishment, and executions for serious law violators (Martinson, 1974, 22). In the words of President Ronald Reagan, "Right and wrong matter; individuals are responsible for their actions; retribution should be swift and sure for those who prey on the innocent" *(Justice Assistance News*, 1981, 1).

In foreign policy, realism normally translates into diplomacy backed by force. Statements such as "force is the only thing they understand over there" are consistent with the realist perspective, and the idea that the U.S. should work mainly, or only, through international organizations, such as the UN, is anathema to realism. In the realist perspective, it would be unwise to negotiate with rogue leaders such as Saddam Hussein simply because they can't be trusted. In foreign policy as well as domestic, coercion then becomes the chosen policy tool.

Roots of realism can be seen in the American Judeo-Christian heritage. The prophet Jeremiah (17:9) declares, "The heart is deceitful above all things and beyond cure," obviously suggesting that humans are naturally bad. Similarly, Jesus is quoted by Matthew (7:19) as saying, "For wide is the gate and broad is the road that leads to destruction, and many enter through it," once again suggesting that the majority of people are more bad than good.

A quick read of almost any newspaper in America on any given day may act to vindicate the realists. One glance at American crime statistics suggests that there does indeed appear to be a lot of bad present in American society. Furthermore, some deviant behavior, such as that of Jeffrey Dahmer, who killed people and ate them, simply cannot be learned from anyone in society and reflects a depraved nature of humanity. For a larger historical example, who on earth, with even rudimentary knowledge of the Holocaust, could conclude that human beings are basically good?

IDEALISM

In contrast to the realist view is the idealist or "nurture" view that is generally viewed as the liberal view of human nature. Idealists believe that human nature is mostly a product of environment. Idealists have a more positive view of human nature, arguing that humans are naturally good, but corrupted by society. Since, in this perspective, all behaviors, both good and bad, are learned, idealists' prescriptions tend to be education-oriented; for instance, idealists typically favor counseling, rehabilitation, and other educational treatment programs for violators of public law, as opposed to incarceration and capital punishment. Idealists defend their positions by noting the innocence of human newborn babies. Perhaps very few individuals can hold a newborn baby in their own arms and declare that the infant is inherently evil and in need of salvation. Society, they believe, obviously corrupts these wonderful, innocent children and turns them into something else long before adulthood.

Both realism and idealism are actually simplifications; human beings are not as uncomplicated as either perspective might suggest. Instead, all people clearly are products of a combination of both genetics and socialization, and both perspectives are therefore lacking. Realists clearly must admit that socialization or learning does affect human behavior; otherwise, there is no reason to listen to the very conservative Dr. James Dobson's Focus on the Family. If children are destined to turn out good or bad based entirely on genetics, and it is impossible to fight this human nature, then all parenting is wasted effort. This is hardly the position taken by Dobson, nor by millions of other social conservatives who advocate "family values." Furthermore, Dobson's ministry openly supports conservative politics; hence, it is obvious that American conservatives often mix some idealism with their realism. Similarly, liberal idealists in the United States argue for stiffer penalties for hate crimes, suggesting that many liberals support the same types of coercive measures in some cases as do their conservative counterparts. The real question, then, is not whether it is nature or nurture that shapes human behavior, but instead which factor is more dominant, since both are significant. In the end, those who view "nature" as more dominant tend to be conservatives, and those who view "nurture" as more dominant tend to be liberals. The debate continues unabated.

2

Traditional Conservatism

Conservative Political Ideology

Samuel Huntington (1957) argues that conservatism is best understood not as an inherent theory, but as a positional ideology. According to Huntington, "When the foundations of society are threatened, the conservative ideology reminds men of the necessity of some institutions and the desirability of the existing ones" (Huntington, 1957, 455). Huntington contends that ideological conservatism arises from an anxiety that develops when people perceive valuable institutions to be endangered by contemporary developments or proposed reforms, and the awareness that perceived useful institutions are under attack then leads conservatives to attempt to provide a defense of those institutions.

Huntington (1957, 456) also explains that conservatism is an extremely situational ideology due to the different societal institutions in different societies at different times that people may desire to conserve. In the words of Huntington, "Because the articulation of conservatism is a response to a specific social situation ... the manifestation of conservatism at any one time and place has little connection with its manifestation at any other time and place." In other words, conservatism is an extremely situational ideology, since conservatives at one time or another have sought to conserve just about every institution ever invented, from monarchies, to aristocracies, to slavery, to tariffs, to free trade, to capitalism, to religion, to the defense of communism in the late 1980s in the Soviet Union.

Conservatism, however, is forced to be selective concerning what traditions and legacies must be retained and which ones may be discarded. In what Edmund Burke referred to as the "choice of inheritance," one may expect disagreement even among conservatives as to which societal institutions are absolutely essential and must be preserved, which ones may be altered and how, and which ones should be abolished completely (Muller, 1997, 31).

In one form or another, then, conservative political thought has existed throughout recorded human history as different individuals and groups in different societies have at times desired to conserve selected societal institutions. For example, the Pharisees, chief priests, and teachers of the Law mentioned so disparagingly in the Gospels of the New Testament were, by Huntington's definition, conservatives bent on retaining long-standing societal institutions against the new teachings of Jesus of Nazareth. Similarly, some of the enemies of Mohammed in the 7th century, who preferred existing traditions over the new teachings of Mohammed, could also be termed conservatives.

The term "conservative" itself, however, dates to 1818 as the title of a French weekly journal, *Le Conservateur*, that was purposed to "uphold religion, the King, liberty, the Charter and respectable people" (Muller, 1997, 26). If President George W. Bush is inserted for the word "King," and "Constitution" is inserted for the word "Charter," then one may see that the fundamental elements of conservatism in France in 1818 are still present in the U.S. in the 21st century. Other aspects of conservative thought that have remained constant throughout the centuries are presented below.

DIVERSITY AND CONSERVATIVE IDEOLOGY

As previously discussed, conservatism in general is an extremely diverse area of political thought, and American conservatism is no exception to this rule. While some facets of conservatism, as well as some individual conservatives themselves, are more ideological than others, it could be argued that most American conservatives are driven by ideology rather than analysis, whether it is one coherent ideology or a combination of several. In the words of Winston Churchill concerning conservatism, "It is stirred on almost all occasions by sentiment and instinct rather than by worldly calculations"(quoted in Manchester, 1983, 3). Similarly, Clinton Rossiter argues that the American conservative "feels more deeply than he thinks about political principles, and what he feels most deeply about them is that they are a gift of great old men" (Rossiter, 1982, 74). To the extent that conservatism is ideologically driven, then it is important to understand those underlying ideologies within the diverse body politic that makes up American conservatism.

Traditional Conservatism

Emerging as perhaps the most important major conservative ideology prevalent in the Republican Party in the late 20th and early 21st centuries is the ideology known as traditional conservatism. Traditional conservatism in American history emerged out of the foundations set by the Pilgrims and Puritans of the 17th century and has continued as an ideological force in American politics through the Christian Coalition and other social conservatives of the present. Traditional conservatism has not always dominated American politics, and from time to time it has taken a significant back seat to classic liberalism, but its influence always has been noticeably present even when it has not been dominant. The central tenets of traditional conservatism are presented below.

NEGATIVE VIEW OF HUMAN NATURE

Traditional conservatives tend to espouse the "realist" or negative view of human nature and a low view of the average person's intelligence. In other words, traditional conservatives tend to view humans as naturally bad, uncooperative, untrustworthy, and in some instances, just plain stupid. As a consequence, traditional conservatives tend to view government and politics (both permeated with those corrupt and dull-minded people) with great skepticism (Schumaker, Kiel, and Heilke, 1996, 90). After all, if people are naturally bad, they can be expected to be worse when they are entrusted with political power. The popular quote from Lord Acton that "power tends to corrupt, and absolute power corrupts absolutely" is consistent with traditional conservative ideology. Christian religious conservatives in the contemporary U.S. tie the negative view of human nature to the doctrine of original sin as based on the teachings of the Bible. In this perspective, the argument is that human nature has been flawed ever since sin first came into the world in the Garden of Eden. In this perspective, it is impossible for humans to be good without divine assistance (Muller, 1997).

SKEPTICISM OF ALTRUISTIC EFFORTS

It is because of this belief in a flawed human nature that conservatives in general also view human attempts to create a just society through reason, as Plato prescribed in *The Republic,* as unrealizable. Thus, movements such as secular humanism are viewed by conservatives as doomed to failure, if not immoral as well. Traditional conservatives typically oppose liberal moral "do-gooders" and scoff at the efforts of those who attempt to improve the lives of those less fortunate. In general, traditional conservatives argue that such efforts only encourage laziness and dependency among the recipients. Furthermore, traditional conservatives argue that such efforts have unintended and unforeseen negative consequences. For instance, a government welfare program that increases aid based on the number of children in a family may be designed to eliminate malnutrition, but would be expected by traditional conservatives to lead to the birth of more welfare-recipient children as people have more children to take advantage of the larger government stipend (Hoover, 1994).

Traditional conservatives typically view income inequalities as legitimate and natural and therefore attempts at redistribution to the poor are a violation of the natural order (Muller, 1997, 18). This attitude is reflected in the majority opinion of Justice Brown in *Plessy v. Ferguson* in 1896: Brown stated, "If one race be inferior to the other socially, the Constitution of the United States cannot put them upon the same plane."

Emphasis on History and Existing Institutions

Traditional conservatives place a major emphasis upon history and the history of human institutions. For conservatives in general, the survival of a human institution throughout history, whether it be religion, marriage, aristocracy, or the free market, proves that the institution itself must serve a human need (Kristol, 1983, 161). The need that is met by the institution, however, may not necessarily be the need for which the institution was created. For example, the practice of the burial of deceased human bodies may have arisen for purposes of sanitation; however, the institution of the funeral and burial serves the purpose of aiding the psychological well-being of the living. The fact that people at any given time may not recognize the utility of an existing institution is seen as a reflection of the limited understanding of the institutions' critics rather than of the limited usefulness of the institutions themselves. The ongoing existence of the institutions is sufficient to indicate their superiority in meeting human needs.

Traditional conservatives typically point to the family as the most important societal institution, but a major emphasis is also placed on religion. Conservatives typically defend religion for its socially stabilizing tendencies, and may ignore or rationalize the fact that religion from time to time throughout history has been abused to cause much discord and oppression. For traditional conservatives, it is sometimes less important whether religion is true or false, and more important that it offers people hope and thus helps to diffuse discontent that could disrupt the societal order (Muller, 1997, 13).

Consistent with their theme of humans as flawed beings, traditional conservatives typically argue that there are limits to human knowledge which should act as a limit on attempts at societal innovation. Governments are believed to lack the wisdom and knowledge necessary to intervene in the free market in order to remedy poverty or income inequalities without producing unintended negative consequences (Quinton, 1978, 17). Consequently, utopian societies envisioned by philosophers (such as Karl Marx, for instance) are impossible to attain. In the words of conservative political theorist Glen Tinder (1989), "To pursue the ideal of perfect justice is to ignore our fallenness."

Instead, traditional conservatives argue that change, if it is merited, should take place gradually, come from experience, and occur within the bounds of existing customs and institutions. Societal change most certainly should not be derived from abstract theories contained in a prescriptive rule book. As such, conservatives distrust intellectuals, whether sociologists, political scientists, historians, psychologists, or economists, who would reform society based on intellectual arguments (Kirk, 1982, 13–20).

SOCIETY IS IN DECAY

Traditional conservatives view the current society as in decay, depraved, and decadent. The government within that society in the here and now is equally flawed, but the government and society of the past are often viewed as virtuous and glorious. As such, traditional conservatives have disdain for current politicians such as the immoral Bill Clinton, who is a product of the current flawed society, but reverence for the politicians of the past, such as George Washington, Abraham Lincoln, and Thomas Jefferson (Hoover, 1994, 47–51).

DEMONIZATION OF ENEMIES

Traditional conservatives also tend to demonize their enemies. Whether the enemy is Bill Clinton or Saddam Hussein, the enemy is not only despised, but demonized, dehumanized and condemned not only as a political opponent, but as evil by very nature (Berlet, 1998). An example of such "demonization" is Osama bin Laden's ability to portray America as such an evil infidel that Allah will be happy with his "martyrs" for flying airplanes into buildings and killing thousands of innocent people. Osama bin Laden and his followers are the traditional conservatives of the Islamic world.

A closer look at the more extreme traditional conservatives in the

U.S., however, reveals some striking similarities. For example, the Web site of Westboro Baptist Church in Topeka, Kansas (www.godhatesfags. com/) denounces homosexuals not only as "workers of iniquity" and "abominable," but also includes a memorial celebration of the number of days that Matthew Shepard, a gay man murdered by exposure in Wyoming, "has been in hell." In such a mindset there is only good and evil, white and black, with us or against us, and no grey areas or anything in between. Osama bin Laden and the Taliban are striking examples of this ideology, but then so is the Westboro Baptist Church in Topeka, Kansas. (It must be noted, however, that Westboro Baptist Church is an independent congregation not affiliated with the Southern Baptist Convention. Furthermore, the Westboro Web site claims that "God hates America," a view that is inconsistent with traditional conservatism in America in general and suggestive that the views of Westboro Baptist Church are exceedingly extreme compared with those of most traditional conservatives.)

The views of Westboro Baptist Church, however, are not unique in American society. For example, in a letter to the Editor of the *Amarillo Globe News* on June 28, 2004, a local traditional conservative complained that Senator Edward Kennedy (D-Mass.) should be executed for treason for his statement that "Abu Ghraib prison is still open, all that has changed is the management." Furthermore, the writer goes on to argue that the Iraqi people are a "bunch of animals" and that the alleged torture at Abu Ghraib prison was therefore fitting punishment for them. Obviously, political enemies, according to this traditional conservative, are so dehumanized that they are not only considered to be "animals," but should be tortured and executed. When the enemy is thus dehumanized, torture and killing are prescribed with little violation of conscience.

LOW SOCIAL TRUST

The negative view of human nature espoused by traditional conservatives also translates into low social trust. As a consequence, traditional conservatives tend to favor rule through coercion and advanced security measures through a strong military, a strong police force, and an emphasis on personal self-defense. For traditional conservatives, a strong military is necessary because foreign entities cannot be trusted not to attack. A strong internal police force is also needed because people, being naturally bad, cannot be trusted to behave themselves otherwise. Measures for personal defense, such as the right to bear arms, are required for the same reasons (Hoover, 1994, 60–61).

Policies for dealing with crime heavily emphasize retribution and punishment, with incarceration, corporal punishment, and capital punishment favored over rehabilitation programs. Essentially, since humans are naturally bad, the only thing they might understand is pain or loss of freedom (Territo, Halstead, and Bromley, 1989, 387–388). The traditional conservative view of punishment is reflected in numerous passages in both the Koran and the Bible. In the words of Mohammed in the Koran (5:38): "And the man who steals and the woman who steals, cut off their hands as a punishment for what they have earned." Similarly, Moses writes in Exodus 21:23–24: "If there is serious injury, you are to take life for life, eye for eye, tooth for tooth, hand for hand, foot for foot, burn for burn, wound for wound, bruise for bruise."

In spite of the negative view of human nature and the disdain for the government and politics of the present, traditional conservatives have a reverence for symbols, institutions, and history, both religious and patriotic (Dunn and Woodard, 1991, 31, 48). Traditional conservatives in the United States generally view the U.S. as the greatest country in the history of mankind, the American form of government the greatest ever invented (if not handed to us directly from God himself), and those who criticize the American form of government as not just critics, but as potentially traitorous. Furthermore, the great figures of American history, such as Lincoln, Washington, Jefferson, and Franklin, were endowed with brilliance, leadership, wisdom, integrity, and virtue that simply cannot be matched in our present time. Historical figures are placed on a pedestal, and the "revisionist" historians who would write things such as the accusation that Jefferson had a mistress who was a slave, or that George Washington was not a great general, and also had a mistress, are not only wrong, but perhaps even deliberately deceitful (the DNA evidence on Jefferson and Sally Hemmings supposedly having been invented by liberal scientists). Furthermore, the suggestion to the traditional conservatives that the First Amendment protects burning the American flag as an exercise of free speech is preposterous. For the traditional conservative in the U.S., America could never be wrong, and those who might say otherwise are not true Americans.

RETURN TO A BETTER, VANISHED TIME

Traditional conservatives are often accused of wanting to return society to a mythical, better, vanished time (Eatwell, 1989, 69). To the traditional conservative, there was apparently once a time of virtue, but today's society has strayed from the country's original founding principles, and what is needed is a return to those original principles and virtues. As a consequence, traditional conservatives in the U.S. can be expected to frequently call for a return to what the Founding Fathers intended. In religion, traditional conservatives tend to hark back to the original principles supposedly in place when the religion was founded (Dunn and Woodward, 1991, 77). For traditional conservatives in fundamentalist Protestantism, this tends to mean a return to the Bible or the principles of the first-century church. For the Taliban and Osama bin Laden, the call is for a return to the Koran and the practices of Mohammed in the 7th century A.D.

In order to return society to that better, vanished time, traditional conservatives believe that a good government resembling that of the past can be reconstructed as long as it is directed by good people with the correct set of values and the correct ideology. In the traditional conservative mindset, there are indeed those who know best, and it is those people who must be put in place to rule (Hoover, 1994, 49). For the traditional conservatives of radical Islam, this ideal means rule by Islamic clergy. For the traditional conservative Christians of the Middle Ages, it meant rule by Christian nobility, guided by the Pope and the Catholic Church. For the traditional conservatives of the United States in the last several decades, it means that "good Christian" leaders should be elected. As a consequence, the Christian Coalition distributes voter guides that inform prospective voters as to which positions are held by which candidates in a given upcoming election.

In this vein, Tim LaHaye, an influential traditional conservative due to enormous sales of his fictional *Left Behind* series, also argued for the election of "pro-moral, pro–American, and Christian" politicians in his 1980 book, *The Battle of the Mind*. In this work, LaHaye argued that what America needed was "pro-moral leaders who will return our country to the Biblical base upon which it was founded" (LaHaye, 1980, 36). In other words, LaHaye is calling for a return to the mythical better, vanished time. LaHaye (1980, 39) further added that the American system of separation of powers and checks and balances was borrowed directly from Scripture. LaHaye then exhorts "Bible-believing pastors" to encourage their congregations to vote. LaHaye is not, however, evidently in political agreement with all of those who call themselves Christian, since he also mentions that there is a "well-known parallel between the social positions of the Methodist Church and the Communist Party" (LaHaye, 1980, 164). In the appendix to his book, LaHaye includes a questionnaire for submission to political candidates that is intended to determine whether they are moral and Christian. Questions include: "Do you favor the passage of the Equal Rights Amendment?" "Except in wartime or dire emergency, would you vote for government spending that exceeds revenues?" "Do you favor a reduction in Government?" (LaHaye, 1980, 164).

GOVERNMENT TO KEEP ORDER AND CORRECT HUMAN WEAKNESSES

The purpose of government in traditional conservatism is to keep order and correct human weaknesses (Schumaker, Kiel, and Heilke, 1996, 86, 93). Classic liberals are congruent with the traditional conservatives concerning the "keep order" function, but they are greatly at odds with traditional conservatives concerning the "correct human weaknesses" function. Whereas classic liberals are generally less concerned with the regulation of homosexual behavior, abortions, alcohol, drugs, pornography, and other "human weaknesses," traditional conservatives make these not only areas of government responsibility, but areas of focus. For example, traditional conservatives in the United States in the last several decades pushed for laws to end abortions and favored laws against sodomy, pornography, prostitution, alcohol, and other "human weaknesses." Similarly, under more extreme forms of Islam in the Middle East, families may stone to death other family members who have "dishonored" the family. For example, if an unmarried woman gets pregnant, the family members may stone her to death for this "dishonor" to the family (*Economist*, 2003). Similarly, Old Testament laws call for executions of those who curse their parents, commit adultery or sodomy, or have sex with animals (Leviticus 20:9–15). Furthermore, in the case of sexual relations with animals, not only the human participant must be put to death, but the animal involved in the sex act must be killed as well (Leviticus 20:15–16).

MORAL ABSOLUTES

The use of government to "correct human weaknesses" by traditional conservatives is tied to their views of moral absolutes. To traditional conservatives, there most definitely *are* moral absolutes that can most definitely and definitively be known and practiced (Hoover, 1994, 50). As a consequence, it is irresponsible to allow people the freedom to do things that are morally wrong and therefore harm society. Freedoms, including academic freedoms, are therefore limited to these "basic truths" or moral absolutes (Nash, 1979, 40).

Generally, traditional conservatives have a source for their moral absolutes, and that source is very likely to be a religious book. In the Middle East, the vast majority of the people are Muslims; hence, the primary source of moral absolutes for most traditional conservatives in that region is the Koran. In the United States, the religion of the majority is Christianity; hence, the primary source of moral absolutes for most American Traditional Conservatives is the Bible. In either case, traditional conservatives call for governmental enforcement of the moral absolutes found in their holy books. Hence, Osama bin Laden calls for governments to adopt *sharia*, the Islamic religious laws, and make those Islamic laws into governmental civil laws as well. Similarly, traditional conservatives in the U.S. push for the incorporation of Biblical morality (such as anti-sodomy laws) into the laws of the U.S. and call for federal enforcement.

GOVERNMENT TO SUPPORT SOCIETAL BUILDING BLOCKS

In furtherance of their goal to create a good and moral society, traditional conservatives argue that government should reinforce the main societal building blocks of church and family (Freeden, 2003, 88). In Iran, Sudan, and Afghanistan under the Taliban, what this came to mean in practice was theocracy, or rule by religious leaders. In the United States, President George W. Bush has pushed for "faith-based initiatives" or the provision of government goods and services through religious institutions. Traditional conservatives in the U.S. have also fought to eliminate the "marriage penalty" tax, and some states have developed new, more stringent marriage laws that eliminate incompatibility as a cause for divorce (Loconte, 1998).

OPPOSITION TO SOCIAL CHANGE

In general, the adherence to moral absolutes tends to create a resistance to social change among traditional conservatives (Freeden, 2003, 88). In the United States at present, gay rights and gay marriage are among the latest in a series of social changes opposed by traditional conservatives that perhaps date back to the very beginning of human existence. Traditional conservatives over the centuries also opposed women's rights, the end of slavery, racial integration, the Protestant Reformation, and the teachings of Jesus, to name a few. (The Pharisees were clearly the traditional conservatives of their society, claiming the knowledge of moral absolutes, calling for the application of those moral absolutes to all society, and opposing Jesus of Nazareth, who violated their conception of moral absolutes by healing and picking corn on the Sabbath, etc.) In the

Middle East, traditional conservatives currently oppose equality of the sexes, western dress, western music, western movies, and other "abominations" such as women without veils and men with clean-shaven faces. In short, traditional conservatives can be expected to resist most social changes unless those changes, such as those imposed by the Taliban, are a return to a discarded dogma or tradition of the past.

Problems with Traditional Conservatism

PROBLEMS OF MORAL ABSOLUTISM

One major problem for traditional conservatism is that large and complex societies do not have unanimity on what constitutes moral absolutes. No matter what one faction within society may call a moral absolute, there is always another faction in society (sometimes even other traditional conservatives) that will argue against such a categorization. For example, Osama bin Laden opposes the shaving of facial hair, but Saddam Hussein, also a Muslim, did not. Orthodox Jews are careful not to clip the hair on the sides of their heads and do not trim the edges of their beards (as commanded in Leviticus 19:27), but other Jews may trim both. Similarly, Protestant fundamentalists in the U.S. tend to condemn alcohol consumption, but the Catholic Church makes use of wine in the sacrament of communion. The Catholic Church opposes all forms of birth control, while Protestant fundamentalists do not. Examples of such disagreement are perhaps endless, even when traditional conservatives all agree on the same source, such as the Bible, for moral absolutes.

The validity of the traditional conservative view of morality, however, is also challenged by contemporary liberals in society. For example, traditional conservatives typically oppose all abortions, yet they also typically oppose welfare programs that address the needs of children after they are born. Liberals argue that it is incongruent for traditional conservatives to claim to care so much for the unborn, yet have no compassion for those who are already born. What purpose is there to save the fetus if its destiny is to starve? How can it be absolutely immoral to abort a fetus, yet not absolutely immoral to oppose government support for children who already have been born? What is the basis for such an inconsistent moral judgment?

As previously stated, in American society, the primary source reference for most traditional conservatives on moral absolutes is the Bible. In the Middle East, it is the Koran. Unfortunately, it turns out that it is difficult to pin down some moral absolutes even when these religious books are the primary guides. This is partially because, as noted, different Muslim and Christian sects differ on interpretation of the same holy books, but also partially because some of the moral precepts and commands presented in the Bible and the Koran are inconsistent with accepted norms and morals of 21st century Western society.

Consider, for example, the Bible teachings on slavery, an institution generally disparaged in recent decades, which is accepted by the authors of the various books of the Bible. In Ephesians 6:5, for example, Apostle Paul commands, "Slaves, be obedient to those who are your earthly masters, with fear and trembling, in singleness of heart, as to Christ." In contrast with Paul, most Americans in the 21st century, including most traditional conservatives, can be expected to oppose slavery on moral grounds. This opposition is in spite of the fact that many American Founding Fathers, such as Thomas Jefferson, were slave owners, and the "father" of the American nation, George Washington, owned almost 400 slaves, none of whom were freed during his lifetime.

Furthermore, traditional conservatives tend to call for a return to what the "Founding fathers intended, the assumption being that the founders were exemplary Christians" (Murrin, 1990, 19). Since many of the Founding Fathers were slaveowners, and slavery is generally condemned in Christendom in the 21st century, traditional conservatives must judge them by their time. That position, interestingly, is generally regarded as a liberal argument—namely, that morals are not absolute, and instead are determined by, and change with, society. Traditional conservatives tend to counter with arguments that the Bible's teachings must also be understood in their historic context; but the closer one inspects the Bible, the more difficult it is to find a moral absolutist position against slavery. For example, in Leviticus 25: 42–46, the God of Israel instructs the Israelites concerning the subject of slavery and condones the enslavement of non–Israelites by the Israelites. There is a bit of a double standard, however, because the Hebrews' God specifically commands that the Israelites themselves may not be sold as slaves. Evidently, it is very good to be God's "chosen" people, and not so good for the "unchosen." The entire passage is presented below:

> Because the Israelites are my servants, whom I brought out of Egypt, they must not be sold as slaves. Do not rule over them ruthlessly, but fear your God. Your male and female slaves are to come from the nations around you; from them you may buy slaves. You may also buy some of the temporary residents living among you and members of their clans born in your country, and they will become your property. You can will them to your

children as inherited property and can make them slaves for life, but you must not rule over your fellow Israelites ruthlessly.

That slavery is clearly allowed here by the God of the Israelites is indisputable. That it is allowed for one group and not for another is also indisputable. That God isn't particularly concerned with equal rights for non–Hebrews is also apparent. Whether it is moral, however, is entirely another issue. Were it found somewhere other than the Bible (such as the Koran, for instance), one suspects that most Bible fundamentalists of the 21st century might consider its teachings immoral. If, however, slavery was a moral practice in ancient Israel because God allowed it, and if morals are absolute and unchanging, then liberals, playing devil's advocate, could argue that slavery in the present is also moral, since morality is absolute and does not change, at least according to traditional conservatives.

Similarly, Exodus 21: 20–21 allows slave masters to beat their slaves without punishment as long as they don't kill them. This passage suggests that it is morally acceptable to physically abuse one's slaves as long as one does not go overboard and kill them. The entire passage reads,

> If a man beats his male or female slave with a rod and the slave dies as a direct result, he must be punished, but he is not to be punished if the slave gets up after a day or two, since the slave is his property.

Once again, we may assume that most American traditional conservatives would find the above passage morally objectionable if it were found in the Koran or any other non–Biblical source of moral precepts. One may also assume that most American traditional conservatives do not believe these to be moral principles that apply to Christians in the 21st century; thus, while traditional conservatives argue for the moral absolutes of the Bible, they seem to be very selective and contradictory concerning which precepts are moral absolutes.

Some may argue that a presentation of the above passages in Leviticus and Exodus is misuse of the Bible—that Christians are no longer under the "old covenant" and can therefore ignore some of the Old Testament commands. Somehow, however, traditional conservatives never argued that one could ignore the commandment not to commit adultery while Bill Clinton was president. Once again, it can be argued that traditional conservatives are selective and inconsistent with their moral absolutes from the Bible. Furthermore, the argument that some Old Testament commands can be discarded contains a weakness, because if morals are absolute and unchanging, they should not change from the Old Testament to the New.

In the later context of the Roman Empire, there are statements from the New Testament that appear to be quite accepting of the reality of slavery. For example, the Apostle Paul states in I Corinthians 7:20–24 that:

> Every one should remain in the state in which he was called. Were you a slave when called? Never mind. But if you can gain your freedom, avail yourself of the opportunity. For he who was called in the Lord as a slave is a freedman of the Lord. Likewise he who was free when called is a slave of Christ. You were bought with a price; do not become slaves of men. So, brethren, in whatever state each was called, there let him remain with God.

In this passage, Paul is obviously telling his fellow Christians that Christianity does not release individuals from slavery. Instead, if one were a slave at the time of conversion to Christianity, that person should remain a slave. Similarly, in Colossians 4:1, Paul addresses slave owners with the following command: "Masters, treat your slaves justly and fairly, knowing that you also have a Master in heaven." Note that in treating slaves "justly and fairly," Paul doesn't mention anything about freeing them.

As for the slaves themselves, the Apostle Paul commands the following in Ephesians 6:5–9:

> Slaves, be obedient to those who are your earthly masters, with fear and trembling, in singleness of heart, as to Christ; not in the way of eye-service, as men pleasers, but as servants of Christ, doing the will of God from the heart, rendering service with a good will as to the Lord and not to men, knowing that whatever good any one does, he will receive the same again from the Lord, whether he is a slave or free. Masters, do the same to them, and forbear threatening, knowing that he who is both their Master and yours is in heaven and there is no partiality with him.

Clearly, Paul does not advocate freeing the slaves in any of these passages. Instead, whether one is slave or free is immaterial because this world is not the one that matters to Paul. For Paul, the only thing that matters is the "next world" in the afterlife. For the slave, he is to remain a slave upon his conversion to Christianity and be obedient to his master as to Christ. As for the slave owner, Paul does not tell him to release the slaves, but only to treat the slaves justly and fairly. These passages raise serious questions concerning slavery and moral absolutes. If slavery is sinful, why does Paul not condemn it? Does sin not matter in this world? Paul certainly offers plenty of condemnation of sinful activity elsewhere (Galatians

5:19–21 is a good example). It is difficult to conclude anything from these passages other than that Paul did not view slavery as sinful or morally wrong in itself.

Paul continues with his tacit support for the institution of slavery in the epistle to Philemon, where Paul addresses the problem of Onesimus, a runaway slave who has since converted to Christianity. He tells Philemon, the slave's owner, that he is sending the slave back—though he should be received as "no longer a slave but more than a slave, as a beloved brother." In Philemon 12–16, Paul states:

> I am sending him back. You therefore receive him, that is, my own heart, whom I wished to keep with me, that on your behalf he might minister to me in my chains for the gospel. But without your consent I wanted to do nothing, that your good deed might not be by compulsion, as it were, but voluntary. For perhaps he departed for a while for this purpose, that you might receive him forever, no longer as a slave but more than a slave, as a beloved brother.

Based on these writings of Paul in Ephesians, Corinthians, and Colossians, it appears inconsistent that Paul's "no longer a slave" statement in Philemon means that Paul is declaring the freedom of the slave. Instead, a logical conclusion is that the slave is returning to his former condition of servitude (the condition he was in when he was called), but he is going to be treated like a "brother" while enduring that servitude. There is no suggestion whatsoever that owning one's "brother" might be morally wrong.

Some may argue that this passage should be interpreted instead to mean that the slave Onesimus has been freed. If this is so, then why is he then being sent back, since the passage at least implies that returning to Philemon was not Onesimus' choice, but Paul's? Further evidence that Onesimus remains a slave is found in verse 14, where Paul informs Philemon that "without your consent I wanted to do nothing." This suggests Paul recognized that it was the slave owner Philemon who has control over the destiny of Onesimus. This is far from a condemnation of slavery, and this is not the "old covenant" here, but the New Testament and the Apostle Paul, the most prolific writer of New Testament epistles.

In the final analysis, if one is to hold to the moral absolutes of the Bible and argue that morals are constant and unchanging, it is difficult to conclude anything other than that slavery is moral and permissible for Christian believers both then as well as now. If one must hold to moral absolutes, the only other possible conclusion is that the Apostle Paul was wrong, and slavery was wrong then as well as now. Accepting this position, however, calls into question the doctrines of Bible literalism and inerrancy, both central to the traditional conservatism of the Christian Coalition within the Republican Party.

Slavery is only one example where American Christians of the 21st century generally differ on a question of morality from that taught in the Bible. Polygamy is another example. In the interest of space, we shall avoid going into as much detail here, but the Old Testament is replete with polygamy that goes unpunished and unprohibited, either by the Hebrews' God or by the Laws of Moses. For instance, in the Book of Genesis, Abraham's grandson Jacob had two wives, the beautiful Rachel and the "sore-eyed" Leah. The story is essentially presented in such a way that one may be caused to feel sympathy for Jacob having to work an extra seven years before he can marry the pretty girl. Instead of being condemned as an immoral polygamist, Jacob is held in high esteem as a "man of God." If immorality is *always* condemned in the Bible, one can logically only conclude that polygamy must not be a moral absolute.

The polygamy in the Bible, however, does not stop with Jacob. King David, "a man after God's own heart," had 14 wives and 10 concubines. Not to be outdone, David's son Solomon, reputedly the wisest man who ever lived, had 700 wives and 300 concubines. While it is true that the Hebrews' God in the Bible punished King David for adultery with Bathsheba (not to mention the murder of her husband), there are no condemnations against David for his many wives and concubines, only for taking his pleasure with the wife of someone else and murdering her husband. In fact, God even helped David's polygamy by striking dead the husband of David's second wife (Abigail) so that David could marry her himself (I Samuel 25:36–44). If morals are absolute and unchanging, one should conclude from the life of King David that polygamy is perfectly moral. The only other possible conclusion, if morals are absolute and unchanging, is that polygamy is morally wrong at present, and that it was also morally wrong for King David circa 1000 B.C. Once again, traditional conservatives might argue that perhaps we must judge King David by his time, when polygamy was accepted. If so, however, morals are not absolute and are instead determined by society, a position that liberals espouse and traditional conservatives vehemently argue against.

MORAL ABSOLUTES LIMIT TECHNOLOGICAL PROGRESS

In spite of the fact that society, including the traditional conservatives themselves, cannot agree on moral absolutes, traditional conservatives sometimes use their moral absolutism to limit academic freedom and therefore hinder technological progress. There is perhaps no greater example than the thousand-year stunting of technological growth in Europe under the auspices of the Catholic Church after the fall of Rome in A.D. 410. During this time period, the Church monopolized learning and made an effort to quash ideas that conflicted with the Church's official view of the Bible. A stagnation of knowledge resulted, with few new discoveries made for centuries. As a result, the aqueducts, plumbing systems, and toilets established by the Romans essentially vanished; the Roman road system fell into disrepair and remained so until the 18th century. The Church taught that all aspects of the flesh should be reviled, and therefore discouraged washing of the body; the Middle Ages were fraught with epidemics partially due to poor sanitation (Ellerbe, 1995, 43–44).

In Pagan and free-thinking Greece in the sixth century B.C., Greek scholars developed thousands of ideas that are now accepted as sound scientific principles, but were later lost after the Catholic Church gained control of knowledge. For example, Pythagoras had first developed the theory, contrary to the Aristotelian or geocentric model of the cosmos, that the earth was a spinning sphere that revolved around the sun. Related to this discovery, Pythagoras concluded that eclipses were natural phenomena rather than special dispensations of Providence. Pythagoras also argued that the earth's surface hadn't always been just as it was, but that what was then sea, had once been land, and vice-versa; that some islands had once formed parts of continents; that mountains were forever being washed down by rivers and new mountains formed; that volcanoes were outlets for subterranean heat rather than surface entrances into Hell, and that fossils were the buried remains of ancient plants and animals turned into stone (Wheless, 1997, 327). Similarly, Aristarchus (220–143 B.C.) correctly calculated the inclination of the earth's axis at 23.5 degrees, and thus verified the obliquity of the elliptic and explained the succession of the seasons. Erastosthenes (276–194 B.C.) knew that the earth was round, invented the imaginary lines of latitude and longitude, and calculated the circumference of the earth at 28,700 miles, seventeen centuries prior to Columbus. Democritus developed a theory of atoms, or constituents of matter too small to be cut or divided, in 460 B.C. Anaxagoras (500–428 B.C.) was the first to trace the origin of animals and plants to pre-existing germs in the air and "ether," more than 2200 years before Charles Darwin. Hero of Alexandria (130 B.C.) discovered the principle of the working power of steam and developed a steam engine 1900 years before steam engines tamed the American West (Wheless, 1997, 327–333).

After the Catholic Church (read here as traditional conservatives) monopolized learning with the fall of Rome, however, the knowledge of the ancients was all but locked away. It would be the 16th century before Copernicus, more than 2000 years after Pythagoras, would reintroduce the theory that the earth revolved around the sun. Galileo, aided by the telescope, later made observations that supported Copernicus, and in 1615, traveled to Rome to defend the Copernican theory. Unfortunately, he had also stated that people should be allowed to read and interpret the Bible for themselves, a heretical view that caused Copernican theory to suffer from "guilt by association." A committee of advisers to the Inquisition declared that holding the view that the sun is the center of the universe, or that the earth moves, is absurd and formally heretical. As a consequence, Cardinal Bellarmine warned Galileo not to hold, teach, or defend Copernican theory. In 1633, Galileo was sentenced to prison for an indefinite term for continuing to teach Copernican theory and forced to sign a formal recantation. Galileo was then allowed to serve his term under house arrest.

Galileo also asserted that all objects fall at the same rate, another scientific fact denied by the Catholic Church. Galileo, to prove his theory, ascended the Leaning Tower of Pisa, from which he dropped two iron balls of different weights. When both struck the ground at the same instant, Christian authorities (again, read as traditional conservatives) refused to accept the results of the demonstration and drove him out of the city of Pisa (Wheless, 1997, 329). Two hundred years later, in 1835, the Church finally took Galileo's works off the list of banned books. Finally, in 1992, the Catholic Church formally admitted that Galileo's views on the solar system were correct. Unfortunately, the apology was a few centuries late to do much for Galileo.

Traditional conservatives in the U.S. at present also now accept that the earth revolves around the sun. However, they tend to argue against Darwin's theory of evolution, which is, in the 21st century, mainstream science and generally rejected only by Christian fundamentalists. Similarly, traditional conservatives in the U.S. tend to oppose stem-cell research because they believe it constitutes human experimentation. Moral debates aside, it is impossible to know what medical breakthroughs may be stunted by limits on stem-cell research; perhaps none. But it is also possible that future historians will place those who oppose the teaching of evolution and stem-cell research in the same bin with the trial of Galileo and the Flat Earth Society. Time will tell, of course, but the best predictor of future prospects is probably past performance, and the past performance of traditional conservatives in the area of science is often a source of later embarrassment.

LIMITS ON FREEDOMS MISUSE RESOURCES

The limits on freedoms imposed by an adherence to moral absolutes also tend to waste, or at least misuse, resources, both human and otherwise. For example, throughout human history, how many great discoveries has the human race not had because half the population—women—was told to stay home, raise babies, and ask no questions? What was lost in Afghanistan under the Taliban as educated women were told to return to their homes and to attend to traditional "wifery"? What was lost in the United States when blacks were kept in slavery and legally denied education? The answers to these questions, of course, are incalculable, but to argue anything other than that technological advancement was surely hindered by traditional conservative ideology is to ignore thousands of years of evidence.

SORDID HISTORY OF TRADITIONAL CONSERVATISM

The adherence to moral absolutes that drives traditional conservatism has a sordid history over the centuries. For example, traditional conservatives opposed the Civil Rights movement of the 1960s in the U.S. During this same time period, American traditional conservative religious leaders, such as Jerry Falwell, preached against integration and civil rights from the pulpit (Conason and Lyons, 2000, 141). Traditional conservatives also opposed the women's rights movement of the 1960s, as well as the women's suffrage movement of the early 20th century. In the case of women's suffrage, Protestant fundamentalists argued that God had set aside a traditional place for women in the home as man's "helper," and that place did not include politics. As a consequence, traditional conservatives argued that women's suffrage would lead to divorce and the destruction of the family (Brinkley, 2003, 586).

Almost as ominous as what traditional conservatives have opposed over the years are the policies they have favored. For instance, traditional conservatives typically favored the war in Vietnam and the McCarthy "witch hunts" of the 1950s, as well as the "Red Scare" of 1919 and the KKK of the 1920s. The KKK considered itself a Christian organization, and membership was open only to white Protestants (Haas, 1963, 52). Traditional conservatives also favored Prohibition because they viewed alcohol as sinful and drunkenness as condemned in the Bible. This condemnation of alcohol was in spite of the fact that Jesus' first miracle was in making approximately 180 gallons of wine at a wedding feast.

Traditional conservatives are also typically anti-immigrant since they prefer to conserve American culture as it is, or as it was in the past, and immigrants tend to bring and blend new cultures with the existing ones. In the early 20th century, traditional conservatives were able to combine their racist and nativist tendencies with their opposition to alcohol and thus blame alcohol abuse on immigrants and minorities when calling for its prohibition. According to the *Baptist Standard* in 1917, Prohibition was "an issue of Anglo-Saxon culture versus the inferior civilization of niggers in the cities" (Calvert et al., 2002, 307).

Traditional conservatives also favor prayer in schools and the teaching of "creationism," but opposed flying (if man were meant to fly, he'd have wings) in the early 20th century. Furthermore, traditional conservatives opposed the abolition of slavery, favored the Tories in the American Revolution, favored the Salem witch hunts (as well as the rest of the "witch hunts" in both the U.S. and Europe), and, evidently, also favored the crucifixion of Jesus of Nazareth if the Pharisees may be considered (as they should be) the traditional conservatives of their time.

WHO ARE THE "GOOD PEOPLE"?

Another major problem for traditional conservatives is that it is unclear just who are the "good people" that should rule. For example, the Taliban in Afghanistan certainly considered themselves to be the "good and Godly people" who were obligated to rule over the people in Afghanistan and correct societal "weaknesses." Meanwhile, most of the rest of the world denounced those same Islamic clerics as evil tyrants and a government that harbored terrorists. Similarly, the Catholic Church killed thousands of people for witchcraft for centuries in Europe, but these actions are now almost universally denounced as morally wrong even by most Catholics. Furthermore, even the Catholic Church admitted that they were wrong in opposing Galileo's astronomical conclusions.

Closer to home, in 2003, George W. Bush referred to the regime of Saddam Hussein in Iraq as part of an "axis of evil" and accused Saddam of brutality and of killing his own people. In the 1980s, however, the U.S. had been aiding that same dictator in his war against Iran. Furthermore, at this writing, there are American troops in Iraq and Iraqi civilians are among those losing their lives in ongoing upheaval, but traditional conservatives do not view the American occupying army and their Commander in Chief as evil. Traditional conservatives might argue that the U.S. military only kills Iraqis who are loyal to the "evil" al Qaeda or Saddam Hussein (who evidently has only really been evil since his invasion of Kuwait in 1990; otherwise he surely would not have been aided by the good and moral Reagan Administration). Regardless, to the families of the dead Iraqis, it probably matters little whether it was "good" Americans or "evil" supporters of Saddam Hussein that killed their family members. In the final analysis, just the fact that there are insurgents against the American occupation may suggest that many Iraqi people are unable to recognize that the American troops are "good and moral." In the spring of 2004, reports surfaced of American actions of torture and humiliation at Iraq's Abu Ghraib prison, certainly clouding the issue of "good and evil" for many Iraqi citizens. Traditional conservatives may argue that the insurgents are evil themselves, and the torture and humiliation was therefore justified, but in any case, there certainly is no universal agreement on who is evil and who is not.

Finally, traditional conservatives themselves do not appear to be consistent in choosing their own "good" leaders. For example, the Christian Coalition argues for the election of Christian leaders, but in 1980 traditional conservatives overwhelmingly supported a former Hollywood actor in his second marriage (Ronald Reagan, the only divorced American President) over the Southern Baptist Jimmy Carter in his first and only marriage. Similarly, Newt Gingrich, who led the Republicans back to power in the House in 1994, had extramarital affairs and announced to his wife that he wanted a divorce while she was in the hospital recovering from surgery (Franken, 1999). Additionally, the wife of frequent presidential candidate and social conservative Pat Buchanan gave birth to a child two months after they were married, despite the traditional conservative taboo against premarital sex. Meanwhile, traditional conservative Bill Bennett, best-selling author of *The Book of Virtues*, admitted a serious gambling habit, another anathema to traditional conservatives, in 2003 (Franken, 2003).

Traditional conservatives have not even been consistent with their support for President George W. Bush. Although the Christian Coalition supported him for president in 2000 and has continued that support ever since, those same traditional conservatives within the Republican Party in Texas just four years earlier prevented some of George W. Bush's delegates from attending the Republican National Convention because Bush was too "soft" on abortion (Maxwell and Crain, 2002, 200).

George W. Bush is also representative of the incongruence between what traditional conservatives say they revere in terms of the self-made man and the work ethic. Traditional conservatives tend to support sobriety and hard work and argue that people should be rewarded based on that hard work; however, George W. Bush actually worked very little in his life before becoming governor of Texas in 1995, was a heavy drinker until age 40, and set a record for the number of vacation days by a president in his first year in office. By April 15, 2004, George W. Bush had made 33 trips to his ranch at Crawford, Texas, for recreation and relaxation. All told, Bush spent almost eight months of his first 38 months in office at Crawford (*Economist,* April 17, 2004). The previous record for vacation days was held by the traditional conservatives' previous champion, Ronald Reagan. Conversely, traditional conservatives typically loathed Lyndon Johnson, Jimmy Carter, and Bill Clinton, all three noted workaholics during their time in the White House.

INTOLERANCE AND DEMONIZATION OF ENEMIES

The adherence to moral absolutes creates intolerance among traditional conservatives against those who think differently and leads to demonization of their perceived enemies. Those that think differently may be considered not only political opponents, but, in extreme cases, as evil individuals who may be exterminated. The very meaning of the word "heresy," for which the Catholic Church executed, tortured, and brutalized thousands for centuries, is "thinking differently." Extreme examples of 21st century traditional conservatives who kill others because the others think differently include Osama bin Laden and the Islamic extremists who carried out the 9/11 attacks on the U.S.

On the subject of the type of traditional conservatism that produces religious terror, Bruce Hoffman (1995) argues that religious terrorists are not constrained by the same factors that inhibit other types of terrorists. They see their world as a battlefield between the forces of light and darkness. Hoffman argues that holy terrorists see killing as a sacramental act and the purpose of their operation is to kill. Pointing to Islamic terrorism as an example, Hoffman argues that the purpose of religious terrorism is to kill the enemies of God. In doing so, religious terrorists demonize their enemies. This makes murder much easier because the enemies are no longer people, but are instead equated with the ultimate source of evil. Enemies are devilish and demonic and in league with the forces of darkness. It is not enough to defeat them. Instead, they must be completely eradicated. Similarly, Chip Berlet (1998) argues that the demonized enemy becomes a scapegoat for all problems and it becomes possible for the group to believe that all evil is the result of some sort of conspiracy involving their scapegoat and the evil entity.

PLOT MENTALITY

The "plot mentality" is the ultimate result of a mindset in which the world is seen as a cosmic struggle between the forces of good and evil

(Eatwell, 1989, 71). In this construct, the evil forces are always plotting to destroy society. The McCarthy hearings and investigations of the 1950s very well fit this type of traditional conservative behavior. Liberals in the U.S. argue that the Whitewater investigation of Bill Clinton by Kenneth Starr was a similar "witch-hunt." Perhaps George W. Bush's targeting of Iraqi leader Saddam Hussein should be similarly categorized. In Bush's arguments for invasion, Saddam Hussein was not portrayed merely as a poor leader or a threat, but as an evil person plotting to destroy the American way of life with weapons of mass destruction (WMDs). For Saddam Hussein's supposed WMDs to be a threat, one had to assume not only that Saddam had them in his possession—an assumption proved false when WMDs failed to materialize—but that he was also evil enough to use them against the United States for the express purpose of killing thousands of innocent Americans without provocation and was secretly plotting to do so.

This plot mentality, however, is not limited to George W. Bush or the American side of the so-called war on terror. In the case of Islamic terrorism, the plot mentality is a major driving force behind the actions of the terrorists. According to Berlet (1998), fanatic Muslims blame all of the world's problems on a conspiracy between the U.S. and Zionists in Israel. This thinking holds that the U.S. is not merely trying to eliminate terrorism or terrorists, but is instead determined to stamp out Islam itself. As a consequence, religious terrorists are not necessarily seeking a wider audience, as other terrorists often are. Instead, their purpose is the defense of Islam and God himself; hence, their play is for God and God alone. Whether other humans condemn their actions as immoral is immaterial as long as God is pleased.

APOCALYPTIC THINKING

Indiscriminate killing by intolerant and demonizing religious traditional conservatives is aided by apocalyptic thinking (Eatwell, 1989, 71). In the Koran, for example, Mohammed speaks of a final judgment against evil; a similar story is found in the Biblical book of the Revelation. In this conception, both Islamic terrorists and bombers of abortion clinics are soldiers of God aiding him in his judgment. All deterrents to violence are rendered meaningless by the promise of a new age that invites terrorists to fight as holy warriors in a period of fanatic zeal when the deity is about to bring creation to an end. What difference does it make if a mess is made of this world if it is going to end tomorrow anyway? Furthermore, since God rewards the faithful, if innocent people are killed this morning, surely the dead will be in a better place in heaven this afternoon, so what's wrong with that? Finally, if evil people are killed, then this world is a better place; the sooner that God can cast the evil ones into hell, the better.

MYTH OF THE "BETTER, NOW VANISHED, TIME"

If there is any constant in history, it is basic human nature. As a result, almost every era could be categorized as both the best of times and the worst of times. For example, traditional conservatives often imagine a golden age in the United States in the early years following the American Revolution. A closer look reveals that things were not quite perfect. Most African Americans at the time were in bondage; therefore, it seems reasonable to conclude that most African Americans of the era did not think of it as a golden age. It is true that not all blacks were slaves in 1776, and that manumission, or legal release from servitude, was widely practiced during the American Revolution. Manumission, however, was extremely uneven across the states. While 10,000 slaves were voluntarily freed in Virginia during the Revolution, North Carolina passed a law in 1778 to prohibit manumission. The statute assigned "countenance and authority in violently seizing, imprisoning, and selling into slavery such as had been so emancipated" (Andrews, 1995, 35). Once again, though there are undoubtedly positives to be celebrated surrounding the time of the birth of the United States, it hardly could be construed by slaves in North Carolina as a golden age.

Similarly, the American Indians of the time of the American Revolution surely could not have thought that things were so golden either as they were being forced off of the land they had occupied for centuries. The Cherokee Nation signed a 1791 treaty with the U.S. that recognized and delineated their territory as a sovereign nation within the State of Georgia. A few years later, gold was found within the designated area of the Cherokees, and shortly thereafter (1830), Congress passed the Indian Removal Act to move the Cherokees further West and off of the land they had been promised by the 1791 treaty. The Cherokees appealed to the federal government to uphold the 1791 treaty (treaties under the U.S. Constitution could supersede other domestic laws), and the U.S. Supreme Court ruled in favor of the Cherokees, but the tribe was evicted from their homes anyway and marched to Oklahoma along the Trail of Tears. The only gold in this age for the Cherokees was found in the land that was taken away from them (Perdue and Green, 2005, 1–19).

Furthermore, since political participation was limited, for the most part, to white male landowners, it stands to reason that all was not viewed as marvelous by the women, nonlanded men, and other disenfranchised minorities of the time. For example, Abigail Adams, the wife of one president and mother of another, wrote a letter to her husband, John Adams, in 1776 asking him to "remember the Ladies" and not to "Put unlimited power into the hands of Husbands." Abigail goes on to declare to John, "That your Sex are Naturally Tyrannical is a Truth so thoroughly established as to admit of no dispute" (Quoted in Andrews, 1995, 33). John responded by essentially ignoring his wife's pleas and helping forge a country that limited politics to wealthy white men and left the women out of the political processes. Perhaps this golden age of America should be viewed as the "better, vanished time" for wealthy white men, sexists, and racists.

Another time that traditional conservatives tend to revere is the years immediately following World War II. It was during these years that the United States had emerged from war as the greatest military power in the world. Sixty percent of Americans attended church on a weekly basis, the highest religious participation of any time in American history. A closer inspection of those "golden years" of the 1950s, however, reveals that African Americans were relegated to second-class citizenship in a segregated society and women were generally denied equal opportunity in the workplace. Meanwhile, greater church attendance did not apparently translate into sexual chastity. Alfred Kinsey (1948), in his revealing study of American culture entitled *Sex and the American Male*, revealed at the time that 67 percent of college-educated males and 84 percent of non college-educated males had engaged in sex outside of the bonds of marriage, whether premarital or extra-marital. Furthermore, 37 percent of American males surveyed revealed that they had experienced some type of homosexual activity (this included mutual masturbation) and 18 percent of rural American males had experienced sex with animals.

CORRECTING HUMAN WEAKNESSES INCREASES GOVERNMENT

Traditional conservative ideology is essentially in conflict with itself in that it tends to call for less government, while simultaneously calling for an expansion of government to correct human weaknesses. Prohibition, for example, was an attempt to correct a human weakness through government that led to expansion of governmental coercive structures such as the Federal Bureau of Investigation (FBI) and the Bureau of Alcohol, Tobacco, and Firearms. Similarly, if abortions and gay sexual activities were prohibited, as advocated by traditional conservatives in the U.S., enforcement would require new divisions within the FBI (if not entirely new bureaucratic entities) charged with ensuring that these human weaknesses are curtailed. Such an increase in government power not only conflicts with the traditional conservatives' own "less government" mantra, but also conflicts with the views of classic liberals within the Republican Party who do not view such correction as within the proper scope of government.

Concluding Remarks

Obviously, there are problems and contradictions within traditional conservatism, and therefore the policy prescriptions that can be expected to arise from this ideology can be expected to be fraught with problems and contradictions as well. After all, this is the group in American politics that boycotts the Harry Potter novels because they promote witchcraft, is seriously concerned about the sexual orientation of a Teletubby (a fictional puppet character on a television show for small children), and spent the 1970s spinning rock and roll records backwards in a fruitless search for reversed satanic messages. These concerns, though misplaced, are probably largely benign. The same cannot be said, however, for the Red Scare of 1919, the McCarthy witch-hunts of the 1950s, the opposition to Civil Rights in the 1960s, the support for the Vietnam War in the 1970s, or the Clinton impeachment. The dangers posed to the world by traditional conservatism are what make the study of ideology perhaps as important as any other subject in political science.

3

Classic Liberalism

Classic Liberalism

Classic liberalism is one of the dominant ideologies within both conservatism and the Republican Party of the early 21st century. Classic liberalism, however, is very different from current liberalism and should not be confused with "liberals" within the contemporary Democratic Party. Classic liberalism is essentially the liberalism of 1776 that was espoused by Thomas Paine, Thomas Jefferson, Benjamin Franklin, and many of the other leaders of the American Revolution. In 1776, "liberal" generally meant a belief in representative government, the free market, and greater equality under law. The "equality" component in 1776, however, should not be overstated. Women and minorities, as well as landless white men, were generally prevented from political participation in 1776 by the laws of the states in which they lived. Furthermore, there was no provision in the Articles of Confederation (or later the Constitution of 1789) that provided for universal suffrage. That being the case, the representative government that the classic liberals espoused in 1776 was largely representative only of land-owning white males. This limiting of political participation to white male property owners is certainly not considered liberal by today's standards, but it was very liberal in 1776 when the international norm was rule by autocratic monarchy.

The ideas of classic liberalism have their roots in the Age of Reason that produced John Locke, Baron Charles de Montesquieu, and Adam Smith, who published *The Wealth of Nations* in 1776 during the American Revolution. The ideas of Locke on natural rights may have been as influential on the thinking of the American Founding Fathers as the ideas of any other political theorist. Similarly, Adam Smith is not only considered a major contributor to the ideology of the Founding Fathers, but he is also considered perhaps the father of free-market capitalism, which is as essential to liberalism as limited, republican government.

In *The Wealth of Nations,* Smith argued that society should be organized around a limited, representative government and a free marketplace. In this classic liberal construct, people pursue their own self-interests within a set of rules that maximizes personal freedom and the free marketplace. The aggregation of all individuals working to secure their own self-interests is what drives economic growth. All society, rich and poor alike, benefits from individual competition in the free market. In Smith's conception, great capital accumulation by people seeking wealth is a benefit to society as a whole, and the income inequality that results therefore must be tolerated. The wealthy capitalist will both consume and invest excess capital, thus creating economic growth and employment for the working classes as well. As a consequence, the natural actions of the wealthy with their capital will end up benefiting not only the wealthy, but all segments of society and the situation of the poor and working classes will improve along with that of the rich. In the words of Adam Smith, "A rising tide lifts all boats."

Leaders in the classic liberal framework, both political and economic, arise based on merit and competition. Classic liberals utilize the "milk-vat analogy" arguing that the "cream rises to the top," meaning that the best, hardest working, and brightest will achieve the most economic and political success.

Wages and prices in the classic liberal framework will be determined according to Adam Smith's "invisible hand" of supply and demand. The free market also determines which goods will be produced in what quantity, and how and to whom those goods will be distributed. In general, if demand exceeds supply, prices will rise, but if supply exceeds demand, prices will fall. In this construct, labor is treated as just another commodity. If there is an oversupply of workers in any particular sector, wages in that sector can be expected to fall; consequently, workers will abandon that sector for a higher-paying sector of the economy and wages will improve in the sector that has been wage-depressed. Similarly, if there is a sector of the economy that is labor-short, wages will rise in that sector and thus attract workers and eventually place downward pressure on the inflated wages in that economic sector.

GOVERNMENT FOR SECURITY AND ORDER

The role of government under the classic liberal construct is to provide the security and order necessary for the efficient operation of the free market. If the free market does not have sufficient security and order, the entire free market system may collapse or become chaotic (Hoover, 1994, 18–19).

Free Trade Benefits All Countries

Another major tenet of classic liberal ideology is a belief that free and unfettered trade benefits all countries (Smith, 1776). Classic liberals argue that countries should import goods where they hold a comparative disadvantage and export goods where they hold a comparative advantage. Included below is a hypothetical figure to illustrate the classic liberals' arguments that trade benefits all countries. In this fictitious construct, each country shifts labor into industries where they hold a comparative advantage and shifts labor away from industries where they hold a comparative disadvantage. The countries then each trade their excess comparative advantage goods for the goods they need to meet their shortfall in goods where they hold a comparative disadvantage. After the trade, both countries are better off economically than they were before trade took place.

In our hypothetical model, the United States has a comparative advantage with Mexico in the computer industry due to a better education system and a better-developed high-tech sector, but Mexico has a comparative advantage with the United States in citrus-growing, due to a climate in some parts of Mexico that is more suited to citrus fruits. In such a scenario, if the United States can shift labor away from citrus-growing, where it is less efficient, to the high-tech sector, then the U.S. can produce an excess of computer products that can be traded to Mexico in exchange for the citrus products where it is comparatively inefficient. The shift of labor out of citrus production to the high-tech sector would obviously produce a citrus shortage in the U.S. if not for the fact that Mexico could easily meet America's citrus needs by shifting workers out of their own high-tech sector (where they are less efficient) to the citrus-growing sector (where they are comparatively more efficient). Mexico should then produce a citrus surplus that could be traded to the U.S. in exchange for computer goods to meet the needs of their deficient high-tech sector. The fictitious scenario in Figure 1 (see next page) illustrates how both the U.S. and Mexico can economically advance through trade.

In our fictitious construct, both the U.S. and Mexico increase their wealth by shifting labor to economic sectors where they hold a comparative advantage and engaging in trade for products where they hold a comparative disadvantage. Classic liberals are quick to focus on the fact that models similar to those in Figure 1 are suggestive of universal economic benefits for free trade.

Figure 1: Free Trade Example:
U.S./Mexico Citrus for Computers

Hypothetical worker output per hour:

	U.S.	Mexico
Computers	9	4
Citrus	3	2

U.S. Output per 100 Workers		*Mexico Output per 100 Workers*	
Computers	900	400	
Citrus	300	200	

U.S. Shifts 10 Workers   *Mexico Shifts 20 Workers*
to Computers   *to Citrus*

	U.S.	Mexico
Computers	990	320
Citrus	270	240

Trade

U.S. Exports 80 excess Units of Computers to Mexico->
<-Mexico Exports 30 excess Units of Citrus to the U.S.

After Trade

	U.S.	Mexico
Computers	910	400
Citrus	300	210

Problems with Classic Liberalism

Perhaps the most glaring problem for classic liberalism is found in the very nature of the free market merit system itself. In other words, by its very nature, the free market creates income inequality because people are not all endowed with equal talents and abilities. Furthermore, the free market does not provide an equal reward to all talents and abilities. Classic liberals, therefore, whether knowingly or unknowingly, acknowledge that the free market creates income inequality through their argument that the best and most talented will succeed through competition. It follows that if the societal cream rises to the top, as classic liberals argue, there must also be a bottom, and the least talented in society or societal "scum," to continue the milkvat analogy, can be expected to fall to the bottom and stay there. This social "scum" does not necessarily consist of criminals or moral degenerates, but instead includes those who lack the talents monetarily rewarded by society. For example, the janitor may work just as hard today as the physician, and his job may even be more physically demanding, but janitorial services are not rewarded greatly in the free market; hence, the janitor earns much less than the physician due to the laws of supply and demand.

Even Adam Smith (1776) recognized this fact and argued for some luxury taxes and redistribution of wealth to the poor. Evidently Smith's "rising tide" does not lift all boats equally.

According to Herrnstein and Murray (1996), the best predictor of individual economic success is ACT scores; hence, those who score very well on standardized tests (supposedly smart people) tend to do very well economically, while those who score poorly on standardized tests (supposedly less-smart people) tend to experience much less economic success. Herrnstein and Murray essentially argue (not without controversy) that the intelligence measured on such tests is genetic; therefore, the best and brightest succeed in the free market because they were born with greater talents, while the "dimmer bulbs" tend to fail because they were born with less mental capacity (which is hardly their fault). As a consequence, as the United States became increasingly free-market oriented during the Reagan-Bush years, income inequality in the U.S. also increased and the real buying power of the working class and poor simultaneously declined when adjusted for inflation. Furthermore, since income inequality also has been linked to slower economic growth, the inequality may have the long-term effect of harming even the wealthy through slower economic growth (*Economist*, 1994).

MERGERS AND MONOPOLISTIC CAPITALISM

A further problem with classic liberalism is that the free market often leads to merger-mania and monopoly capitalism. Karl Marx argued that capitalism contains the seeds of its own destruction in the form of a constant pressure for expansion driven by the profit motive. Capitalists constantly attempt to increase their market share, in turn creating downward pressure on both wages and prices. Essentially, the capitalists will try to increase sales and market share by cutting prices. Consumers will then purchase more from the capitalistic enterprise with the lower prices, thus increasing the sales and market shares of the lower-priced merchants. In order to turn a profit at the new lower prices, however, the merchants must cut their costs, meaning that wages will be cut for the laborers within the organization. The low-price merchants' competitors will attempt to regain the lost market share by retaliating with reductions in prices, and therefore lower wages, of their own. In order for the first discounting merchant to regain the market advantage that had been gained from the original price-cutting, prices, and therefore wages, must be slashed again. In turn, the lower wages in the marketplace lead to diminished buying power on the part of the workers and eventually to a decline in the aggregate demand for goods, since the workers earning less must therefore consume less. The decline in demand then leads merchants to again cut prices to increase sales, and wages again are cut to ensure a profit. In the Marxist framework, the scenario continues in a downward implosive spiral until capitalism collapses.

Obviously, Marx's theory leaves a few items unexplained, since capitalism has not imploded in the time since his 19th century writing; therefore, classic liberals delight in concluding that Marx's theory was void of substance. That said, there does appear to be at least a grain of truth in Marx's arguments. One need only look at the American economy in the late 19th century, when John Rockefeller had a monopoly on oil, Andrew Carnegie a monopoly on steel, and the E.C. Knight company a monopoly on sugar manufacturing, to see that American capitalism had moved toward monopoly capitalism in numerous sectors, and that the economy was beset with tremendous income inequality. The situation was not corrected until the federal government under Theodore Roosevelt, and later William Howard Taft and Woodrow Wilson, intervened into the free market and broke up the monopolies.

Furthermore, a quick glance at the changes in the American economy since World War II reveals that the 19th century economic scenario may be repeating itself. For example, a visit to any antique car museum will reveal the movement in the American automobile industry away from competition toward an oligopolistic, if not monopolisitc, market. Whatever happened to Hudson, Packard, Rambler-Nash, Studebaker, Maxwell, and Stanley Steamer of the early 20th century? By the early twenty-first century they were all gone, and all that remained were the "Big Three" American automakers. To make matters even worse, it is unclear whether Chrysler still should be considered an American automaker at all, since the corporation is now controlled by the German company, Daimler-Benz.

The American retail business is in similar shape. Montgomery Wards, Woolworth's, and Gibson's Discount Centers all seem to have gone the way of the Stanley Steamer. Even Kmart has filed for bankruptcy in the face of the near-monopolistic growth of the Wal-Mart retail department store chain. Furthermore, just as Marx predicted, wages in the retail department store industry have dropped precipitously since the 1960s. In the 1960s, workers in American department stores were likely to be full-time employees with benefits packages, but by 2004, department store workers were often part-time employees with low wages and minimal benefits packages. It appears that competition in the retail department store industry has driven down wages and prices to the point where few persons in the industry can actually make a living. The industry appears to be moving toward monopoly capitalism, just like Marx predicted.

TYRANNY OF THE MAJORITY

Another problem with classic liberal ideology is that it allows for tyranny of the majority. American history is replete with supporting examples, including, but not limited to, slavery, Jim Crow laws, and the denial of equal opportunity to women. In 1956, 80 percent of Texans voted for a nonbinding referendum that would have made interracial marriage illegal. On that same ballot, 80 percent of Texans voted for two other measures that were designed to prevent school integration. One might argue that the U.S. has advanced since these times of oppression of minorities, but more recent examples suggest that the majority would still exact its tyranny on the minority if there were no constitutional protections.

For example, some communities in the United States would perhaps vote to disenfranchise gay Americans were it not for constitutional protections. A case in point was made in 1998, when a mayoral candidate in Springdale, Arkansas, stated as part of his campaign that he favored the placement of a road sign on the outskirts of town with the words "No Fags" printed on it. The campaign stirred a controversy that revealed the willingness of many in the Arkansas community to strip gay Americans of their constitutional rights. In Fayetteville, the municipality that borders Springdale, the city council voted 6-to-2 to adopt a resolution that prohibited city officials from discriminating against applicants for city jobs based on their sexual orientation or familial status. Fayetteville Mayor Fred Hanna vetoed the resolution, saying it was divisive and "contrary to the public interest of the citizens of Fayetteville." The city council then voted to override the veto during their meeting of May 5, 1998. This prompted a group opposed to the resolution to begin collecting signatures to bring the matter to a public vote. The measure, put on the ballot in November 1998, was defeated with 58 percent voting against, and 42 percent voting for, the resolution to prevent discrimination based on sexual orientation (*Northwest Arkansas Times*, 1998). In short, it appears that a solid majority in Fayetteville, Arkansas, favored discrimination against homosexuals in municipal hiring in 1998. It is perhaps unlikely that Fayetteville is completely unique. If there were no Bill of Rights, and no powerful national government to enforce its protection of gay Americans, there might be nothing preventing the majority from exercising their tyranny over the homosexual minority in Fayetteville. A national government with such power is inconsistent with the "limited government" aspect of classic liberalism.

INEQUALITY OF OPPORTUNITY

Similarly, the free market may create, or at the very least allow, inequality of opportunity. Once again, the examples of Jim Crow laws, and the informal system of discrimination in employment against minorities and women prior to the institution of affirmative action, are testimonies to the inequality of opportunity that often exists in the free market society. These inequities were only remedied through government intervention into the free market in a manner (i.e., affirmative action) inconsistent with the "limited government" creed of classic liberalism.

UNSAFE, UNHEALTHY, AND IMMORAL PRODUCTS

The free market also allows for unsafe, unhealthy, and immoral products. For example, prior to the intervention into the free market by Theodore Roosevelt with the Federal Meat Inspection Act, it was estimated that one-third of the meat sold in America was unfit to eat, and any number of contaminants, including animal feces and urine, commonly could be found in meat sold in the U.S. (Carson, 1997, 75). Upton Sinclair created a political firestorm with his documentation of the unsavory conditions in the Chicago meat packing industry at the turn of the Century in his 1906 novel *The Jungle*. Sinclair described spoiled hams treated with formaldehyde and sausages made from rotten meat scraps, rats, and other refuse (Nash et al., 1998). The presentation in Sinclair's work was so graphic that it caused President Roosevelt to push for policy change. Roosevelt's initial reaction to Sinclair's book was satirically captured by one of his White House servants at the time (quoted in Carson, 1997, 75):

> Tiddy was reading Upton Sinclair's novel, toying with a light breakfast an' idly turnin' over th' pages iv the'new book with both hands. Suddenly he rose fr'm th' table, an'cryin': 'I'm pizened,' begun throwin sausages out iv th' window. Th' ninth wan shtruck Sinitor Biv'ridge on the head an' made him a blond. It bounced off, exploded, an' blew a leg off a secret-service agent, an' th' scatthred fragmints desthroyed a handsome row iv ol' oak-trees. Sinitor Biv'ridge rushed in, thinkin' that th' Prisidint was bein'assassynated be his devoted followers in th'Sinit, an discovered Tiddy

engaged in a hand-to-hand conflict with a potted ham. Th'Sinitor fr'm
Injyanny, with a few well-directed wurruds, put out th'fuse an'rendered
th'missile harmless. Since thin th' Prisidint, like th' rest iv us, has become
a viggytaryan.

Thousands of other Americans had similar (though less violent) reactions to that of Roosevelt upon reading Sinclair's novel; consequently,
Sinclair's book created a groundswell of support for government regulation of food products that continues through the present. Meat, of course,
is not the only food item that is regulated by the government. Rodent
droppings, for instance, most assuredly would be present in breads and
cereals without government regulations. The classic liberal arguments
against government regulation of business would, if carried to extremes,
allow rodent contamination of grain products to the extent that public
health would be seriously endangered.

Tainted food, however, is not the only product problem allowed by
an unregulated free market. Child pornography, for example (included
here as an example of an immoral product), would also be present in abundance in an unregulated free market, since such materials, though illegal,
are still available on the black market. Essentially, the laws of supply and
demand that govern the free market mean that for every vice for which
there is a societal demand, the market will produce a supply. Consequently,
the unregulated market will have prostitutes, mind and body destroying
drugs, and pornographic books and films. Obviously, even the regulated
market has all of these things, but the problems are likely to be worse
without government regulations.

In addition to allowing products that violate public morals, the
unregulated free market allows profits to unscrupulous businesses that will
sell all manner of products and make all kinds of false claims in order to
make a profit. This was the case before government got involved in the
business of regulating such things, and it still is. Consider the following
article from 1905 (quoted in Nash et al., 1998, 751).

> Gullible Americans will spend this year some seventy-five million dol-
> lars in the purchase of patent medicines. In consideration of this sum it
> will swallow huge quantities of alcohol, an appalling amount of opiates
> and narcotics, a wide assortment of varied drugs ranging from powerful
> and dangerous heart depressants to insidious liver stimulants; and, far in
> excess of all other ingredients, undiluted fraud. For fraud exploited by the
> skillfullest of advertising bunco men is the basis of the trade.

So it was in 1905, prior to government regulations, but the general
trends appear to have continued somewhat even with regulations. For

example, the marketers of a food supplement known as Enzyte claim that their product will enlarge penis size up to 41 percent. Advertisements for Enzyte state that "87 percent of women secretly revealed they wouldn't mind if their partner had added size. Enzyte can take you there." There are also similar products on the market that are purported to increase the size of women's breasts. Evidently, little has changed since the Pure Food and Drug Act of 1905, and advertisers still make questionable (if not just plain false) claims despite classic liberals' complaints of government over-regulation. Clearly, such false advertising could be much worse in the absence of government oversight.

FREE MARKET DISLOCATIONS

A further problem with classic liberalism is that the market produces harsh dislocations and hardships such as unemployment. In truth, not all unemployment is due to the fact that there are some lazy people that do not want to work. Instead, investment in the free market can be expected to produce new technologies that have the negative, if temporary, result of displacing workers. For instance, many a wagon wheel manufacturer was put out of work in the early 20th century after the introduction of the automobile. Similarly, the ice man who delivered blocks of ice to private residences was quickly put out of work after the invention of electric refrigeration. In either case, the unemployment that resulted had nothing to do with the willingness of people to work, and everything to do with free market-driven changes in technology that displaced workers.

PROBLEMS WITH FREE TRADE

Another facet of classic liberalism that is fraught with problems is the doctrine of free trade. This is not to say that all free trade is negative, and indeed it is not; however, it is also far from problem-free. For example, the laws of comparative advantage may shift employment in any given country to low-wage industries. In our fictitious free trade example presented earlier, for instance, Mexico would shift labor away from computers and into citrus farming, while the United States would shift labor away from citrus farming and into computers. Obviously, the shift of workers in Mexico from the high-tech sector to citrus agriculture would involve a shift from a higher-wage industry to a lower-wage industry, and thus could be expected to depress wages, consumption, and growth in Mexico, as well as to slow technological advancement. In general, empirical studies suggest that more workers in the agricultural sector in any country seems to correlate more with economic underdevelopment than with development, thus the long-term impact of such a shift due to free trade may be negative (Wheeler and Muller, 1986, 314).

A further problem with free trade is that it often leads to dependence on unreliable foreign sources for goods. For example, the OPEC oil embargo of 1973 sent oil prices soaring and contributed to double-digit inflation in the United States. The embargo did not end until Secretary of State Henry Kissinger made a visit to the Middle East to warn the Saudis that the U.S. would not tolerate a continued embargo. The embargo ended thirty days later, but not before significant economic upheaval (Jones, 1996, 637).

4

Libertarianism

Libertarianism is a form of conservatism that is often considered separate from the more mainstream conservative ideologies, partially because it is a bit more extreme, and partially because libertarians often separate themselves from other forms of more mainstream conservatism. In fact, libertarians, unlike traditional conservatives and classic liberals, have their own political party in the United States and run their own candidates for office separate from the Republican Party, the party generally recognized as the party of mainstream conservatism.

Unlike classic liberalism and traditional conservatism, libertarianism is not generally recognized as a dominant ideology in the U.S., and the Libertarian Party remains a small splinter party that can be expected to garner less than two percent of the vote in national elections. This figure may be a bit misleading, however, since a 2000 Rasmussen Research poll (www.lp.org/organization/history) revealed that up to 16 percent of Americans might be ideologically libertarian even if they tend to vote for Republican political candidates instead of libertarians. If these survey data are valid, it suggests that the libertarians, though much smaller as an organized political party in the U.S., are nonetheless a significant ideological force in American politics.

Individualism and Choice

Libertarianism is essentially an offshoot of classic liberalism where the basic premises and fundamental centers of attention have been altered from the free market to individual choice. Libertarianism is in many ways similar to classic liberalism, but more extreme in its call for limited government, celebration of individual rights, and adherence to the free mar-

75

ket. In the libertarian construct, unlimited consumer choice tends to crowd out or demote other values championed by classic liberals and traditional conservatives. Essentially, libertarians are individualist conservatives whose primary political objective is the minimization of government, and consequently the maximization of personal freedom and choice (Hoover, 1994, 66–68).

Libertarianism is a hyper-individualist ideology: libertarians view themselves as the "true believers" in individual freedom and emphasize that government, by its very nature, limits freedom. Individual freedom is valued above all else, and it is assumed that the greater the individual freedoms, the greater the common good.

FOCUS ON PROPERTY RIGHTS

A major segment of the libertarian celebration of individual freedom is the freedom and control over one's own property. For libertarians, individual property rights are virtually inviolate, and property owners should be free to do whatever they please with their own property regardless of concerns for the common good. In turn, libertarians tend to view the freedom over one's own property as an encapsulation of the common good in itself.

The libertarian position on private property is explained in detail by Robert Nozick (1974) in *Anarchy, State, and Utopia*. Nozick argues that individuals are entitled to their property and that everything in society flows from this property entitlement. For Nozick, individual freedoms and property rights are inextricably intertwined. Consequently, individuals cannot be deprived of their rights to their property without their consent or without just compensation. Furthermore, government cannot make policies that place limitations on individual freedoms or deprive persons of their property because any governmental actions should require the consent of the individuals affected by those actions.

Libertarians also share some similarities with traditional conservatives, in that libertarians tend to hark back to a "better, vanished time," but not necessarily to the era of the Founding Fathers. Instead, libertarians idealize the time before the era of "big government" in the U.S. that is generally viewed as beginning with the New Deal of Franklin Roosevelt in the 1930s. Hence, libertarians view themselves as conservators of an earlier political and economic tradition, even though that earlier tradition was really the era of classic liberalism and the U.S. has never really had a truly libertarian era (Hoover, 1994, 70).

Role of Government

The only appropriate role of government in the libertarian perspective is for security, especially security against threats from other countries. In other words, libertarians may favor a strong military so as to prevent foreign invasion, but that is the extent of their support for governmental activities (Sargent, 1993, 189). In fact, libertarians are likely to view the military, like other facets of government, as wasteful of taxpayer money and a potential danger to individual freedoms. Hence, though a strong military may be necessary, it too should be subjugated to the overriding principle of limited government (Dunn and Woodard, 1991, 42–42). Some libertarians, however, such as Murray Rothbard (1975), even argue against a large military, favoring instead the privatization of national defense. Similarly, in foreign policy, libertarians tend to be isolationists and oppose American intervention in the affairs of other nations. Such "globalism," libertarians argue, can only expand the power and scope of the national government and therefore should be avoided.

In the libertarian perspective, even security against domestic dangers should be limited and police protections can be privatized. Optimally, individuals can arrange for their own protection, either by defending themselves personally or through the hiring of private security firms (Rothbard, 1975). In other words, every avenue should be pursued to ensure that governmental police protections are kept to a minimum. Similarly, other services that one may normally think of as governmental such as education, sanitation, public health, etc., would be delivered by private entities and paid for by the users of the services. Those who do not utilize the services available would therefore not have to pay anything. In this construct, for example, the only people paying to support schools would be the students or their parents or guardians. Those not using the schools would pay nothing and no one would be coerced to pay anything for the benefit of anyone other than himself. Ideally, school costs for the indigent would be paid for by voluntary gifts from philanthropists. Persons who do not attend schools, and are not responsible for persons attending schools, would pay nothing toward the support of education for others unless they chose to do so voluntarily (Muccigrosso, 2001, 103–104).

PREMIUM ON THE FREE MARKET

Libertarians are generally in agreement with classic liberals in seeking free-market solutions to societal problems. In the libertarian vision, wages, prices, employment, and distribution of goods would be properly determined by the invisible hand of supply and demand. Any government intervention into the free market for any purpose is anathema. Libertarians may admit that such a system may produce great inequalities of income and wealth due to inequalities of abilities; however, they generally argue that incomes that are gained from just processes of the free market are moral and proper regardless of any inequality that may result. Furthermore, libertarians argue that the state has no right to redistribute goods that were justly obtained through the free market (Schumaker, Kiel, and Heilke, 1997, 54). In the words of Robert Nozick (1974) in *Anarchy, State, and Utopia*:

> There is no central distribution; no person or group entitled to control all the resources, jointly deciding how they are to be doled out. What each person gets, he gets from others who give to him in exchange for something, or as a gift. In a free society, diverse persons control different resources, and new holdings arise out of the voluntary exchanges and actions of persons. There is no more a distributing or distribution of shares than there is a distributing of mates in a society in which persons choose whom they shall marry.

Nozick simplifies this theme with a play on Marx's famous dictum, "From each according to his abilities, to each according to his needs," and instead provides his libertarian version: "From each as they choose, to each as they are chosen." In other words, governmental redistribution programs are viewed as violations of property rights and individual liberties and therefore unacceptable. Furthermore, any governmental solution is assumed to be inherently inefficient as well as a violation of the rights of taxpayers to do what they want with their own property. Taxes in general necessarily must be kept to an absolute minimum, since government is kept to an absolute minimum; thus the rights of property owners to control their own assets are maximized. Libertarians argue that the best method for remedying the inequalities produced through the free market is through voluntary action. Libertarians admit that inequalities will remain, but assume that the societal "haves" will be charitable enough of their own volition to prevent starvation among the societal "have-nots." In no case can such charity be coerced by the state.

Libertarians and Human Nature

The libertarian view of human nature is generally congruent with the negative views of human nature espoused by traditional conservatives.

Libertarian Albert Nock (1931) for example, in his *Theory of Education in the United States*, argued that the average person is incapable of higher learning and simply uneducable. Consequently, some libertarians take the realist position that people are naturally bad, uncooperative, stupid, selfish, and untrustworthy. As a consequence, any government led by these "naturally bad" human beings is likely to reflect the negative character of human nature. The minimization of government therefore also minimizes the problem of these bad, uncooperative, selfish, and untrustworthy individuals having oppressive authority over others.

Unlike traditional conservatives, however, libertarians do not favor restrictions on personal behavior or the use of government so as to correct societal weaknesses. In the libertarian construct, individual behaviors will be regulated by the natural consequences of destructive behaviors. Drug abuse, for example, would not be worse because the drugs themselves are destructive and most people therefore seek to avoid drug addiction so as to improve their lives. Conversely, a minority of persons can be expected to abuse drugs. Since drug abuse exists despite governmental restrictions and controls, the imposition of such controls only raises taxes, limits freedom, and does little to curb drug abuse. Libertarians point out that compliance with laws is for the most part voluntary; hence, coercive measures to restrict personal behavior are of little effect.

Libertarians also have a tendency to disdain written law, including the U.S. Constitution. Albert J. Nock (1936), for instance, argued that the U.S. Constitution betrayed the spirit of individual liberties embodied in the Declaration of Independence by aiding and abetting the rise of state power.

History of Libertarianism

The historical roots of libertarianism are traced essentially to some of the same roots as classic liberalism and traditional conservatism. Libertarians, like classic liberals, celebrate the writings of Adam Smith and his free-market laissez-faire capitalism. Libertarians are also persuaded by Thomas Paine's argument in *Common Sense* (1776) that oppressive governments are the greatest threat to individual liberties. Libertarians, however, generally apply Herbert Spencer's (1851) essentially "social Darwinist" argument to the free market. Writing almost a decade before Darwin's *Origin of the Species*, it was Spencer who coined the term "survival of the fittest." Spencer believed in the evolution of society through free-market competition. In this view, the market is essentially a means of "natural selection" among human beings, and the "fittest" are the brightest, hardest working, and most talented individuals who would achieve success in the free market. The weak, slow-minded, and lazy, would fail in such a system, but this is natural and essentially unavoidable in any competitive system. Spencer also emphasized (like Hobbes) that people are naturally competitive, rather than cooperative, and free-market competition is essentially identical to the "state of nature." Spencer argued, however, that free-market competition would produce a better society in the long run, even if the weak and disadvantaged were forced to suffer in the short run. In any case, Spencer eschewed any form of governmental intervention to alleviate the suffering of the less talented.

Taking the Hobbesian negative views of human nature and principles of limited government a step further, Friedrich A. Hayek (1944) argued that the state, even if acting for the purpose of security, could lead to tyranny, since reliance on the state would lead to a breakdown in the system of individual self-reliance on which a natural society was based. In Hayek's view, it was this breakdown of individual self-reliance and its replacement with reliance on the state for security that led to the rise of the Nazis and the destruction of liberties in Germany in the 1930s. Hayek's theme that statism is destructive to self-reliance was also central to the writings of Ayn Rand (1966), Tibor Machan (1974), and Albert J. Nock. Nock (1936, 3), argued in his book *Our Enemy the State*:

> If we look beneath the surface of our public affairs, we can discern one fundamental fact, namely: a great redistribution of power between society and the State.

In Nock's view, democracy had ceased to function properly because, instead of the government being directed by the people, the people were being directed by the government. Nock had been a progressive Democrat and supporter of Woodrow Wilson prior to World War I, but the expansion of government power during the war caused Nock to become disillusioned with progressivism and turn philosophically in the opposite direction. Nock essentially became a libertarian in the 1920s before there was such a movement, and argued that the blame for the depravity of human beings should be laid at the feet of an overgrown, inept government and its laws. Nock published a journal in the early 1920s known as *The Freeman* that championed what would now be termed as libertarian positions (Muccigrosso, 2001, 76–78).

Nock and other libertarians became important as a political force in the 1930s as part of the conservative backlash against the New Deal. Nock juxtapositioned "social power," defined as the power of individuals and private associations, and state power. Nock and the libertarians essentially equated capitalism with individual freedom and democracy and argued that the expansion of the state under the New Deal would be destructive to all three. Nock (1936) argued that the state by nature is exploitive, bent on confiscation of property, and exists to further the interests of one class over another. The New Deal, in Nock's conception, was a manifestation of this statism, and was therefore antisocial in character. As a consequence, libertarians were part of the partnership of conservatives in 1934 that formed the American Liberty League, an organization that was formed as a pressure group representing opponents of the New Deal. The American Liberty League condemned both FDR and his policies and compared him to the notorious authoritarian dictators of the time: Hitler, Mussolini, and Stalin (Muccigrosso, 2001, 75–76). Nock (1936) and Ralph Adams Cram (1937), in his work titled *The End of Democracy,* took the extreme position that the rise of statism would eventually destroy both capitalism and democracy.

In 1943, libertarian thought received a boost when Ayn Rand published her novel *The Fountainhead,* a libertarian work of fiction that essentially defined the human moral purpose as the unfettered quest for one's own betterment and happiness. Rand, like Nock and Cram, argued that freedom and capitalism were inextricably linked, and to drive the point home, sometimes gave public lectures while wearing a dress covered with dollar signs. Rand was passionately anti-communist and a defender of private property rights, libertarian themes that have continued through the present (Muccigrosso, 2001, 86–87).

After World War II, libertarianism received another intellectual boost from what is known as the Austrian School or Chicago School of economics. Ludwig von Mises, an Austrian economics scholar who immigrated to the U.S. in reaction to the calamity of Nazism in central Europe, argued against any form of statism, whether Nazi or otherwise. Mises argued that statism, including government economic planning and intervention, is incompatible with capitalism (Muccigrosso, 2001, 86). Mises' younger Austrian colleague, Friedrich A. Hayek, who taught at the University of Chicago, concurred with Mises' analysis of statism, but focused more on the "evils" of socialism. In 1944, Hayek published *The Road to Serfdom,* in which he blamed the totalitarianism in Europe on socialist trends from the previous decades. Hayek argued that once the state controls portions of the nation's economy, it starts society down a slippery slope toward the complete control of society by the state. The slide toward state control would be gradual, but nonetheless ruinous to individual freedom and democracy in the end.

In the 1950s, the libertarian anti-statist theme was continued by Frank Chodorov, an associate of Albert J. Nock. Chodorov railed against statism and taxation in his 1954 work, *The Income Tax: Root of All Evil,* and founded an essentially libertarian interest group known as the Intercollegiate Society of Individualists, dedicated to ending what he viewed as the dominance of New Deal statism at American universities. In furtherance of their goals, the Society distributed libertarian and other conservative publications on college campuses. Eventually, the organization became the Intercollegiate Studies Institute that distributes conservative literature and publishes *Campus*, a national conservative newspaper written and edited by students. Libertarianism received another boost in the 1950s with the revival of Nock's libertarian journal, *The Freeman*, which included contributions from Hayek and Mises (Muccigrosso, 2001, 85).

In the early 1960s, the Chicago School of Economics grew in importance with the ascendancy of Milton Friedman, a student of Friedrich Hayek. In 1962, Friedman published *Capitalism and Freedom*, where he argued that capitalism and freedom were inextricably linked and that both are better served when the role of government is minimized. Furthermore, for what state power is necessary, Friedman argued that it was best placed at the state and local levels, rather than the national level.

Friedman also argued against the Keynesian economics of the New Deal and disputed the claim of contemporary liberals that the Depression had been caused by defects in capitalism. Instead, Friedman argued that the Great Depression was the result of government mismanagement through misguided monetary policies of the Federal Reserve. Friedman was elected president of the American Economic Association in 1967 and received the Nobel Prize in Economics in 1976. Friedman, however, did not limit his commentary to the economic realm; he also argued for the elimination of military conscription and the implementation of a school voucher system for parents who wanted to use their tax money to send their children to private schools (Muccigrosso, 2001, 101–102).

Libertarians largely remained within the Republican Party until military conscription during the Vietnam War of the 1960s that violated the Libertarians' celebration of individual choice as the fundamental basis for society (Tucille, 1970). As a consequence, a movement toward the establishment of a Libertarian Party as a viable alternative to the Republicans gained momentum. The American Libertarian Party began in 1971 in Colorado as a group of disillusioned Republicans, and others disenchanted with the major parties, set out to provide an alternative. Libertarians were at odds with other conservatives within the Republican Party over the issues of conscription, personal drug use, and the Vietnam War in general. Libertarians such as Murray Rothbard argued that the Vietnam War and globalist policies promoted statism and thus deprived the individual of liberty. Karl Hess, former speech writer for Barry Goldwater, argued:

> Vietnam should remind all conservatives that whenever you put your faith in big government for any reason, sooner or later you wind up as an apologist for mass murder [quoted in Muccigrosso, 2001, 103].

Hess was also appalled by government efforts to coerce its citizens through federal law enforcement agencies and compared the FBI with the Soviet KGB (Muccigrosso, 2001, 103).

By 1980, the Libertarian Party was on the ballot in all 50 states, and Libertarian presidential candidate Ed Clark received almost a million votes. Libertarians continued to be appalled at America's globalist foreign policies, the continued expansion of state power, and the continuation of the Cold War under Presidents Carter and Reagan. As a consequence, the Libertarian Party continued to gradually grow in size. Over the next two decades, the Libertarian Party grew until over 300 libertarians were serving in elected public offices across the country by 2001. In 2002, the Libertarian Party ran 1,642 candidates for public office, the largest slate of candidates for office from any third party in American politics since the Second World War (www.lp.org/organization/history).

As the movement gained steam, some libertarians, most notably Karl Hess, advocated not only separation from the Republican Party and the formation of a third party, but separation from the community at large. Hess argued that a better society could be forged through self-reliance on the neighborhood community level and that society should therefore be decentralized into self-sufficient neighborhoods. Hess's ideas, as he outlined them in *Community Technology* (1979), spawned a separatist libertarian community in a Washington, D.C. neighborhood. Though the libertarian community in the nation's capital was a failure within five years, the ideas of neighborhood-level self-help as strategies for fighting urban decay became adopted by the Reagan administration in the 1980s. They are also reflected in George H.W. Bush's vision of "1000 points of light" and accompanying calls for volunteerism at the end of the decade.

Problems with Libertarian Ideology

Libertarianism suffers from all of the same problems and contradictions stemming from the free market as classic liberalism. Essentially, the unregulated free market produces inequalities, unsafe products, environmental degradation, and profits to unscrupulous merchants, to the detriment of the common good. Furthermore, there is no historical example that supports the libertarian contention that volunteerism can adequately solve the problems of poverty and extreme income inequality that tend to result from the free market in a large, industrialized society. Even Hess's small-scale libertarian neighborhood experiment in Washington, D.C., in the 1980s quickly failed.

The libertarian focus on individual security also appears to be problematic. After all, the very reason that governments are formed in the first place is that people are unable to provide for their own security on an individual basis. All too often, a society without sufficient government becomes Thomas Hobbes' savage jungle, where life is "nasty, brutish, and short." In general, libertarians are victims of what Jean-Jacques Rousseau termed as the "Law-Freedom Paradox." Essentially, while libertarians are correct in their assertion that law limits freedom, it also appears that there is little freedom without law.

Individualism by its very nature also clashes with the restrictive positions on social issues taken by traditional conservatives. Libertarian individualism essentially celebrates choice as its highest value. Some individuals in such a system can be expected to choose activities, such as homosexuality, substance abuse, abortions, and sexual promiscuity, that are abhorrent to traditional conservatives. Consequently, the individualism and minimal government positions of libertarians (much like those of classic liberals) also clash with traditional conservatives, who would use government to rid society of activities they view as human weaknesses. Ayn Rand (1962), for example, criticizes traditional conservatives for their failure to wholeheartedly embrace unfettered capitalism. In the words of Rand:

> The plea to preserve 'tradition' as such, can appeal only to those who have given up or to those who never intended to achieve anything in life. It is a plea that appeals to the worst elements in men and rejects the best: it appeals to fear, sloth, cowardice, conformity, self-doubt—and rejects creativeness, originality, courage, independence, self-reliance.

Similarly, libertarian pundit Russell Kirk (1982) argues that because of the libertarians' beliefs in "moral freedom" for individuals, they oppose restrictions on abortion as restrictions on individual freedoms. Traditional conservatives respond with criticism of libertarians for their lack of concern for customs, traditions, history, and societal institutions such as church and family (Dunn and Woodard, 1991, 108–109). Libertarians have also been accused by traditional conservatives (and contemporary liberals) of following an ideology that is without morality due to their emphasis on individualism that essentially celebrates selfishness as a virtue. Furthermore, if all persons are selfishly seeking their own good, and no one is seeking the common good, it should not be surprising if the common good does not result.

Libertarians counter these charges with the contentions of Ayn Rand in *The Virtue of Selfishness* (1961), where she argues that societal moral decay was not due to selfishness, but due to a tendency to equate morality with altruism. Rand accepts the Hobbesian negative view of human nature and argues that human nature does not allow people to sacrifice for others. As a consequence, altruistic morality is a nice idea, but people are unable to pursue it in practice. In contrast to what they therefore view as truly futile moralities espoused by traditional conservatives, the libertarian view of a moral person is one who simply respects the rights of others, pursues the best things for his own life, and does nothing that discourages others from becoming equally self-reliant. The problem with Rand's argument, unfortunately, is that if one accepts the libertarian premise that people are naturally bad, then they cannot be expected to live up to the libertarian view of the moral person, and instead can be expected to trample on the rights of others when it suits their own selfish motives.

Libertarians have also criticized traditional conservatives for what they view as inflexible, archaic, and authoritarian value systems and structures that they view as hindering liberty. H.L. Mencken, a writer for the *Baltimore Sun* during the 1920s and 1930s and a leading libertarian critic of the New Deal, also criticized fundamentalist Protestant religions and rural American values. Mencken once declared that the American farmer did not belong to the human race and that the American South was ruled by "Baptist and Methodist barbarism." Obviously, such a position places the libertarians at odds with much of the core support for the Republican Party.

Finally, in the minds of many, libertarianism was effectively discredited by the Great Depression and World War II. Contemporary liberals argue that if there is any lesson to be learned from the Great Depression, it is that sometimes government intervention into the free market is necessary to alleviate free-market harshness. Similarly, the World War II experience suggests that security is impossible without collective action; hence, libertarianism is doomed to failure both in the area of security and in the areas of economic and social welfare.

Concluding Remarks

Libertarianism continues to be a growing ideological force in American politics and an important influence in the Republican Party. As the Republican Party under George W. Bush (as well as the Democrats) have continued to violate the libertarian principles of less government, one might expect libertarianism to continue to grow in the near future as a reaction to government expansion. Another severe free market economic downturn where governmental solutions become popular, or another major security threat, however, may again partially discredit the movement, but ideologies tend to be resilient in spite of being exposed as deficient time and time again. Perhaps just as plausible, libertarianism may experience greater growth in the coming years in reaction to what many view as the folly of George W. Bush's military globalism.

5

Conservative Extremism

Conservative extremism is not a dominant ideology in the United States, but it is neither absent nor impotent. In fact, the Oklahoma City bombing in 1994 by conservative extremist Timothy McVeigh suggests exactly the opposite. Similarly, the rise of the Nazis in Germany from an insignificant splinter party in 1928 to the control of the government in 1933 is a testimony to the powerful potential of conservative extremism as an ideology that can mobilize the masses. If such a takeover could happen in Germany in 1933, then it is conceivable that it could happen in the exceptionally rural and religious United States in the 21st century.

The World War II experience largely discredited conservative extremist ideologies under the names of Nazism and fascism; consequently, if conservative extremism is to become dominant in the United States, it is perhaps most likely that it would resurface under another name, whether it be the citizen militia movement in the U.S., or a more militant version of the religious right. In any case, it would be foolish to accept the position that the U.S. or any other advanced industrial democracy is immune to such a movement.

Conservative extremism, like other facets of conservatism, is not monolithic, but diverse; as a result, there is less common agreement among scholars about the use of terms to describe conservative extremism as opposed to other ideologies (Eatwell, 1989, 68). For example, McCarthyism in the U.S. in the 1950s is quite different from Nazism in Germany in the 1930s because McCarthyism did not feature a focus on anti–Semitism. Therefore, should these movements be considered ideologically similar, or different? There is, however, a commonality among conservative extremist ideologies in that they tend to be viewed as ideological aberrations from the norm, and there is a tendency in society at large to associate a pejorative meaning with the labels attached to the movements themselves (Eatwell, 1989, 68).

Conservative extremism also differs from other ideologies in that it lacks its own version of a Karl Marx or some other grand theorist to whom all conservative extremists turn for guidance. Adolf Hitler's *Mein Kampf*, most scholars would argue, does not qualify. In the words of Michael Billig (1979, 148):

> *Mein Kampf* is better categorized as a mish-mash of self-serving autobiography, psychopathic hatred and prejudice, should not be considered as an intellectual work of political theory. The mystery is how such nonsense became to be taken seriously by so many people.

If there is any stream of writing to which conservative extremists tend to draw their ideas, however, it is the writings in the pseudo-science of eugenicists, who argue that there are genetic differences between peoples and races with the natural result that some races are superior to others (Poliakov, 1974, 14). Writers such as Madison Grant, in the *Passing of the Great Race*, argue that a particular race of people (normally white Anglo-Saxons) is superior to all others and that race therefore must be kept pure. In cases of intermarriage between the preferred race and those of the "inferior" races, so argue the conservative extremists, the children always go to the "lower case," thus diluting and destroying the "superior" race. As a consequence, conservative extremists argue for severe immigration restrictions so as to prevent such interracial "mixing," and segregationist policies and apartheid-style inequalities under law are championed.

Central Tenets of Conservative Extremism

Conservative Extremism, whether it be termed as fascism, Nazism, or the white supremism of the KKK, is a combination of racism, nationalism, and authoritarianism that has a tendency to center on a belief in the superiority of a specific group of people (Mosse, 1964, 70). Conservative extremism rests on a fear of foreigners and immigrants among indigenous members of the population. The target of the conservative extremists' wrath and fear, however, is not always the same, because as immigration patterns change, it is not always the same "foreigner" who is being denigrated. Furthermore, the form of the conservative extremist hatred at differing times is similar, but the object may differ because the ideologies allow "substitutability of targets" (Billig, 1979, 151). The conservative extremism of Adolf Hitler in Nazi Germany, for example, had as its basis a belief in the superiority of the German people, while the conservative extremism of Japan during the same time period celebrated the superiority of the people of Japan. Similarly, the conservative extremism of the KKK in the U.S. in the 1920s was based on "purer Americanism" and the "God-given right of white Protestant males" in addition to the assumed inferiority of African-Americans and other non-white, non-Protestant individuals (Alexander, 1965, 14). Conservative extremists in the U.S., however, could easily shift the focus of their wrath from African-Americans to Latin Americans or Asians depending on shifting cultural and immigration patterns and political events. After the terrorist attacks of September 11, 2001, for instance, it would not be surprising if American conservative extremists designated Muslims as their new objects of vilification.

Conservative extremists accept the proposition that different persons have different levels of talents and abilities, a point with which classic liberals, traditional conservatives, and libertarians would agree. Conservative extremists, however, take this principle a step further and generalize it to groups of people based on ethnicity, nationality, religion, or some other demographic category. In other words, conservative extremists generally argue that different groups of people have differing levels of talents and abilities as groups, in addition to individual differences. Conservative extremists can be expected to view the talents of their own group as superior to those of all others, and view the world as a hierarchy of groups of peoples with their own group rightfully situated, or belonging, at the top. In the conservative extremist construct, race, ethnicity, or nationalism is normally the motivating and unifying force, and purity of the group is the guiding precept of the community (Cassels, 1968, 23–25).

Conservative extremist ideologies are also typically reactionary in character. The KKK, for instance, developed as a reaction to the end of slavery and the Southern defeat in the Civil War. Similarly, Nazism in Germany developed as a reaction to the German loss of World War I and as a response to the threat of socialism. Fascism in Italy under Mussolini also arose at least partially due to a perceived threat from socialism, as did McCarthyism in the U.S. in the 1950s (Cassels, 1968, 23–25).

PRIORITY ON MYTH

Conservative extremism generally places a high priority on myth, and like traditional conservatives, the conservative extremists may hark back to the symbols and heroes of a better, vanished time as a motivating force. Conservative extremist ideologies also typically aggrandize selected historical figures to mythical and heroic proportions. The heroes of the past are then connected to an aggressive and romantic vision of nationalism that becomes, in the conservative extremists' vision, (to borrow a phrase popularized by Rush Limbaugh) "the way things ought to be." In this view, the present is viewed as decadent, often with little or nothing to "conserve." The conservative extremism of Osama bin Laden and al Qaeda, for example, preaches the decadence of the current society, calls for its complete destruction, and urges a return to the 13th century teachings of ibn Tamiyya (Benjamin and Simon, 2002, 38–52).

Typically, conservative extremism includes leadership by a charismatic authoritarian leader who takes on mystic, "messiah-like" characteristics. Osama bin Laden and Adolf Hitler are excellent examples of the charismatic leader. Without such a strong leader, the movement may not be able to gather momentum. For example, Benito Mussolini, the leader of Fascist Italy in the early twentieth century, once remarked, "What would Fascism be, if I had not been" (quoted in Ingersoll, Matthews, and Davison, 2001, 213). The strong leader is expected to unite the people and return society to the truer version of the past. The charismatic leader in conservative extremism typically becomes an authoritarian leader who not only assumes policy leadership, but also takes a leading role in constructing and perpetuating the myths on which the ideology is based and in identifying and condemning heretics and heresies (Eatwell, 1989, 69–70). Pursuant to these goals, Osama bin Laden has issued religious fatwas calling for holy war on the West. Bin Laden has also called for the overthrow of "apostate" Islamic rulers, such as Saddam Hussein and the Saudi Royal family, whom bin Laden views as straying from the principles of pure Islam (Benjamin and Simon, 2002, 38–42).

CONSPIRACY THEORY

A central component of conservative extremism is often conspiracy theory. Senator Joseph McCarthy's assertion in the 1950s that there was a communist conspiracy to undermine the U.S. government and American society, and Adolf Hitler's assertion that the German defeat in World War I was because Jewish traitors betrayed Germany, are prime examples. Western culture is perhaps especially susceptible to conspiracy theories since its monotheistic Christian beliefs simplify world conflict for people into a struggle between God and Satan, or good and evil. Since in Christianity, there is a general belief in invisible forces of evil plotting against the forces of good, whether those evil forces be witches, demons, or the Devil himself, it is then very easy to believe that there are invisible human plots as well.

Outsiders to the conservative extremists' preferred group (Jews in

Nazi Germany, for example) are demonized and cast as societal scapegoats for all of the multiple ills that beset society. Consequently, conservative extremists generally argue that these outgroups must be purged, expelled, or at least controlled, if not completely eradicated, in order for society to advance. The most important societal problems are attributed to the scapegoat groups and to those within the preferred group itself who have adopted the ways of the scapegoats. For example, in Nazi Germany, the German defeat in World War I was explained as a result of Jewish officers who betrayed Germany at Versailles and other German officials who collaborated with the Jewish traitors (Bell, 1986, 78–79).

The conspiracy theories of conservative extremism help provide a common sense of identity for the extremists themselves, who view themselves as having true revelation about the dark and evil forces that lurk in the world while others unwisely ignore their warnings. The conservative extremists then view themselves as the last bastion of hope against the hidden, evil, and corrupting forces that are loose on society (Eatwell, 1989).

Conspiracy theories also allow conservative extremists to resolve dissonance. In other words, the ideology allows conservative extremists to explain away any and all factual evidence that appears to be in conflict with their beliefs. For instance, a conservative extremist may be able to believe that the Holocaust never happened because the media and academia are dominated by Jews, liberals, and communists who have forged and perpetuated intricate lies to deceive the people (Eatwell, 1989, 72).

Conspiracy theories in conservative extremism, however, do not stop with the enemy scapegoats. Conservative extremists often see conspiracies among those even within their own organizations. For example, Adolf Hitler purged many a dedicated Nazi out of paranoia, and Joseph McCarthy at one time even accused Republican president and hero of World War II, Dwight Eisenhower, of being a communist (Brinkley, 2003, 794–795).

The preferred group itself becomes a central focus in conservative extremism and the group itself takes on glorious, a mystical, almost religious, character. For the Nazism of Adolf Hitler, the focus was on the "Volk" or German people, and the nature of the group was founded on blood nationalism and sacrifice (Eatwell, 1989, 72). In Fascist Italy, the focus was on the nation-state itself. In the words of Mussolini (quoted in Somerville and Santoni eds., 1963, 192):

> The State, as conceived of and as created by Fascism, is a spiritual and moral fact in itself, since its political, juridical, and economic organiza-

tion of the nation is a concrete thing; and such an organization must be in its origins and development a manifestation of the spirit.

ROLE OF THE STATE

The role of the state in conservative extremism includes the provision of security, both internal and external; however, the state is also, in the words of Mussolini (quoted in Somerville and Santoni, eds., 1963, 194), "the custodian and transmitter of the spirit of the people." In other words, the role of the state in the conservative extremist construct includes developing and perpetuating the ideological myths on which the group is predicated. History is interpreted by the state in conservative extremist ideological terms, and events and symbols of the glorious past of the people are linked with the people of the present. The group of the present is the manifestation of the glory of the people of the past.

Conservative extremists place a premium on societal order over individual freedoms and argue that unrestrained individualism leads to disorder. Whereas classic liberals and libertarians assert that the state is subservient to the individual, conservative extremists argue that such individualism leads to conflict, disunity, and chaos. Conservative extremists argue that such a society constructed on selfishness and conflict is an affront to order, progress, and morality (Ingersoll, Matthews, and Davison, 2001, 219–220). Instead, conservative extremists argue that there is no freedom without order, and that it is in a "morally pure" and orderly society that freedom is the greatest. As a consequence, individuals essentially have no rights, but only whatever privileges are granted them by the state or preferred group entity. As a consequence, no parties, interest groups, religions, or other institutions that are deemed to be in conflict with the good of the preferred group (as defined by the charismatic leader or governing authorities) are allowed. The only societal groups allowed are those so designated by the governing authorities, since it is they who determine what is in the interest of the common good (Ingersoll, Matthews, and Davison, 2001, 220–221). The social structure that emerges is one that is termed as "corporatism," where certain societal representative groups are granted monopolies on representation for different segments of society and incorporated into the state itself.

Although conservative extremism shares a tendency toward authoritarianism with Leninist communism, conservative extremism is in other ways antithetical to communism in that communism constructs a society based on class, regardless of race, ethnicity, religion, or heritage. In conservative extremist ideologies, a pluralist society cannot be classless because ethnic minorities, minority religious groups, and other minority groups designated as substandard by the authorities, cannot be placed on equal footing with the preferred group. Furthermore, class interests could be expected to conflict with group unity and therefore may conflict with the common good. As such, it is not accidental that Mussolini's Fascists came to power in Italy at a time that the middle and upper classes feared the growing political power of Italy's communists (Ingersoll, Matthews, and Davison, 2001, 220–221).

MILITARISM

Conservative extremism has typically contained elements of Spartan machismo and militarism and lent itself toward military adventurism. Typically, the conservative extremists view military conflict as inevitable and even desirable and right, since it is only natural that the stronger and "better" people should rule over the weak (Woods, 1989, 126–127). Essentially, if the preferred group is to be better than all others, it follows that the preferred group may prove their superiority on the battlefield. By testing themselves against other groups or nation-states, the preferred conservative extremist group can assess their progress in their quest to become the superior people encompassed in their own mythology. Some conservative extremists, however, may become isolationists and anti-internationalists because of their lack of trust for outsiders and their reverence for their preferred group (Woods, 1989, 126–127).

ANTI-INTELLECTUALISM

Conservative extremism also contains a strain of anti-intellectualism due to its preference for emotion over substance. If the charismatic leader is to mobilize the masses, he must move them through emotive symbols rather than sound analysis. After all, sound analysis is unlikely to support the notion of the superiority of the preferred group in the first place. Additionally, the conservative extremists typically value action as more important than ideas anyway. Consequently, there is little reason to study the great questions intently when faster solutions to society's problems can be achieved through action (Ingersoll, Matthews, and Davison, 2001, 219–221).

The anti-intellectual and action-based focus of conservative extremism is echoed by political theorists Nietzsche and Sorel. Sorel (1969) argued that action was a necessary part of political activity and that thought was mere rationalization. Sorel therefore called for action (including violence), not thought, as a prerequisite for overthrowing what he viewed as the hedonistic, materialistic, liberal democratic state. Similarly, Nietzsche argued that rationalism was bankrupt as a means for political change and that instead, at rare moments in history, an exceptional leader could emerge who could lead the people to correct societal problems.

The action is necessary because conservative extremists view the entire existing society as decadent and in need of total abolition and replacement with a newer, better society (Muller, 1987, 29–30). As a consequence, the typical conservative preference for minimal government is replaced by the urgent need to install the "correct" political program before the forces of darkness completely destroy society. An ideology that has as its basis the need for abolition of an existing order is particularly inclined to stress the "spirit" of a new political order rather than its content; hence, action is placed over substance (Woods, 1989, 127). As such, conservative extremism typically becomes anti-democratic in character. In this construct, democratic rights and liberties will have to be limited in order to protect the good of the preferred group. After all, democracy allows the possibility that leaders will be elected who do not subscribe to the views of the conservative extremists. In order to ensure that right-thinking individuals of the preferred group are elected, it is therefore necessary to limit political participation to the preferred group itself. Furthermore, rights of those who are not in the preferred group will necessarily have to be limited to ensure that those in the preferred group also occupy the preferred positions in society. As a consequence, Hitler revoked the rights of the Jews in Nazi Germany, and conservative extremists imposed segregation and Jim Crow laws on African-Americans in the American South following Reconstruction.

Problems with Conservative Extremism

SORDID HISTORY

Obviously, the largest problem for conservative extremism is its sordid history of intolerance, narrow-mindedness, injustice, brutality, holocausts and witch hunts that have permeated its presence throughout human history. From the Salem witch hunts, to the KKK lynchings, to the bombing of abortion clinics, to the death of Matthew Shepard, to the Oklahoma City bombing, to the attacks of 9/11, conservative extremists have repeatedly proven to be dangerous to their fellow human beings. In the twentieth century, conservative extremist ideologies came to power in a number of countries with disastrous results. Most notably, conservative extremism led to the military expansionist policies of Nazi Germany, Imperial Japan, and Fascist Italy in the 1930s, and to the oppressive regime of the Taliban in Afghanistan at the end of the century. Rights were trampled everywhere the conservative extremists took over, nations and peoples were conquered by the conservative extremist regimes, and enemies of the regimes were massacred by the millions. With the Holocaust in Europe, the Bataan Death March in the Pacific, and the great calamity in general that was World War II largely blamed on conservative extremists by the rest of the world, conservative extremism was effectively discredited as of 1945. After the photographs of the Nazi concentration camps became public knowledge, the idea of the great state built on racial supremacy could no longer be innocently supported (Billig, 1979, 157–158). As a consequence, conservative extremist groups have been relegated to the fringes of the political spectrum with very limited support, and their parties and ideas are typically shunned by more mainstream conservatives (Billig, 1979, 152–153). Furthermore, no conservative extremist party has risen to power in any developed industrial democracy in the six decades following World War II. The closest that any have come is Jean Marie LePen's second-place electoral showing in France in 2003, but Le Pen was trounced in the national election for president against Jaques Chirac, gaining only 18 percent of the vote. Although LePen's second-place showing is certainly significant, it is difficult to say that he was near winning an election when he lost five votes out of six.

Conflict with Classic Liberalism and Libertarianism

Although the legacy of the past is undoubtedly its biggest problem, conservative extremism also has another impediment to its success in that it conflicts with the individualism of libertarianism and classic liberalism. In conservative extremism, the good of the preferred group takes precedence over any individual rights. In the words of Mussolini (quoted in Somerville and Santoni, eds., 1963, 426),

> The Fascist conception of life stresses the importance of the State and accepts the individual only insofar as his interests coincide with those of the State.

As a consequence, conservative extremist ideas can be expected to be shunned as anathema by the more "mainstream" classic liberals in the

Republican Party, as well as by libertarians, who place a premium on the individual.

Conservative extremism also created very large, powerful, and coercive states in Germany, Italy, and Japan in the 1930s. Such a state is completely at odds with the limited government ideals of classic liberals and libertarians. Similarly, the coercive states in Germany, Italy, and Japan of the 1930s created corporatist structures, command economies, and tremendous governmental intervention into the social order, to the degree that even individual thought was a concern of the state. The space between public and private spheres became blurred or destroyed with the result that the state was entitled to regulate all aspects of economic, political and social life (Freeden, 2003, 91). All of these state intrusions are abhorrent to classic liberals and libertarians.

Conservative extremism also tends to break down the rule of law and replace it with rule by the whim of the charismatic leader. The distinctions between legality and illegality become blurred so that ordinary citizens (especially those who do not belong to the preferred group) are unable to discern which side of the law they are on and whether or not the state is their friend or foe. This breakdown of the rule of law is in direct conflict with the premises of classic liberalism and therefore hinders the ability of conservative extremists to expand their appeal in contemporary liberal democracies.

INACCURATE VIEWS OF HISTORY AND REALITY

Conservative extremism has also often been criticized for championing inaccurate portrayals of reality and history. For instance, Jean Marie LePen in 1987 all but denied the Holocaust during World War II. In the words of LePen:

> I ask myself a certain number of questions. I'm not saying that gas chambers did not exist. I have not been able to see any myself. I have not specially studied the question. But I consider it a matter of detail in the history of the Second World War.... I say that some historians are debating these questions (*Observer*, 1987).

If LePen's perspective were unique, then one could discount it as a function of LePen's individual personal ignorance and psychology. Instead, however, Holocaust denial has become prevalent in conservative extremist literature. For example, Richard Harwood wrote a pamphlet in 1974 denying the Holocaust titled *Did Six Million Really Die?* The pamphlet became widely circulated among conservative extremists all over the world and led to the publication of similar works (Billig, 1989, 157). Soon, Holo-caust denial even began to spread marginally over into mainstream con-servative American politics. For instance, Pat Buchanan, a former speech writer for President Richard Nixon and frequent candidate for the pres-idency, essentially denied some aspects of the Holocaust in an article he wrote in the *New York Post* in 1990. In this article, Buchanan discusses what he termed as a "Holocaust Survivor Syndrome" that involved what he labeled as "group fantasies of martyrdom and heroics." Buchanan went on to deny that people were killed in Nazi death camps from toxic fumes produced by diesel engines and pumped into sealed rooms, thus essen-tially denying known historical facts while simultaneously displaying an ignorance of diesel engines. More recently came the publication of Arthur R. Butz' 2003 book titled *The Hoax of the Twentieth Century: The Case Against the Presumed Extermination of European Jewry.* The title itself per-haps tells the reader all one needs to know.

The denial of the Holocaust, as incredible as it may seem, is not merely an attempt to rewrite or deny one isolated event in history, but is part of the "plot-mentality" paranoia that tends to afflict conservative extremists. The Holocaust-denying extremists are essentially arguing that recorded history is a lie and a myth that has been fed to the people as part of a global plot, in this case by the Jews and liberals who control the media, the universities, and, in their view, just about everything and every-one else. The conservative extremists in this case view the whole world as hopelessly duped, while they alone possess the wisdom and understand-ing to see through the plot for what it is (Billig, 1989, 158). To the rest of the world, however, the plot-mentality conservative extremists merely appear to be either stupid, willfully ignorant, mentally unstable, or all three.

Concluding Remarks

Whether it be African-American Jesse Owens winning a sprint in the 1936 Olympics in Berlin, African-American Joe Louis winning a boxing match, or Soviet tanks rolling into Berlin, Adolf Hitler was faced with constant reminders that his myth of Aryan supremacy was in real-ity just that: nothing but myth. Obviously, the inglorious deaths of both Hitler and Mussolini did little to perpetuate the myths of their superior leadership. In essence, all racial superiority myths and leader-cult myths are doomed to failure because all human groups and all human leaders suffer from human flaws and imperfections, not to mention their own mortality. Those flaws and imperfections are easily revealed when the preferred group is challenged, thus eventually exposing the conservative extremist myths for what they are. The only real question is how many people can be deceived by the myths, and for how long. Unfortunately, in the cases of Germany, Italy, and Japan in the 1930s, it was too many people for too long, and the result was the death of millions. No such charismatic leader has yet arisen in the United States with a legitimate chance at taking power, but if it were possible for conservative extremists to take over in Japan, Germany, and Italy in the 1930s, it is conceivable that they could take over in the United States, a nation that is historically predisposed to conservatism in comparison to other developed democracies. In fact, many American liberals try to draw numerous parallels between President George W. Bush and the most notorious conservative extremist of the last century, Adolf Hitler. Columnist David Lindorff (2004), for instance, in *This Can't Be Happening!*, compares Bush's War on terror to Hitler's rampage across Europe, equates what he sees as propaganda from the Bush administration to the Hitler/Goebbels propaganda of the 1930s, and compares John Aschcroft's Justice Department to the former East German police state of "citizen spies." Although Bush's popularity in Europe is the lowest of any American president in recent memory, he achieved reelection in 2004 with a majority of the popular vote, suggesting that majority of Americans are exceptionally conservative in comparison to their European counterparts and the liberal critics of the Bush administration in the U.S. This exceptional American predisposition to conservatism is clearly related to the people and traditions that have permeated its unique history of individualism, religiosity, immigration, and frontier.

6

Contemporary Liberalism

The third major ideology in the American political landscape is known as contemporary liberalism or reform liberalism. Reform liberals are the liberals of the present and are generally those referred to when contemporary Americans use the word "liberals." Reform Liberals or contemporary liberals have also tended to be members of the Democratic Party since the 1930s.

Contemporary liberalism as it is known in the U.S. emerged out of the populist and progressive eras of the late nineteenth and early twentieth centuries and became labeled as "liberal" with the New Deal of Franklin Roosevelt in the 1930s. Roosevelt and his supporters purposefully selected the term "liberal" to describe their New Deal programs in order to connect with America's free-market classic liberal traditions, but also to connect with progressives, who had been important on the American political left for the previous three decades. The word "liberal" also had the added advantage of disassociating Roosevelt and his programs and supporters from socialists and communists, even though many New Deal programs were, in fact, socialist or communitarian in character, and contemporary liberalism shares many of the ideas of socialism (Skocpol, 1983, 87–104). Contemporary liberalism in the United States is also generally associated with welfare state capitalism and social reform movements, whether for civil rights, gay rights, protection of animals, or protection of the environment.

Government as a Solution

The basic idea behind the New Deal, which remains perhaps the central tenet of contemporary liberalism, is the idea that government can provide the solutions to the societal problems left unsolved by the free

99

market. Contemporary liberals generally accept the classic liberal notion that the free market is most efficient; however, they view the free market as also extremely harsh and fraught with problems that do not necessarily serve the common good. As a consequence, contemporary liberals desire to use government wherever necessary to intervene into the free market and make corrections in the interest of the common good and the less fortunate (Dolbeare and Dolbeare, 1976, 72–75).

The use of government to intervene in the free market in the interest of the common good and the common person has its roots in the populist movement of the late nineteenth century in the United States. The populists favored the use of government to establish what political scientists term "positive liberty." Whereas classic liberals, with their adherence to limited government and the free market, sought to provide "negative liberty," or the removal of governmental or societal barriers to their freedom of choice, the populists went a step further to use government to provide the means for the overcoming of deficiencies and other societal impediments to the exercise of free choice. The basic idea is that even with every obstacle to freedom of choice removed (such as special privileges for nobility), many people may lack the means or opportunity to exercise their freedom of choice due to the unavailability of jobs, physical handicaps, the effects of racism or sexism, or their own inability to fund the education necessary to exercise their choices. A very bright person with the intellectual ability and test scores to get into medical school, for instance, may not be able to achieve the desired goals if that person is from a low-income family and lacks the economic means to pay for school. Contemporary liberals argue that government is therefore needed to step in and provide the solutions, whether they be the means for education, job training programs, child care, or rules that mitigate the effects of racism and sexism (Hoover, 1994, 83).

VICTIMIZATION

Contemporary liberalism often includes a strain of victimization, where people, often of lower income or ethnic minority status, feel victimized by specific groups and entities within society. For example, the agricultural populists of the late nineteenth century suffered economic hardship as a result of low prices for agricultural commodities during the time period, as American farmers produced more agricultural goods than the global market could absorb. The populists, however, believed that they were being victimized by railroads, grain elevators, banks, and crooked politicians who were profiting at their expense. Although much of the victimization was imaginary and the farmers' problems often had more to do with free market forces than human corruption, it was also true that some of the railroad practices, such as charging higher prices where they lacked competition and lower prices where competition was present, were debatably unscrupulous. As a result, the populists pushed for government regulation of railroads, banks, and grain elevators, including government-set railroad rates, government loan programs, and inflationary monetary policies intended to drive up the price of agricultural goods (Garraty, 1991, 603–605).

The quest for "positive liberty" did not die with the populist movement, but continued to influence the successive political-left movements of the twentieth century that followed, including the progressives of Theodore Roosevelt and Woodrow Wilson, the New Dealers of the 1930s, the Fair Deal of Harry Truman, and the Great Society of Lyndon Johnson in the 1960s. Progressives in the early twentieth century, for example, pushed for more regulation of railroads, greater labor rights, limits on child labor, anti-trust legislation, government regulations of food and drug industries, better sanitation in the workplace, and numerous government reforms aimed at the elimination of corruption so as to eliminate the oppression of the "little people" (Brinkley, 2003, 576–583). In the 1930s, the reform liberals of the New Deal pushed for government programs to help the victims of the Great Depression with public works programs and direct relief. The New Deal also brought the beginning of federal entitlements with the introduction of Social Security (Freidel, 1964, 76–91). In the 1960s, reform liberals focused on removing the oppression of minorities and women with the Civil Rights Act of 1964, the Voting Rights Act of 1965, and the introduction of affirmative action programs designed to bring "positive liberty" to both academia and the workplace. All of these directions of liberalism mirrored the populists of the late nineteenth century in that they sought to protect the "little people" who believed, correctly or incorrectly, they were being victimized by more powerful forces (Skidmore, 1993, 37).

GOVERNMENT AS A REMEDY
TO FREE-MARKET HARSHNESS

In their pursuit of positive liberty, contemporary liberals make a serious break with classic liberalism in their argument that government must intervene in the free market to alleviate harsh dislocations such as economic recessions and unemployment. Whereas classic liberals view the free market as the solution to most problems, contemporary liberals view the free market as in constant change and fluctuation driven by the laws of supply and demand. Inevitably, some of the fluctuations will have negative effects on some segments of the population. In other words, instead of solving all problems as classic liberals suggest, contemporary liberals argue that the free market creates numerous problems of its own. Contemporary liberals essentially argue that Adam Smith's rising tide does not lift all boats: some are prevented from rising due to heavy anchors and chains attached to them by more powerful boats. Contemporary liberals therefore argue that government intervention is the appropriate tool to adjust for shifts and fluctuations of the free market for the benefit of all society. Contemporary liberals have not abandoned all of the principles of the classic liberal free market, but instead favor a mixed economy with some goods and services delivered privately and some publicly, but all government sectors regulated to ensure the common good (Sargent, 1993, 100).

Contemporary liberals argue that the introduction of new technologies, while producing new employment in some economic sectors, may create unemployment in others. For example, the invention of refrigeration in the early twentieth century clearly created employment in a new economic sector that did not previously exist (refrigerators and air conditioners). Simultaneously, unemployment quickly developed in the home ice delivery business. Rather than just let the ice delivery person starve, contemporary liberals favor government intervention in the form of an unemployment insurance program and/or job training and education programs that will prevent displaced workers from starving while they retrain and subsequently find new employment. The programs are supported by taxation and therefore lead to market inefficiency, since taxation depresses consumption and investment. But contemporary liberals place what they view as the common good, in this case the elimination of the harshest effects of unemployment, over market efficiency or lower taxes as a desired end (Hoover, 1994, 84–88).

The types of government intervention supported by contemporary liberals and designed to alleviate the harshness of the free market are numerous. Worker's compensation insurance that compensates workers for on-the-job injury is a good example. Workplace safety laws that are designed to prevent workplace injuries in the first place are another, as is unemployment insurance. Environmental laws, many of which clearly make the free market less efficient, are further examples of government intervention into the free market in the interest of producing a public good rather than profit.

Intrinsic Equality

Contemporary liberals typically accept the idea of intrinsic equality, or the equal value of each human life regardless of talents, assets, or other capacities. Consequently, contemporary liberals attempt to construct institutions that reflect and reinforce the belief that no person is inherently superior or inferior to another (Dahl, 1989, 84–88). Contemporary liberals also argue that the free market, by nature, produces income inequality, which they see as a violation of this core value. As previously discussed in the section on the problems of classic liberalism, contemporary liberals point out that in a pure merit system, if the "cream" rises to the top, as classic liberals say that it does, then there must also be a "scum" that falls to the bottom. Clearly, there are those in society who are born with greater talents than others, and the free market can be expected to reward them accordingly; hence, economic inequality is a certain result of the free market. Whereas classic liberals are not necessarily concerned with great income inequalities, contemporary liberals are much more in agreement with Plato's assertion that no one in a society should make more than five times that of anyone else. The preference for a more equal society in terms of income has a long history in the United States, and was well enunciated by Ben Franklin, who argued:

> The Combinations of Civil Society are not like those of a Set of Merchants, who club their Property in different Proportions for Building and Freighting a Ship, and may therefore have some Right to vote in dispositions of the Voyage in a greater or less Degree according to their respective Contributions; but the important ends of Civil Society, and the personal Securities of Life and Liberty, these remain the same in every Member of the society; and the poorest continues to have an equal Claim to them with the most opulent, whatever Difference Time, Chance, or Industry may occasion in their Circumstances [quoted in Lynd, 1982, 71].

In order to remedy what they see as the injustice of gross income inequality where the wealthy live in the world's greatest opulence while the poor starve in squalor, contemporary liberals favor income redistribution plans (welfare) in an attempt to alleviate the suffering of the "have-nots" (Freeden, 2003, 83). Such programs have to be funded, obviously, by the "haves"; hence, contemporary liberals favor shifting the tax burdens to the rich and redistributing that income to the poor. In short, contemporary liberals see themselves as essentially modern-day Robin Hoods, who tend to take from the rich and give to the poor, but they are perhaps much less popular than Robin Hood for doing so. Contemporary liberals point out, however, that even the champion of the free market, Adam Smith, favored some luxury taxes and redistribution of wealth to the poor (Prewit et al., 1991, 76).

Contemporary liberals also argue that the free market allows inequalities of opportunity and tyranny of the majority. The fact that African Americans were denied equal rights, including economic rights, in the United States until well into the twentieth century is a case in point. The continued (though greatly reduced) income disparity between men and women, and the fact that women could not vote in federal elections across the country until 1920, is another. As a consequence, contemporary liberals favor programs such as affirmative action that are designed to reduce inequalities of opportunity. Similarly, contemporary liberals champion the equal protection clause of the Fourteenth Amendment as an avenue toward the protection of the rights of minorities against the tyranny of the majority (Hoover, 1994, 87).

No Moral Absolutes

On the subject of morality, contemporary liberals are greatly at odds with traditional conservatives, essentially producing a "culture clash" within the American body politic. Contemporary liberals typically view the world in natural or secular rather than religious terms, and view the role of God in the universe and in human existence as irrelevant to the construction of a sound political system. Contemporary liberals hold that there are no moral absolutes and that whatever morals are present are established by society. Similarly, social arrangements are not ordered by God or nature, as traditional conservatives might suggest, but socially created by human societies (Schumaker, Kiel, and Heilke, 1996, 275). Slavery and polygamy, for example, morally accepted in antiquity but now generally viewed as immoral (as discussed in chapter 3), are two prime examples, but further examples are legion. For instance, in Afghanistan at present, it is generally considered immoral for women not to wear veils, while in the U.S., it generally is not. In the United States, however, it is generally unacceptable for women to expose their breasts in public, even at most beaches, while topless women on beaches are very common in Europe with no social stigma. Similarly, President Clinton's indiscretions in the Oval Office contributed to a rift in American politics not seen since Reconstruction, i.e., the impeachment of a President; while the European reaction to Clinton's indiscretion was much more muted (Vaisse, 2001).

The abandonment of moral absolutes as a guide leads contemporary liberals to espouse the expansion of individual liberties and choice. In other words, if one chooses to consume alcohol, that choice should be protected as long as it does not harm the public good, and there certainly should not be a constitutional amendment preventing such a choice. Similarly, if an individual chooses a homosexual lifestyle instead of a heterosexual one, that choice should also be protected because there is no authority to judge for certain that it is morally wrong. The same can be said for the choices to gamble, use mind-altering drugs such as marijuana, and engage in sexual activity outside of marriage (Galston, 1986, 131).

REJECTION OF FATALISM

Partially as a result of their secular approach to human problems, contemporary liberals tend to be much less fatalistic than traditional conservatives and believe that people have the capacity to shape their own future. Contemporary liberals tend to argue that nothing in human history or the future is predetermined by God, nature, or any other non-human entity, but the events of history are the result of human actions and decisions. The great reform liberal economist, John Maynard Keynes, for example, argued that the belief that there was some "law of nature" that precluded human intervention in the free market was "nonsense" (Keynes, 1980, 90–91).

Contemporary liberals do argue, however, that the progress of society requires the fostering of certain liberal values, including a commitment to social justice, a respect for the rights of others, and a willingness to protect liberal rights and values, such as freedom of speech and equality under law. Contemporary liberals argue that these core values of liberalism must be protected by the power of the state (Galston, 1989, 93). If society is allowed to abandon these core values, contemporary liberals believe that society may regress. In short, contemporary liberals believe that people have the ability to shape a just and moral society, but may choose injustice and tyranny instead.

Contemporary liberals tend to believe that people do not all celebrate the same values and that individuals may continuously alter their own values to conform to new information and experiences. Consequently, all persons may not choose values that are consistent with a liberal capitalist system; hence, government must go beyond merely protecting liberal values, and should also play a role in teaching and dispersing them (Schumaker, Kiel, and Heilke, 1996, 275–276). This position obviously sets up contemporary liberals in a position to clash with traditional conservatives, who desire to use the government to teach and enforce what they see as moral absolutes, some of which may be illiberal in character.

Communitarian Perspective

Contemporary liberals also tend to be more communitarian than their conservative counterparts and tend to view the group, whether society as a whole or a smaller group within society (such as women, for instance) as the basic social unit. Consequently, contemporary liberals have a tendency to search out the good of the entire community first, rather than first seeking the good of the individual (Freeden, 2003, 83). In general, this perspective can be summed up as a belief in the greatest good for the greatest number. Contemporary liberals, much more than classic liberals or traditional conservatives, view human existence in terms of relations with other human beings as well as relations between people and their environment (Freeden, 2003, 83). In this perspective, it is perfectly moral, for instance, to break up corporate monopolies, whether they be John Rockefeller's oil monopoly of the 19th century or Bill Gates' not truly monopolistic software empire of the 21st century, regardless of whether the company in question has intentionally and maliciously violated laws, as long as the common good is served.

ENVIRONMENTALISM

Similarly, contemporary liberals believe that individuals may be prevented from damaging the environment in the interest of the common good, even if it infringes on their rights to do as they please with their own property. Environmentalists argue that unregulated capitalism will lead to the destruction of the environment for the benefit of wealthy elites at the expense of the common good (Naess, 1984, 28). Environmentalists also tend to argue that finite resources on the earth are endangered by unrestrained capitalism and therefore must be protected with government intervention to produce cleaner technologies (Schumacher, 1973). In general, "liberal" Democrats tend to favor greater environmental protection even at the expense of economic gains, while "conservative" Republicans tend to favor using more of the natural environment in the interest of economic advantage. American environmental policies since the 1960s reflect this political struggle.

Environmental concerns were not high on the American national agenda for most of the nation's history, but rose to a prominent place in the United States during the volatile 1960s (Shabecroff, 1993, 34). The new visibility of environmental concerns that developed in the 1960s gained impetus from an abundance of scientific evidence that suggested America's industrial prosperity and technological advancement had come at the expense of the environment. An absence of any national strategy for environmental preservation had left the country with severe air and water pollution and problems with solid waste removal that were easily noticeable by the general public. All that was needed was a precipitant to mobilize the public into political action.

In 1962, marine biologist Rachel Carson wrote *Silent Spring*, a book about the impact of pesticides on the environment, which became a best seller and piqued the awareness of many Americans about the destruction of the environment. Carson focused on the poisoning of the environment with the pesticide DDT, but she broadened the inquiry to examine how carelessly applied science and technology were destroying the environment in general, leading ultimately to the destruction of human life. Carson raised the question of whether advanced industrial societies could survive over the long term if they destroyed their own environments and essentially answered that they could not.

What followed Carson's work was an environmental movement that seemingly sprouted from everywhere in the U.S. Americans were urged not to pollute through magazine and television advertising placed in the national media by various groups. Among the most famous and effective was an ad placed in 1971 by the Advertising Council, a political arm of the advertising industry, which showed a "Native American" (actually an Italian American actor) in a canoe meandering through a river littered with refuse. At the end of the commercial, a tear rolled down the "native's" cheek, sending the message, "If we don't clean up America, it won't be America any more" (Shabecoff, 1993, 42).

The environmental movement was also given another boost by Ralph Nader's 1965 book, *Unsafe at Any Speed*, a book that attacked the automobile industry with a focus on unsafe automobiles, Nader included in the book a chapter on air pollution from automobiles, in which Nader argued that automobile manufacturers were "using the atmosphere as a septic tank." Nader formed private state and national public interest research groups and included environmental protection as one of their stated goals (Paniccia, 1996, 15).

The 1960s also witnessed several sensational environmental events, including the shocking fire that burned on the Cuyahoga River in Cleveland; because the river was so polluted with petroleum products and other chemicals, it was able to ignite. Another disaster was an oil spill off the coast of Santa Barbara that presented Americans with TV images of dead birds washing up on the oil-slicked shores (Crispino, 1996, 29).

By the 1970s, another offshoot of environmentalism gained momentum in the form of opposition to the use of animals for scientific experimentation. Peter Singer, in his 1975 book titled *Animal Liberation*, detailed poor conditions and unnecessary pain inflicted on laboratory animals. Tom Regan (1983, 393) took the argument a step further and argued for animal rights on the basis that no living thing should be treated as if it is merely there for the use of others. Regan argued that just as people should not be harmed for the benefit of others, neither should animals be harmed; he thus called for rights for animals on par with those of human beings.

These works and events combined to create a political climate where concern for the environment became politically expedient for both major parties. Congress responded to the new public environmental awareness by taking on an environmental leadership role, and the result was the environmental "revolution" of the 1970s, a slew of congressional statutes and new federal rules and agencies, including the Environmental Protection Agency (EPA), purposed to protect the environment. Critics charged, however, that the new federal government concern for protection of the environment often came at the expense of individual property rights, corporate profits, and economic well-being. The sacrifice of individual rights and economic advancement for the environmental good therefore placed contemporary liberals in the position of a values clash with classic liberals and libertarians, who oppose such infringements on individual rights and economic efficiency.

Idealism

Contemporary liberals adhere to an idealist view of human nature and argue that people are naturally good and cooperative, but corrupted by society and their own socialization experiences. Contemporary liberals argue that all human behaviors, both proper and improper, are learned. Consequently, criminals can be taught proper behavior, and can learn to avoid and to cease their participation in criminal behavior. The liberals' prescriptions are generally much less retributive in character and geared more toward treatment or rehabilitation. In the area of crime, liberals again focus on the idea of creating positive liberty by eliminating the social conditions, such as poverty, low education levels, handguns, racial injustice, and substance abuse, that correlate with criminal behavior (Vold and Bernard, 1986, 210).

The reform liberal view of crime, which became the policy guide in the late 1960s until the mid–1970s, is reflected in the 1967 report of the Presidential Commission on Crime. The Commission concluded that crime was the result of disorganization in American society and a lack of resources dedicated to law enforcement, adjudication, and corrections. The Commission also concluded that rehabilitation had been insufficiently emphasized in the treatment of offenders, and therefore corrections should be reoriented away from retribution and toward rehabilitation. Consequently, the Commission recommended focusing on the elimination of social conditions that contribute to crime and focusing on the elimination of racial injustices (Clear and Cole, 1990, 33).

Premium on Labor

Contemporary liberals place a premium on labor, rather than capitalist investors or corporations, as the fundamental element around which society is structured. Contemporary liberals also view the workplace as another area where government intervention to produce positive liberty is required, since the unfettered market of the late nineteenth century allowed scores of abuses, such as unsafe work places, company scrip, company stores, and child labor. As a consequence, contemporary liberals champion protections for workers against tyranny in the workplace, including workplace safety, unemployment insurance, workers' compensation insurance, protections against discrimination based on sex and ethnicity, and the right to bargain collectively (Freeden, 2003, 83). Contemporary liberals are therefore more likely than classic liberals or traditional conservatives to view labor unions as a positive force in society for the protection of common people against the tyranny of the rich and powerful.

Liberation Ideologies

Among the more radical strands of contemporary liberalism are the liberation ideologies of feminists, gays, and ethnic minorities. Both ethnic and women's liberationists, along with gay rights advocates, view themselves as victims in a system that contains structural impediments to their advancement. As a consequence, liberationists, whether based on ethnicity or sex, place a premium not only on providing negative liberty, but on using government to secure positive liberty for their own particular group. Undoubtedly, American political society has a history of structural impediments to the advancement of gays, minorities, and women; consequently, the tendency of these groups to categorize themselves as victims has a solid foundation in historical facts. African Americans in particular need go no further than the issue of slavery to prove their point. Women can point to the fact that they did not have the right to vote in nationwide federal elections until 1920. Gays need look no further than the Web site of Westboro Baptist Church in Topeka, Kansas (godhatesfags.com), to prove that there are those in the U.S. who oppose their very existence. Similarly, other minorities, including the Irish, Catholics, Jews, and Asians who suffered from the anti-immigrant and anti–Catholic backlash of the 19th century, the Japanese who were interned in concentration camps during World War II, and Arab Muslims of the present who may be more subject to searches at airports, may all point to their own histories and instances of victimization (D'Emilio, 1983).

The African American liberation movement of the twentieth century is a textbook model of liberation ideology. African Americans viewed themselves as victimized and envisioned liberation as the abolition of race-based barriers to their individual freedom (Hamilton, 1972). The movement also developed a significant degree of pride in African American ethnicity and identity. African Americans argued that racism in the United States had been internalized by whites and blacks alike, to the extent that blacks, who had been taught that they were inferior, came to believe in their own inferiority (Sargent, 1993, 127). As a consequence, the movement in the 1960s developed the slogan "black is beautiful" to assert that their own values and culture were equal or superior to others. The basic idea is that in order for an oppressed minority to develop the self-confidence necessary to stand up to discrimination and to achieve liberation, a healthy measure of pride and self-worth is required (Grier and Cobbs, 1968). Typically, liberation ideologies seek the end of stereotypes and the creation of a society that is neutral to ethnic minority status. In turn, the elimination of stereotypes is purposed to secure freedom of choice for the oppressed group. In particular, liberation ideologies tend to target forms of economic discrimination and advocate the use of government to eliminate their economic impediments (Hoover, 1994, 197–198). In more extreme cases, however, those who subscribe to liberation ideologies may argue for separation of their group from the community as a whole (Hoover, 1994, 219).

Liberation ideologies also tend to focus on raising the consciousness of group members, but also of society as a whole toward identifying practices that hinder the liberty or rob the dignity of the minority group. Liberation ideology may target customs and practices that society as a whole does not necessarily view as oppressive, but which the minority group does, even if the oppression is unconscious (Grier and Cobbs, 1968). For example, many African Americans object to the Confederate flag as a symbol of slavery and oppression, while some others may simply view the flag as a harmless symbol of Southern pride.

Good examples of a black liberation ideology would include the theses of black ministers James Cone and Albert Cleage during the black liberation movement of the late 1960s and early 1970s. In *Black Theology and Black Power* (1969), Cone argues that Christianity is a religion of liberation and that the struggle of oppressed African Americans for political, social, and economic justice is a central component of Christ's message. Furthermore, Cone (1969, 113) criticizes African American Christian churches for their adoption of what he refers to as the "white lie" that Christianity is primarily concerned with life after death. For Cone, Christianity is not primarily about salvation of the soul in the next life, but instead is all about black liberation. Similarly, Albert Cleage (1972, xxviii), minister of the Shrine of the Black Madonna in Detroit, argues that whites introduced blacks to Christianity for their pacification and for the purpose of supporting the imposed authority of white supremacy. Cleage argues that the Christian message was given to blacks so that they could endure suffering at the hands of whites in this world due to promise of reward for their suffering in the next world. Cleage (1972, 8) draws his inspiration from Marcus Garvey, a radical black leader in the late 1920s who organized the African Orthodox Church and developed the idea that God, Jesus, Mary, and the angels were all black. Cleage (1972, 4) argues that Christians must accept the fact that Jesus was black and that his purpose was that of a black revolutionary leader seeking to lead blacks to freedom. Similarly, Cone (1970, 120–121) also views God as at least figuratively black and argues that God reveals Himself with His blackness, meaning that "God is identified with the oppressed to the point that their experience becomes his or he is a God of racism." Cone goes on to argue that "because God has made the goal of Black people his own goal, Black Theology believes that it is not only appropriate but necessary to begin the doctrine of God with an insistence on his blackness" (quoted in Cone, 1970, 121).

Another example of black liberation ideology is represented by the Nation of Islam, a black separatist group that stresses not only liberation, but black supremacy, black self-help, and racial separateness. The adoption of Islam as a religion helps separate blacks from others in American society, with worship on Friday instead of Sunday, dietary restrictions, and other customs and traditions central to Islam (although other Muslims in the world do not necessarily accept America's Nation of Islam as "true Muslims"; Johnstone, 1992, 253). The Nation of Islam encourages its members to "buy black," or support black-owned businesses with black patronage, secure education at black universities, and achieve success without help from non-blacks (Johnstone, 1992, 253).

Feminism

Feminism is a liberation ideology that gained widespread appeal in the 1960s as women organized to oppose what they saw as the oppression of women by men. Like other subscribers to liberation ideology, feminists seek to use government to end their perceived oppression. Feminists are also similar to other liberation ideologies in that they tend to engage in consciousness-raising and other exercises to instill a sense of pride in their own identity. Generally, radical feminists argue that gender differences are largely socially induced as females are conditioned by society to accept inferior status and traditional gender roles (Epstein, 1971).

In addition to fighting for equal opportunity for women and demanding equal pay for equal work, feminists tend to identify and condemn symbols of male supremacy and oppression in society. For example, Sharon Neufer Emswiler (1974) condemns what she views as entrenched sexist practices in religion. Emswiler points out that in spite of the fact that most church members are female, most clergy are male and most other important church offices are also held by men. Emswiler claims that even the music in church tends to be sexist in character and dominated by hymns such as "Rise Up, O Men of God" and "Faith of Our Fathers," and that even the popular songs of Christmas, such as "God Rest Ye Merry, Gentlemen" and "Good Christian Men, Rejoice," tend to support the idea of male dominance. Emswiler (1974, 4) explains the difficulties that these songs impose upon her as a woman, stating that:

> As I try to imagine that these songs are speaking to me, but I am not accustomed to thinking of myself as a "man" or a "brother;" and the identification is difficult, and most often impossible. The only way I can find to identify with these masculine words is to attempt either to deny or set aside my femininity. But I do not want to deny that part of my personhood; I want rather to affirm it.

Emswiler (1974, 3–5) argues that women should be liberated from such sexist religious music: new hymns should be written that are gender-neutral, and old hymns should be re-written to remove their sexist content. Furthermore, women should be allowed to perform all of the same roles in worship as men so as to liberate them from male oppression. Going even further than Emswiler, Mary Daly (1972) argued that the religious community was too ingrained in sexism to reform and therefore called for the liberation of women through "exodus," or the departure of women from male-dominated churches. Finally, in her book *Beyond God the Father* (1985), Daly asserts that the true liberation of women requires the "death of God" as a male, as God generally has been represented throughout the Judeo-Christian era, and the replacement of the traditional "male" God with a gender-neutral concept of God. Only in doing so can the true roots of male oppression be eradicated and true gender equality be achieved.

Problems with Contemporary Liberalism

GOVERNMENT ECONOMIC INTERVENTION CREATES INEFFICIENCY

Like all ideologies, contemporary liberalism is not without its problems. First of all, contemporary liberals admit that governmental intervention in the free market creates inefficiency. That being the case, there surely is a point where too much government intervention creates excessive inefficiency, and the contemporary liberals' governmental solutions in such cases may actually create more problems than they solve (Charles, 1995, 114–118). As a consequence, exactly when government should intervene in the free market and how much intervention is prudent are matters of debate, even among the contemporary liberals themselves. Classic liberals argue that the costs of over-regulation of the economy outweigh the benefits and result in nonsensical regulations. For example, Robert Charles (1995, 115–116) argues that 12 percent of local revenues are now devoted to meeting unfunded federal mandates and that overzealous government regulators ignore costs to industry when formulating regulations. As an example of the absurdity of some of the regulations, Charles states that the EPA considers the aroma of baking bread, in particular the nontoxic ethanol created by mixing flour, water, and yeast, to be a "volatile organic compound" banned by the Clean Air Act of 1990.

In addition to the argument that the government has intervened into the economy too much and at too high a cost, classic liberals argue that exactly what types of intervention into the economy are beneficial is unclear. For example, affirmative action, a system of racial and sex-based preferences in employment and academic admission, has been a controversial program since its inception, and it is unclear if it is the correct tool for eliminating discrimination in hiring based on sex or race. Although there can be little doubt that minorities and women suffered discrimination in the workplace prior to the time that affirmative action was first implemented, it is unclear whether the discrimination that remains is severe enough to merit keeping in place such a system of race and sex-based preferences. Furthermore, while it is certain that there remains in the U.S. some forms of discrimination against women and minorities, it is just as true that affirmative action discriminates against white males on the basis of both race and sex. In other words, combating discrimination, which has been identified as a social evil, with affirmative action, which makes distinctions based on race and sex, is tantamount to fighting discrimination with discrimination. Therefore, to defend affirmative action is essentially to argue that two wrongs make a right (Carter, 1991).

PUBLIC PREFERENCE FOR ECONOMIC
WELL-BEING OVER ENVIRONMENT

Unfortunately both for human beings and for all the other life forms with which we share the earth, virtually all economic activity disrupts the natural environment. Even at the most primitive level in hunting and gathering societies, human efforts to subsist are disruptive to the natural environment through human selection of plants and animals for human use. Activities as simple as selecting the best berries off a plant for human consumption leave the plant with a reduced reproductive capacity and alter the natural genetic progress of the plant. If the best seeds are selected for consumption, while the worst seeds are left on the plant, the species will eventually be stuck with a reproductive cycle that produces inferior seeds. Similarly, the hunter is more likely to catch slower prey, over time gradually selecting out slow animals for consumption and leaving the faster ones to breed (Diamond, 1999, 107–113).

Since some disruption of nature is essential for human existence, people must search for the proper long-term balance between their activities and the environment. Classic liberals and libertarians argue that all too often, correction of the environmental problems may cost far too much for the benefits achieved (Charles, 1995, 114–118). Compounding the problem politically is the fact that in general, political leaders in contemporary democracies are largely held responsible by the public for the state of the economy and not for environmental protection (Lindblom, 1977). Furthermore, the American public does not always consider environmental concerns the most important problems facing the U.S. For example, in a 1998 poll that asked respondents to list the most important issues facing the nation, only two percent listed the environment. Similarly, only one percent of respondents in a January 1995 Gallup poll considered the environment to be the "most important problem" facing the U.S. (Bosso, 2000, 56–57). Consequently, political leaders often can be expected to be more zealous in securing a robust economy than in preserving the environment, and this priority has been reflected in the anti-regulatory classic liberal ideology of the Republican Party. Republican control of the presidency during the 1980s and of Congress in the latter half of the 1990s, followed by President George W. Bush and a Republican Congress in the new millennium, predictably produced an anti-regulatory backlash at least partially purposed to limit federal regulation of the environment in the interest of greater economic growth.

EXPANDED GOVERNMENT HINDERS LIBERTIES

One need only visit an airport since the 9/11 attacks to be reminded that government, by its very nature, hinders liberties. As a consequence, the efforts by contemporary liberals to correct for free-market harshness, ensure equality of opportunity, and protect against tyranny of the majority, end up creating government programs that may run counter to their ideological preference for the expansion of individual liberties. Furthermore, contemporary liberals are often selective as to which liberties they want expanded. Contemporary liberals generally champion freedom of choice when it comes to freedom of expression, homosexual lifestyles or the decriminalization of marijuana, but those same contemporary liberals tend to favor statutes limiting hate speech and favoring gun control. Critics argue that if freedoms are weakened for one person or group, then society begins down a slippery slope of erosion of liberties in other areas as well (Strossen, 1995, 227–230).

LABOR UNIONS PRODUCE CORRUPTION AND ECONOMIC INEFFICIENCY

Labor unions in the United States are generally much weaker than in Europe, and no Labor Party exists in American politics as they do in European democracies. The development of American labor is undoubtedly limited by Americans' individualism and preference for classic liberal ideology (Cohen, 2000, 125). Labor in the U.S. has been further hindered by the fact that, in the late nineteenth century, early labor unions were disproportionately made up of recent immigrants, thus causing many in the general population to view labor unions as "foreign" in character (Cohen, 2000, 125). Labor was further hindered by violence that accompanied labor union activities of the nineteenth century, such as the Haymarket riots; labor unions therefore became associated in the minds of American conservatives with "bomb-throwing radicals." Violent clashes between striking workers and "scabs," as well as management and Pinkerton security agents, permeated the history of American labor and exacerbated its dangerous image. Between 1876 and 1896, there were more strikes and more persons injured or killed in labor protests in the U.S. than in any other nation (Cohen, 2000, 125–126). Though such incidents have certainly diminished since World War II, conservatives may argue that the reduction in violence is merely due to a significant reduction in union membership. More recently, labor unions have been associated with organized crime; the disappearance in 1975 of labor leader Jimmy Hoffa, who had been associated with organized crime figures, only reinforced the negative union image. In 1998, for instance, survey data suggests that only about thirteen percent of Americans had "a great deal of confidence" in those running labor unions (Cohen, 2000, 132).

Conservatives also argue that labor unions drive up wages and make American industry less competitive, thus driving jobs overseas (Cohen, 2000, 132–133). Although contemporary liberals correctly point out that American workers cannot live on the wages paid in China, conservatives are also correct that labor unions most certainly play a role in increasing American wages. After all, if they did not, why would workers be interested in joining in the first place? Classic liberals argue that the final result is that businesses flee the American labor market and send jobs overseas, a situation viewed as negative by both liberals and conservatives. How large a role labor unions play in the flight of jobs to overseas markets is a matter of debate, but labor unions and contemporary liberals are assigned their share of the blame nonetheless (Cohen, 2000, 132–133).

Too Much Freedom Leads to Disorder

All societies will have to place some limits on behavior in the interest of order. Otherwise, the end result will be that one has the freedom to do anything in the abstract, but the ability to do nothing in reality due to societal chaos. This is essentially what is known as the "law-freedom paradox" of Jean Jacques Rousseau. Rousseau (quoted in Ebenstein and Ebenstein, 1992) argued succinctly that "law limits freedom, but there is no freedom without law." The criticism of contemporary liberals in this regard is that they err too far on the side of individual freedoms, with the result that freedom actually becomes limited through chaos. For example, conservatives argue, rightly or wrongly, that the rights afforded criminals in the United States lead to situations where murderers are acquitted due to legal "technicalities" and walk free among endangered citizens. Similarly, American intelligence entities were well aware that suspected terrorists were attending flight schools in the U.S. prior to 9/11, but because they had committed no crime, their liberties under the U.S. Constitution prevented their detention (Benjamin and Simon, 2002). Furthermore, traditional conservatives argue that many of the "rights" championed by many contemporary liberals are nothing more than types of moral permissiveness that lead to moral decay.

NONCOERCIVE MEASURES HAVE NOT ELIMINATED CRIME

Based on the arguments of contemporary liberals, states have instituted all types of varied treatments and punishments in the American system of corrections since the 1960s. Despite the existence of job training and education programs, psychological counseling, probation, parole, and other innovative programs, the incarceration rate in the United States remains among the highest of industrialized democracies. In contrast, the crime rate in Singapore, where vandals are beaten with a cane, is much lower. Traditional conservatives tend to argue that the treatment programs prescribed by contemporary liberals do not work, and that the only things the criminals understand are coercive punishments (Martinson, 1974, 22).

The conservative criticism is supported by some empirical data that reveal that virtually all correctional policies advocated by contemporary liberals have met with a significant degree of failure. For example, contemporary liberals often herald probation as a more cost-effective alternative than incarceration, since the repeat offender rates for inmates who receive probation are somewhat better than for inmates who receive incarceration. Conservatives point out studies that have revealed that approximately two-thirds of criminals receiving probation are re-arrested for another crime, and that three-fourths of the new arrests are for serious crimes (Petersilia, et al., 1985). Similarly, parole has come under criticism in recent years since studies that have found that two-thirds of parolees were re-arrested within six years after their release. Consequently, some states have abandoned the use of parole in its entirety (Hoffman and Stone-Meierhoefer, 1979, 215).

Due to these failures, conservatives typically continue to favor longer prison sentences, mandatory minimum sentencing, corporal punishment, and the death penalty, thus conflicting with the views of contemporary liberals. Conservatives also tend to favor greater expenditures on law enforcement agencies as opposed to social programs aimed at preventing crime. President Ronald Reagan perhaps well summed up the conservative position on crime when he stated, "Right and wrong matter; individuals are responsible for their actions; retribution should be swift and sure for those who prey on the innocent" (*Justice Assistance News*, 1981, 1).

REDISTRIBUTIVE PROGRAMS
CONFLICT WITH INDIVIDUALISM

As previously discussed, the U.S. is a very individualistic society, and the dominant American ethos supports the notion of self-responsibility. Under the individualist ethic, each person is responsible for his or her own well-being. If an individual is unable to provide for his or her own well-being, it is not necessarily the responsibility of the rest of the community to attend to those needs. Essentially, conservative individualists tend to argue that economic failure on the part of the individual is often his or her own fault, and is largely attributable to a lack of effort. Poverty is therefore often viewed by conservatives as a phenomenon that is individually caused, rather than produced by the structural forces of the free-market society. In other words, the poor have less because they are lazy, lack motivation, or choose not to better themselves (Lipset, 1967, 51). These dominant values of individualism and self-sufficiency contribute to the unpopularity of welfare programs and helped bring political pressure for welfare reform in the Reagan era (Hasenfeld and Refferty, 1989).

Although critics of contemporary liberalism in the United States are not completely unsupportive of aid to the elderly and disabled, they tend to be vehemently opposed to aid to able-bodied individuals because they believe it provides a disincentive to work. Even Democratic President Franklin Roosevelt, whom many credit (or blame) for the current American social welfare system, referred to cash relief as a "narcotic" (Koon, 1997, 4).

Social conservatives also oppose many social programs that they view as inimical to the traditional family or as hindering the development of traditional family structures (Bane and Ellwood, 1994). For example, welfare benefits for unwed mothers and children born out of wedlock, and Medicaid benefits to AIDS patients, are viewed by social conservatives as anti-marriage and as public support for immorality.

SOCIAL PROGRAMS HINDER
INVESTMENT AND ECONOMIC GROWTH

Furthermore, conservatives argue that government social programs violate sound economics by placing downward pressure on investment, and therefore the gross national product, since they take resources from the wealthier segments of society that would have invested the funds and allocate them elsewhere. Conservatives also generally oppose welfare programs because they contribute to higher taxes, which conservatives vehemently oppose. Additionally, conservatives tend to prefer state and local government as opposed to central government power, hence, they tend to favor state, local, and private efforts to provide poverty relief. These ideological factors, combined with the fact that welfare recipients do not have the resources necessary for a strong political power base, have created a political environment that has been ideologically antagonistic to welfare state since 1970 (Heclo, 1994, 396).

THE LOONY LEFT

Citizen groups exist in the United States for almost every issue that one can imagine, many of which are very narrow, politically extreme, and unrepresentative of Americans as a whole. While the political left certainly does not have an exclusive on these fringe groups (the KKK and the John Birch Society being prime right-wing examples), the left certainly has its fair share, and their presence works to taint the image of the left as a whole. Many of these groups are single-issue oriented and generally out of step with the majority of Americans. For example, there is a group within the People for the Ethical Treatment of Animals (PETA) that advocates equal rights for fish. As PETA's Bruce Friedrich puts it, "Fish have the capacity to feel pain. They have a capacity to suffer. For reasons that defy logic, we allow people to spend their afternoon impaling them on hooks" (Schultz, 2002). Given the popularity of fishing as a sport in America, along with the necessity of commercial fishing, most Americans clearly disagree with such logic. Similarly, the American Civil Liberties Union stepped in to defend the New York City teacher fired for his association with NAMBLA (see Chapter 1), outraging conservatives and associating contemporary liberalism in general with immorality and pedophilia (Etzioni, 1994, 11).

It is not just groups, however, that have contributed to the "loony" image of contemporary liberalism. Far-left individuals have also made their own contributions to the "loony" image with numerous extreme arguments and actions. For example, during the turbulent 1960s, Harvard psychologist Timothy Leary advocated experimentation with mind-altering drugs, including LSD. Leary is credited with coining the phrase "Turn on, tune in, drop out" that became a rallying cry for the drug-oriented counterculture at the time, but a symbol of everything that was wrong with America, and with contemporary liberalism in particular, to American conservatives (www.lib.virginia.edu/small/exhibits/sixties/leary. html.) That the vast majority of America's contemporary liberal professors disagreed with Leary at the time was often ignored by the conservative majority. Similarly, contemporary liberal activist lawyer William M. Kunstler discredited the entire political left in the minds of conservatives during the Vietnam War when he publicly criticized singer Joan Baez for her complaints about human rights abuses by the communist government of North Vietnam. Kunstler considered Baez's criticisms to be inappropriate because the government of North Vietnam was socialist and Kunstler argued that socialist countries should not be criticized for any reason (Skidmore, 1993, 309).

Perhaps as frightening as anything to conservatives, racial minorities and feminists have often behaved in a manner inconsistent with the values of mainstream America. The aforementioned theses of Albert Cleage and James Cone that "God is black," along with the separatism of the Nation of Islam, are cases in point. For another example, one need look no further than certain aspects of the radical women's movement. Naomi Goldenberg (1979) describes her experience at the first National Conference on Women's Spirituality held in Boston in 1976 and attended by several hundred women. Goldenberg (1979, 92–93) states:

> The audience became very active. In tones ranging from whispers to shouts, they chanted, 'The goddess Is Alive—Magic Is Afoot.' The women evoked the Goddess with dancing, stamping, clapping and yelling. They stood on pews and danced bare-breasted on the pulpit and amid the hymnbooks. Had any sedate, white-haired clergyman been present, I am sure he would have felt the Apocalypse had arrived.... In fact, the women were angry at all religions of the fathers and took this opportunity to mock and defy those religions in a Church they had rented for the occasion. The anger was not pretty but it certainly was justified. Why not be enraged with the whole Judeo-Christian tradition for centuries of degradation of the bodies and images of women? Why not display your breasts in a place that has tried to teach you that they are things to be ashamed of, features that make you unlike God or His son? Proclaiming that the 'Goddess Is Alive' in a traditional church setting is proclaiming that woman is alive, that being female is divine. The women in Boston were raising up their images as fleshly female beings to defy their culture's image of God as an

immaterial male spirit. At this opening of the Boston conference the Goddess represented fierce pride in female physical presence and fury at the abuse that presence has taken from male religious authorities. The Goddess was never symbolized as an idol or a picture in this or any other ritual. Instead, She was seen as the force which had motivated each woman to be present at the first national gathering in Her honor.

Perhaps Goldenberg is absolutely correct in her assertions about the "Goddess" as a motivating force for women, but this type of behavior often causes others who lack the same "spirit" to be repelled from such a movement and denounce it as a hall full of loonies. Therefore, regardless of the possible positive impact of such a gathering on the participants themselves or even the consciousness-raising of society as a whole, the political cost of the association of contemporary liberalism with such a gathering is perhaps most likely to be an electoral loser. These types of persons and groups have repeatedly taken political debates to the far-left extremes over the years, with the result that the interests of the political center (where most Americans, including most contemporary liberals, may be on any given issue) are essentially ignored (Moore, 1994). As a result, the mere mention of PETA, the Sierra Club (forever demonized by the right for attempting to save the spotted owl from logging), the Nation of Islam, or the ACLU tends to cause conservatives to associate all contemporary liberals with their most extreme elements and thus damage contemporary liberalism as a whole.

No More Worlds to Conquer

The last major problem we will discuss for American contemporary liberals is less of an ideological flaw than it is a practical one. Essentially, by the 21st century, contemporary liberals have become victims of their own success. If one were to go back a century and look at the laundry list of things contemporary liberals wanted, one would find that almost all of them have been achieved. At the end of the 19th century, for example, contemporary liberals clamored for federal regulation of big business, specifically railroads, the biggest business of the time. In the hundred years since, contemporary liberals also pushed for workplace safety laws, workers' compensation insurance and unemployment insurance, as well as federal regulation of food and drugs, old age pensions, government health care for the indigent and elderly, welfare and public housing for the poor, job-training programs, environmental protection, affirmative action, the end of segregation, and women's rights, just to name a few.

The benefits for society from some of these programs have been nothing short of phenomenal. Children do not starve to death in America because food is unavailable (though adequate nutrition is sometimes lacking). The poverty rate in 1960 prior to the implementation of the Great Society programs was approximately 23 percent. After the passage and implementation of the Great Society in the mid–1960s, the poverty rate declined to approximately 12 percent in 1974. Although the "war on poverty" was not won, significant progress had been achieved. The election of Ronald Reagan in 1980, however, brought an anti-welfare backlash and more classic liberal free-market economics. Simultaneously, the poverty rate increased again, surpassing 15 percent in the early 1980s and during the recession of the early 1990s before returning to 13.6 percent in 1996, the year of the latest major welfare reform (U.S. Census Bureau, 1998). These figures support the position that the greatest inroads against poverty were made when more was spent on welfare, rather than less. Consequently, it is reasonable to expect the poverty rate to rise again in the near future as both the states and the federal government reduce their welfare rolls due to the shift of the political culture away from contemporary liberalism in the George W. Bush era.

Despite the fact that these contemporary liberal programs have undeniably produced some societal benefits, the contemporary liberals are placed in the unenviable position of having to defend their creations, none of which work perfectly. Unfortunately, for almost every government program, there is an associated abuse and criticism. Conservatives argue that many welfare recipients are lazy people who would rather accept welfare checks than work. Some individuals who draw benefits from unemployment insurance or workers' compensation insurance are actually able-bodied individuals who are fraudulently scamming the system. Welfare mothers supposedly have more babies in order to get more welfare (Ozawa and Kirk, 1995, 195). While it is true that unscrupulous persons undoubtedly have faked injuries to collect worker's compensation insurance, remained on unemployment longer than necessary, and traded food stamps for beer money, the fact that such abuses have occurred has often obscured the positives accomplished with the social programs.

Underlining how anti-welfare the American political culture had become, in the late 1980s, the party of contemporary liberalism, the Democratic Party itself, began to turn against some of its own government intervention. By the end of the 1980s, the Democratic Party was in somewhat of a state of disarray after losing three straight presidential elections in 1980, 1984, and 1988 to Republican candidates Ronald Reagan and George Bush, a clear public repudiation of contemporary liberal ideology. As if three straight losses weren't bad enough, the Democrats had lost two of the three presidential elections previous to 1980, giving them losses in five of the previous six elections, Jimmy Carter's 1976 success in the wake of Watergate the lone victory. The defeats convinced some Democratic Party leaders that the party must reformulate their platform that had been so successful for them from the New Deal of the 1930s through the Great Society of the 1960s, but had faltered in the two decades since. In response to the latest electoral losses, a new party leadership group, the Democratic Leadership Council (DLC), was created, which included, among others, Paul Tsongas, Richard Gephardt, Sam Nunn, Bill Bradley, Al Gore, and Arkansas governor Bill Clinton, who chaired the DLC just prior to his candidacy for the presidency (Karger and Stoesz, 1998, 11–12).

The goal of the DLC was to turn the Democratic Party away from traditional New Deal "big government" liberalism and turn the party more toward an agenda that would retain the support of the liberals, but no longer alienate business interests and those who opposed federal social welfare policies on ideological grounds. In 1989, the DLC released the "New Orleans Declaration: A Democratic Agenda for the 1990s," which outlined policy goals that were pro-business, yet "compassionate." To establish their credibility, the DLC sought to distance the Democratic Party from the large-scale federal welfare programs through a promise of reform. The DLC argued for "workfare," time-limited welfare benefits, support for the traditional family, and frugal, responsible government rather than the deficit spending that had plagued the 1980s. The DLC called for replacement of cash assistance programs with investments in education, research, and job training. The DLC also supported free trade and the North American Free Trade Agreement as a means of reducing unemployment and welfare reforms, a position that was vehemently opposed by labor unions, generally thought of as major constituents of the Democratic Party (Karger and Stoesz, 1998, 11–12).

During his presidential campaign of 1992, Bill Clinton echoed the DLC platform when he promised to "end welfare as we know it today." Although Clinton did not immediately announce the details of his welfare reform plan, he did make references to his experience in the DLC and in Arkansas, where welfare was reformed by putting people to work. The idea of "workfare" evidently struck a positive chord with the American public, despite the fact that previous efforts to eliminate welfare through employment had failed to accomplish the desired results. In 1988, Congress had passed the Job Opportunity and Basic Skills (JOBS) program that was formulated based on the same goals, as was the Work Incentive (WIN) program, which passed Congress in 1967; yet the public perception was still that welfare recipients generally did not work. This negative public perception concerning welfare, and the policy proposals that have arisen in response to that perception, are not new developments. In fact, Congress has amended welfare programs in some way in every session of Congress since the Social Security Act in 1935, yet the public remained largely dissatisfied with the system, suggesting the contemporary liberal ideology is at least partially out of step with the individualistic American culture (Dobelstein, 1999, 5).

Obviously, no matter what measures the government takes to reform welfare, there will always be problems and abuses; consequently, there will always be criticisms of the government programs regardless of whatever good is produced. The claims that contemporary liberal welfare programs have wiped out death by starvation in America and reduced poverty can be expected to be ignored (as are other benefits from the liberals' creations), and instead critics can be expected to continue to focus on both real and imagined negatives. The final result is that rather than taking credit for the good things their programs produce, contemporary liberals are often merely blamed for the abuses of the system, and the positives produced are obscured by the negatives.

7

Communism

At the extreme left of the political spectrum is communism, an ideology that gained a significant following in Europe in the nineteenth century and formed the basis for much of the political conflict that permeated the twentieth century. At its most basic, communism is simply the idea of people living and working collectively and holding all property in common, as opposed to owning property individually. In fact, according to the godfather of communist ideology, Karl Marx, "the theory of the communists may be summed up in the single sentence: Abolition of private property" (Marx and Engels, 1848, 1992, 329).

If that is the case, then communism, or the idea that people should hold property collectively, is not a new ideology at all, but has been around for at least two thousand years and was even practiced in some early Christian communities mentioned in the New Testament. For example, it is explained in Acts 2:44 that, "And all those who had believed were together, and had all things in common; and they began selling their property and possessions, and were sharing them with all, as anyone might have need." In a second passage, the writer of Acts (4:32) adds, "And the congregation of those who believed were of one heart and soul; and not one of them claimed that anything belonging to him was his own; but all things were common property to them." Although many American Protestant fundamentalist Christians undoubtedly would prefer that the collective arrangement of the first-century church described in Acts not be labeled "communism," under Marx's definition of communism as "the abolition of private property," it appears that communism would be the appropriate label. Not only did the early Christians evidently abolish private property, but the parallel of Acts 2:44 with Marx's famous maxim, "From each according to his abilities, to each according to his needs," is obvious. Contemporary anti-communist American Christians may argue that the descriptions of the early church in Acts are not "communism" per se, but simply "sharing." Nonetheless, as Marx so succinctly stated, it is these ideas of abolishing private property, sharing, and living collectively that are the very essence of communism. Consequently, communism itself is neither new nor must it be necessarily atheistic in character, though Marx not only popularized the idea of a collectively based society, but also advocated the abolition of religion. Marx was not religious himself, but his reason for abolishing religion had less to do with unbelief and more to do with his contention that religion would serve to pacify the masses and render them content with their inferior economic status, thus serving to hinder proletarian discontent and therefore communist revolution (Marx and Engels, 1848, 1992, 332).

The scope, breadth, and duration of the New Testament Christian "communist" experiments are essentially unknown, but communal living obviously did not develop into a major ideological component of Christianity or a global communist movement in the first century. The first-century church of Acts, however, is not the only American historical and cultural connection to communism. Instead, communism, as defined by the abolition of private property, has been present in American history since the earliest English settlements of North America, beginning with the communist experiment of the Pilgrims at Plymouth in 1620. Though their communist economic arrangement was short-lived, Pilgrim leader William Bradford (1856, 1981, 132–133) discusses how the Pilgrims spent the first two years of their experience in Plymouth in what he called a "common course and condition," where property was held collectively and work responsibilities were collective rather than individual. Bradford also relays, however, that it became necessary in 1623 to transition to a private property system since the communist system was producing discontent and inefficiency. Nevertheless, "communism" clearly was the Pilgrims' initial New World political/economic arrangement. In the words of Bradford,

> The experience that was had in this common course and condition, tried sundry years and that amongst godly and sober men, may well evince the vanity of that conceit of Plato's and other ancients applauded by some of later times; that the taking away of property and bringing in community into a commonwealth would make them happy and flourishing; as if they were wiser than God. For this community (so far as it was) was found to breed much confusion and discontent and retard much employment that would have been to their benefit and comfort. For the young men, that were most able and fit for labour and service, did repine that they should spend their time and strength to work for other men's wives and children without any recompense. The strong, or man of parts, had no more in division of victuals and clothes than he that was weak and not able to do a

quarter the other could; this was thought injustice. The aged and graver men to be ranked and equalized in labours and victuals, clothes, etc., with the meaner and younger sort, thought it some indignity and disrespect unto them. And for men's wives to be commanded to do service for other men, as dressing their meat, washing their clothes, etc., they deemed it a kind of slavery, neither could many husbands well brook it. Upon the point all being to have alike, and all to do alike, they thought themselves in the like condition, and one as good as another; and so, if it did not cut off those relations that God hath set amongst men, yet it did at least much diminish and take off the mutual respects that should be preserved amongst them. And would have been worse if they had been men of another condition. Let none object this is men's corruption, and nothing to the course itself. I answer, seeing all men have this corruption in them, God in His wisdom saw another course fitter for them.

In spite of the fact that the Pilgrims clearly abandoned their early communist experience in the New World as unworkable, the Puritan group that arrived in the following decade practiced some similar collectivist arrangements to those of the Pilgrims. For example, the Puritans laid out their villages in an arrangement around a central pasture or "common" that was a grazing area shared by all (Brinkley, 2003, 87). Some early Puritan communities also farmed in open fields shared by all, and cut firewood from communal woodlands (Nash et al., 1987, 46).

Other collectivist communities in American history include the early nineteenth century Mormon community where no property was owned individually, but property was allocated to each family by the Church (Denton, 2004). Similarly, the Oneida community of John Noyes, founded in 1848 at Oneida, New York (famous, among other things, for the Oneida cookware company that still exists in the twenty-first century), was another religious community that established a collectivist living arrangement. Noyes, however, not only abolished private property, but also abolished monogamous marriage and introduced a system he called "complex marriage," where sex was permitted between any man and woman in the community who had been "saved." Due to this "all sharing all" nature of Noyes' complex marriage relationship, responsibility for child rearing also became the collective responsibility of the community, with every adult equally responsible for the well-being of every child in the community (Roark et al., 2005, 427).

These minor collectivist communities did not, however, lead to major collectivist movements in the United States in the long run. Instead, American history thus far has been dominated by the sanctity of private property. The American Revolution itself was in part a revolt against English interference into colonial private property arrangements through taxation and restrictions on trade. When the American colonies revolted against England and formed their own country in 1776, the Founders wrote a constitution, the Articles of Confederation, that provided little in the way of collectivism outside of the nationalized post office. To that, the Constitution of 1789 would add a collectivized national standing army, but collectivism as a whole remained minimal. Instead, Americans in general have typically remained wary of collectivism, and communism has never become a major political movement in United States. Instead of embracing Marxist-Leninist communism as it rose as a global political force in the twentieth century, reactionary anti-communism became a significant ideological force driving American politics from the time of the Bolshevik Revolution through the present.

Karl Marx

Though communism as a human living arrangement has existed for centuries, communism did not develop as a major ideology and political movement until the writings of Karl Marx in the 19th century. Marx, along with his collaborative partner Friedrich Engels, is generally credited with developing and popularizing communist ideology with his extensive writings, beginning with the *Communist Manifesto* in 1848. Vladimir Lenin would then seize upon the ideas of Marx in tsarist Russia in the late nineteenth century and catapult Marxist communism into a significant global political movement in the twentieth century. Marxist-Leninism by mid-century became the guiding principle for the world's largest countries in both land mass (the Soviet Union) and population (the People's Republic of China), and emerged as one side of the most significant political and ideological struggle in global politics: the Cold War, with America's foreign policy based on the containment of communism.

Karl Marx was born in 1818 in Trier, Germany, the son of a Jewish lawyer who had converted to Christianity. Marx began the path of following in his father's footsteps in 1836 when he began studying law at the University of Berlin. At the university, Marx became interested in philosophy and became acquainted with some of the ideas that he would later transform into what has since become known simply as "Marxism." Marx was awarded a doctorate in philosophy at Jena in 1841 and then took a job at a newspaper, first as a reporter, and then as an editor. The newspaper was suppressed by the Prussian government in 1843, causing Marx to move to Paris to become the editor of a newspaper for Prussian immigrants. Marx was subsequently expelled by the French government at the behest of Prussia in 1845 and migrated to Belgium and then England, which was in the midst of the Industrial Revolution with all of its turbulence (Ingersoll, Matthews, and Davison, 2001, 115).

It was in Paris, however, that Marx became acquainted with his friend and collaborator, Friedrich Engels, who had studied the British capitalist system and was repulsed by what he saw as its exploitive character. Marx and Engels moved to Brussels and became associated with a radical group known as the Communist League. In 1848, Marx and Engels then wrote the *Communist Manifesto* as part of their association with the Communist League (Ingersoll, Matthews, and Davison, 2001, 116). Marx went to England in 1849 and remained there until his death in 1883, but it was during this time that he wrote his crowning achievement, *Das Kapital*. The first volume was published in 1867, and the remaining two volumes after his death, in 1885–95 (Ebenstein and Ebenstein, 1992, 310).

INFLUENCES AND METHODS

Perhaps the greatest influence on Marx were the writings of G.W.F. Hegel, a German philosopher who argued that history had meaning and purpose and that it moved in a set pattern toward a known goal. In Hegel's view, history should be viewed as the progressive unfolding of reason. Hegel contended that all prior reason was incomplete and a limited form of understanding. Furthermore, Hegel argued, borrowing from the Greek philosopher Heraclitus, that there was no permanent reality, except the reality of change. The only reality for Heraclitus was the transitional reality of "becoming," a view that Hegel accepted (Ingersoll, Matthews, and Davidson, 2001, 118–119). Hegel built on the philosophy of Heraclitus and argued that history was a dialectic struggle of higher and lower human forces and that the struggle continued through numerous stages. At the conclusion of each phase of the struggle, a new and higher phase of human evolution replaced the preceding one (Ebenstein and Ebenstein, 1992, 310). Marx would adopt Hegel's dialectic reasoning and argue that the human struggle was on an unstoppable path toward eventual communism. Just as capitalism had replaced feudalism in a dialectic struggle, so would communism eventually replace capitalism. Marx's line of reasoning that economics has been the driving force behind human societies throughout history has been labeled by scholars as "historic materialism" or "economic determinism," though it was followers of Marx, rather than Marx himself, who first used these phrases (Croce, 2004).

Marx also borrowed from Hegel the idea that labor is the principal means through which people achieve self-actualization and realize their value and potential as human beings. Furthermore, Marx argued that human freedom could only be achieved when all people are capable of achieving self-actualization and "rationality," thus the exploitive nature of capitalist labor that denied self-actualization required change for people to achieve their full potential (Ingersoll, Matthews, and Davidson, 2001, 121–122).

Scientific Socialism

Followers of Marx typically employ the term "thesis-antithesis-synthesis" to describe Marx's historical dialectic. Marx described any given dominant historical socioeconomic condition as the "thesis." For example, Marx uses the "thesis" of feudalism as an illustration of a once dominant socioeconomic condition. Feudalism, however, contained the seeds of its own destruction, since the landed nobility who controlled economic and political power in the system desired luxurious commodities; consequently, the bourgeoisie (merchant class) developed within feudal society in order to meet those needs. With the development of bourgeois commerce, capitalism grew to become the "antithesis" that challenged the feudal "thesis": the bourgeoisie developed conflicts with the nobility, largely over the need for common laborers. While the nobility needed the commoners as serfs to cultivate their land, the bourgeoisie needed the same commoners to work in their factories. The final result was the overthrow of the nobility by the bourgeoisie in violent revolution, of which the French Revolution is the prime example. The system that would emerge would be a "synthesis" of the two preceding antithetical ideas; over time, this synthesis would become the new, accepted "thesis" for socioeconomic organization. In the case of the French Revolution, capitalism became the new thesis after its overthrow of feudalism. In Marx's conception, as capitalism matured, communism would eventually then become the new antithesis, and the historical pattern of thesis-antithesis-synthesis, ending in revolution, would be repeated. The final result would be that communism would emerge as the final synthesis toward which all of history had progressed. At that juncture, with a new universal society of creative laborers living in peace and harmony under the communist system, the process of thesis-antithesis-synthesis would end (Heilbroner, 1953, 12–23).

Rather than a moral approach, Marxists claim that Marx's theory is a scientific approach in that his theory was derived not from arguments concerning morality, immorality, or the human relationship to a deity, but through analysis of political and economic history. Marx and Engels essentially argued that the transition from capitalism to communism was inevitable based on the laws of political economy as revealed through history. The argument was not that communism was a choice people should make because it is more moral or less depraved, but that it would be the unstoppable result of powerful economic forces (Engels, 1880, 1959, 79–90).

Communist Manifesto

In the *Communist Manifesto*, Marx and Engels outlined what became the basic creed for communists in the decades (indeed, centuries) to come. They argued that all of human history is the history of class struggle and that class struggle always ended either in the "revolutionary reconstitution of society at large, or in the common ruin of the contending classes" (Marx and Engels, 1848, 1992, 321).

Marx and Engels argued that society is always stratified into two classes directly facing each other, the bourgeoisie, or upper classes, who own the means of production and are fewer in number; and the proletariat, or working classes, who own only their own labor and are much greater in number. Control of production produces wealth for the bourgeoisie, which allows them to control the mechanisms of the state and use it as a tool with which to oppress and control the proletariat. Even though the proletariat are greater in number and may even have equality under the law, they have unequal bargaining power with the bourgeoisie, whose wealth provides them the power to exploit the proletariat. The bourgeoisie force the proletariat to work for subsistence wages and reap vast profits at their expense. The capital accumulation of the bourgeoisie grows ever greater; thus, economic inequality can only increase (Marx and Engels, 1848, 1992, 322–324).

The bourgeoisie use their accumulated capital to invest in innovation and new technology; machines are thereby created that replace human labor, further depressing the bargaining power and position of the proletariat. Competition, however, causes some of the bourgeoisie to go bankrupt and fall to the level of the proletariat themselves. Consequently, the class of the bourgeoisie grows ever smaller while the class of the proletariat grows ever larger (Marx and Engels, 1848, 1992, 322–324).

According to Marx and Engels, the bourgeoisie had essentially created a world culture, with all nations compelled to adopt the bourgeois capitalist model due to capitalism's need for expansion. For Marx and Engels, the very earth itself had even succumbed to capitalism, which cleared continents for development (Marx and Engels, 1848, 1992, 322–

324). The ability of the bourgeoisie to oppress the proletariat is aided by the liberal propaganda of the bourgoisie and the teachings of religions that promise the proletariat a better existence in the next life (Marx and Engels, 1848, 1992, 328–332).

Marx and Engels believed, however, that the bourgeois capitalist system could not stand in the long run. Property and capital in the capitalist system would eventually become concentrated in few hands, thus depressing demand and consumption and bringing overproduction. The existence of excess goods would then force capitalists to seek out new markets, but eventually the market would reach its end as capitalism spread throughout the entire earth. The oppressed proletariat, however, would ultimately organize globally and rise up to challenge their capitalist oppressors (Marx and Engels, 1848, 1992, 324–326). Marx and Engels argued that the proletarian revolution, and with it the abolition of existing property relations, is part of historical destiny, and not a distinguishing feature of communism. As feudalism was inevitably destroyed by capitalism, so capitalism would be destroyed by communism (Marx and Engels, 1848, 1992, 326).

The new structure of property relations that would be established by the proletariat after the overthrow of the bourgeoisie would be communism, or the abolition of private property. Marx and Engels argued that when property is held in common, it loses its class character. They claimed that the elimination of private property will not harm the vast majority of society because by the time of the proletarian revolution, ninety percent will not own any private property anyway, and there will be nothing that can be taken away from them; hence, the transition to communism for the ninety percent can only mean material gain (Marx and Engels, 1848, 1992, 330–331).

As to the argument that the abolition of private property would breed laziness, Marx and Engels argued that such reasoning is a tautology. In the words of Marx and Engels (1848, 1992, 330),

> It has been objected, that upon the abolition of private property all work will cease, and universal laziness will overtake us. According to this, bourgeois society ought long ago to have gone to the dogs through sheer idleness; for those of its members who work, acquire nothing, and those who acquire anything, do not work. The whole of this objection is but another expression of the tautology: There can no longer be any wage-labour when there is no longer any capital.

More radical than the abolition of private property, Marx and Engels proclaimed that the proletariat would abolish family, the foundation of which is capital and private gain. The abolition of capital and private property would therefore abolish family as well since it would abolish the very foundation of family. Marx and Engels explain that

> ... marriage is in reality a system of wives in common and thus, at the most, what the communists might possibly be reproached with is that they desire to introduce, in substitution for hypocritically concealed, an openly legalized community of women (Marx and Engels, 1848, 1992, 331).

Marx and Engels also argued that nation-states, nationalism, and the exploitation of one nation by another will end with the communist revolution, as the global proletariat, with common bonds among them, will end international strife as class antagonism vanishes (Marx and Engels, 1848, 1992, 332).

Finally, Marx and Engels argued that the communists will abolish all existing religion and morality and reconstitute them on a new basis. Religion and morality, they claimed, are mere tools of the bourgeoisie to enslave and pacify the masses by helping them accept their sad state of existence in exchange for the promise of a better experience in the next life (Marx and Engels, 1848, 1992, 332).

Marxist Communism

Marx believed that communism would eliminate all of the exploitation of capitalism and restore the self-actualization for individual workers that had been lost under unregulated capitalism during the Industrial Revolution. Marx also argued that working for the collective would restore meaning to work and make people more productive, so that they could accomplish more in three or four hours than they would in an entire day under capitalism. Furthermore, people would use the rest of their day to be creative, and would develop new technology and better products with their free time (Hoover, 1994, 111–112). Marx argued that under communism, work could be reorganized so as to better match individual skills with the type of work available, and thus humanize labor. The waste that is associated with competition would be eliminated, as would be the anger and resentment associated with the exploitation of workers by overseers (Hoover, 1994, 111).

Concerning the distribution of goods, Marx argued that individuals would receive from the community whatever they needed, since there was not a problem of scarcity in the existing economy, but of maldistribution.

Marx argued that one of the problems with capitalism was that capitalist economists concerned themselves with market prices and did not distinguish between needs and wants or examine the conditions under which the value of products was created by laborers. Such a system obviously would lead to exploitation as the free market would produce goods at low prices based on severe worker exploitation. The use of low-paid child labor to sew garments together would be a case in point (Ollman, 1976, 193–194).

This did not mean, however, that Marx did not expect people to work or that he would tolerate those who were lazy. Persons who refused to work, according to Marx, would have no part in the distribution of goods. In this, Marx is no different from anti-welfare conservatives of the twenty-first century U.S. Again, Marx's basic idea is that communism would eventually cause people to share in such a way that each would produce according to his abilities and give to others according to their needs. The removal of the dehumanizing and exploitive capitalist labor system would produce a system where people achieved self-actualization through work; hence, the disincentive to work would be greatly reduced and laziness would be much less of a problem.

Concerning the notion of individual rights, Marx was particularly unimpressed. Marx argued that individualism and individual rights work against freedom because the bourgeoisie use free speech in a capitalist society to control the media and drown out the voices of proletarian dissent. In this way, the bourgeoisie present private ownership of production as encased in eternal and inviolable natural laws on which society in the abstract is founded (Marx, 1974, 87).

LABOR THEORY OF VALUE

Marx argued that the true value of any particular good was the value of the labor that went into making it. Capitalists, however, are able to extract "surplus value" from their goods by persuading workers to accept much less in wages than the value of goods that they produce. Capitalists can only expand their market share through lower prices, which means they must continually reduce the value of the labor that goes into making goods. If wages are cut, however, the proletariat can then purchase fewer goods, thus decreasing demand and inducing capitalists to attempt to further cut prices, and therefore labor costs, in order to regain the same market share and surplus value. The free market will therefore eventually implode in a downward spiral of wage and price cuts as capitalists drop wages and prices ever lower in attempts to increase market share and profits. Eventually, capitalism itself will completely implode under such a system since proletarian wages will be eventually reduced below subsistence levels, causing a collapse of consumption (Marx, 1978, 285). The proletariat in such a system would see their status and buying power forever dwindling, unemployment would rise, and the proletariat would have no alternative but to become a militant, revolutionary force that would overthrow capitalism in a violent revolution (Marx, 1978, 285).

REVOLUTION

In order to coerce workers into accepting less than the real value of their labor, capitalists will have to dominate the cultural and political environment and repress dissent through manipulation and force when necessary, backed by their control of the state. As capitalism matures, the inequality between the proletariat and the bourgeoisie would become ever greater, as would the proletarian disillusionment. Eventually, the proletariat would develop class consciousness and revolt, but not before all of the bourgeois barriers to class consciousness are eliminated. Marx argued that the capitalists dupe the proletariat into believing that they share the same values and interests of the bourgeoisie. The rejection of this belief by the proletariat will come only after the elements in society that are used by the bourgeoisie to prevent the development of class consciousness are overcome. Factors that hinder the development of class consciousness include not only liberal individualism, but religion, ethnic differences, and regional or sectional geographic separation, as well as bourgeois control of the agents of propaganda (Hoover, 1994, 126–127).

The goals of the proletarian revolution would be the overthrow of capitalism and bourgeois private ownership of production, and its replacement with proletarian ownership of production through the power of the state. In the words of Marx and Engels (1848, 1992, 332), "The first step in the revolution by the working class is to raise the proletariat to the position of ruling class, to establish democracy." Marx and Engels then argued that the proletariat will use their "political supremacy" to "wrest by degrees, all capital from the bourgeoisie, to centralize all instruments of production in the hands of the state, i.e., of the proletariat" (Marx and Engels, 1848, 1992, 332). Capitalism would then be replaced by a new socialist order based on a superior value system that places a premium on providing life's necessities to everyone equally. The proletarian revolution would lead to the development of a classless, socialist society that would pave the eventual way to communism (Marx, 1978, 291–292).

Marx and Engels (1848, 1992, 333) provided a basic ten-step road map for the establishment of the proletarian society.

1. Abolition of property in land and application of all rents of land to public purposes.

2. A heavy progressive or graduated income tax.

3. Abolition of all right of inheritance.

4. Confiscation of the property of all emigrants and rebels.

5. Centralization of credit in the hands of the state, by means of a national bank with state capital and an exclusive monopoly.

6. Centralization of the means of communication and transport in the hands of the state.

7. Extension of factories and instruments of production owned by the state; the bringing into cultivation of waste lands, and the improvement of the soil generally in accordance with a common plan.

8. Equal obligation of all to work.

9. Combination of agriculture with manufacturing industries; gradual abolition of the distinction between town and country, by a more equable distribution of the population over the country.

10. Free education for all children in public schools. Abolition of child factory labour in its present form. Combination of education with industrial production, etc.

DICTATORSHIP OF THE PROLETARIAT

In order to build the socialist society, the workers would have to take control of production and reorganize it along socialist principles; production must be reoriented to meet the needs of society as a whole rather than the needs of the elites and bourgeoisie (Hoover, 1994, 129). During the socialist transition to communism, the bourgeoisie can be expected to attempt a counter-revolution (if not several) in an attempt to restore themselves to wealth and power. Consequently, the proletariat must establish a "dictatorship of the proletariat" that will suppress the counterrevolution by force. The bourgeoisie, however, will wage not only a physical battle, but a battle of words and ideology with the proletariat in an attempt to win the hearts and minds of the people. Consequently, Marx and Engels argued that bourgeois ideas must be attacked and eradicated from society by the proletarian dictatorship and replaced with socialist values. The dictatorship of the proletariat must seize control of art, culture, and education and use them to instill new proletarian values. Workers must come to view themselves as "comrades" rather than competitors. Religion must be thwarted so that it does not delude the people into accepting bourgeois ideas wrapped in the promise of rewards in the afterlife (Hoover, 1994, 130).

During the transition period of proletarian dictatorship, the state will be the tool of the dominant class as before, but in this case the dominant class is now the proletariat, who will use the state to accomplish the proletarian goals. After the state takes over production from the bourgeoisie, the state itself must essentially establish a planned, robust command economy so that goods are produced, distributed, and consumed. All workers will become employees of the state and paid based on what they produce, just as in the capitalist system. The bourgeoisie and other classes would be given jobs that would develop within them the new proletarian values and eventually mold them into membership in the proletariat, so that all classes are eliminated except for the one proletarian class, to which all humanity belongs. The new state-run economy is expected to be more productive than the capitalist society, since elites who did not work previously will be given productive jobs in the socialist society. People will require fewer incentives to work because of their awareness of their important roles in society (Sargent, 1993, 166–167). During this period, the redistribution of wealth and equality of income will create a situation in which the social and ideological remnants of bourgeois society will melt away, to be replaced with new egalitarian communist ideals of liberty and fraternity. As people adopt the new fraternal values, the state will require fewer resources and expend less energy due to the lack of a need for policing crime and regulating capitalism. The state will therefore gradually lose any significant reason for existence and will wither away. The elements of the state that will remain will be planning functions that will be coordinated in response to the people's priorities. In the communist society that will emerge, people will not be constrained by economic necessities, since all will have plenty, based on the idea that the world's resources are plentiful, just maldistributed. Furthermore, under the new socialist freedom, individual creativity will experience a boom due to the availability of more free time. The new socialized economic structures will also operate more efficiently due to the elimination of overlap through planning. Finally, in the new communist social arrangements, a "New Man" will emerge who is completely committed to the communist ideals of egalitarian liberty and fraternity. (Marx, 1959, 111–132). In the end, Marx and Engels argued that when the proletariat has become successful in installing itself as the ruling class, it will have "swept away the conditions for the existence of class antagonisms, and of classes generally, and will thereby have abolished its own supremacy as a class" (Marx and Engels, 1848, 1992, 333). Instead of the bourgeois society of classes and class antagonisms, Marx argues that the elevation of the proletariat will create "an association, in which the free development of each is the condition for the free development of all" (Marx and Engels, 1848, 1992, 333).

VANGUARD OF THE PROLETARIAT

Marx did not, however, view the proletariat as sufficiently educated and capable of understanding their own interests, the intricacies of class struggle, and the necessary steps for building socialism as a transition to communism. Consequently, Marx argued that the proletariat must be led by a "vanguard" of intellectuals who best understand the proper directions. This "vanguard of the proletariat" would then essentially provide the instruction that would help to form proletarian class consciousness, and thus help initiate the revolution and direct the proletariat toward their goals. Marx made it clear, however, that the proletarian revolution would be led by the proletariat themselves rather than the vanguard. In the words of Engels (1888, 1959, 4), "The emancipation of the working class must be the act of the working class itself."

Final Stage of Communism

In the final stage of communism, the "command economy" created in the socialist transition, would largely still exist; but it would no longer be controlled by the state, which had withered away. Distribution of goods would be according to need, and there would be no classes and no exploitation, only one class of happy workers. The need for money or capital as a means of exchange would no longer exist as people received and distributed goods based on need. In other words, the physician would treat the shoemaker for free, and in turn, the shoemaker would provide shoes for the physician for free when the physician was in need of shoes. With the exploitive bourgeois class eliminated and people working more efficiently due to the social incentives of communism, the economy would be more productive, producing abundance for all (Wiles, 1962, 332–333).

Communism would bring major social changes in addition to political and economic changes. Religion, of course, would be completely abolished, since its reason for being, the control of the masses by the upper classes, would no longer exist. Education would be available to everyone and would, of course, be free to all. All crime would disappear because there simply would be no reason for it anymore. Even prostitution and adultery would disappear, and the monogamous marriage relationship based on love would become the only known sexual relationship. Women would be equal with men and enjoy the same occupations as men based on their own abilities (Balagushkin, 1963, 43).

Politically, with the state withering away, an entity would need to develop that would manage the socialist economic system. Marx envisioned "a free and equal association of producers" that would have the authority to direct production and distribution. The association would then collect data and establish priorities and goals for the various economic entities. The association would not be coercive in character, but would merely administer the economy so that manufacturers produced what people needed (Sargent, 1993, 169). The withering away of the state would also mean the withering away of nationalism as the entire world would become communist. The classless nature of the global communist society would then overcome all national and ethnic differences (Sargent, 1993, 170).

Leninism

Vladimir Ilich Ulyanov, later known as Lenin, adopted Marx's ideas in the late nineteenth century and fashioned them into the basis for communist revolution in Russia in 1917. After the success of the Bolshevik Revolution, Lenin became essentially the global leader in the reformulation of Marxist theory since he was the leader of the first successful communist revolution. Leading the Bolshevik Revolution at the time that he did, however, required that Lenin alter some of the major principles of Marxist theory, most notably Marx's notion that capitalism would have to come to maturity before there could be proletarian revolution. Russia in 1917 was essentially still a feudal society, by no means a mature capitalist society in Marxist conception; consequently, it would not have been viewed by Marx as ripe for revolution. Furthermore, Russia lagged behind Western Europe in industrialization, and the proletarian class was therefore comparatively small. Lenin, however, argued that proletarian revolution was possible in Russia before the capitalist phase of the historical dialectic had fully matured. Lenin argued that the Russian peasants were the equivalent of an "agrarian proletariat" under the leadership of industrial workers. Such a revolution, Lenin argued, would require the leadership of an elite, small, disciplined group of revolutionaries—in essence, Marx's vanguard of the proletariat (Baradat, 1989, 46).

Whereas Marx would have had the vanguard provide only the intellectual basis for the proletarian movement, Lenin argued that the intellectual vanguard should direct the revolution itself. Once the revolutionaries took over, the vanguard, in the form of the Communist Party, would direct the new proletarian-led state through the transitions to socialism and eventual communism. Borrowing from Leon Trotsky, Lenin adopted the position that the vanguard could seize control of the state and use its institutions to continue the proletarian revolution until society had passed through all of the necessary historical dialectic eras and enter the communist phase. The vanguard of the proletariat would use their authority during the transition to make what Trotsky referred to as "permanent revolution" until the time that the perfect communist society would emerge (Baradat, 1989, 46–47).

Mao Ze Dong would later adapt Leninist theory to China and lead Chinese agrarian peasants in communist revolutionary overthrow of the Chinese capitalist system. Echoing Lenin, Mao proclaimed the existence of a "People's Democratic Dictatorship" that would unite all anti-imperialists, regardless of class, against the bourgeois elements in communist society. In the words of Mao,

> All classes, strata, and social groups that approve, support, and work for the cause of a socialist construction belong to the category of the people, while those social forces and groups that resist the socialist revolution and are hostile to and try to wreck socialist construction are enemies of the people [quoted in Schram, 1969, 305].

Thus, in Mao's conception, anyone, whether peasant, proletariat, elite, or bourgeoisie, could become a member of the People's Democratic Dictatorship provided that he approved of, worked for, and supported his conception of socialist revolution. Since China at the time was an overwhelmingly rural, agrarian society, Marx, like Lenin, was essentially arguing that the peasants could play a role in the revolution.

LENINIST IMPERIALISM

In his 1916 work *Imperialism, the Highest State of Capitalism*, Lenin argued that as global capitalism matured, the concentration of capital into fewer and fewer hands and the downward pressure on wages and prices due to competition would force capitalists into competition for new markets on a global scale in order to compensate for overproduction and falling prices and profits in their home countries. Capitalism would then transform itself into an assortment of enormous global monopolies that would control the world economy. The monopolies would become more and more entrenched in lesser-developed countries, and would then enrich themselves at their expense by means of profits from cheap labor and mineral resource exploitation (Ingersoll, Matthews, and Davison, 2001, 159–160). The excess profits from imperialistic capitalism could be redistributed somewhat to the proletariat in the developed capitalist states so as to stave off proletarian revolt and forestall the natural historical dialectic progression (Schumaker, Kiel, and Heilke, 1996, 181). The exploited lesser-developed countries could then be expected to launch wars of liberation and unite with communists across the globe to throw off capitalist oppression. Once successful in throwing off the capitalists, nationalist movements in the lesser-developed countries would adopt the Marxist transition to socialism and eventually to Marxist communism. Without the lesser-developed countries to exploit, capitalists would be forced to return to the exploitation of the proletariat in their home countries, with the results that Marx's proletarian revolution would eventually occur in the developed capitalist countries and the entire globe would make the final transition to Marxist communism (Ingersoll, Matthews, and Davison, 2001, 161–162).

STALINISM

Joseph Stalin was general secretary of the Communist Party during the Bolshevik Revolution of 1917, and he remained in that position until his death in 1953. Stalin would parlay his position as head of the party into a position of power that was not envisioned by Marx or Lenin. It is clear that Lenin in particular did not intend for Stalin to become the totalitarian dictator of the Soviet Union: prior to his death, Lenin directed that Stalin should be removed from his post as party general secretary. In the words of Lenin (quoted in Khrushchev, 1975, 414),

> Stalin is too excessively rude and this defect, although quite tolerable in our midst and in dealings among us Communists, becomes intolerable in a secretary-general. That is why I suggest that the comrades think about a way of removing Stalin from that post.

Obviously, Lenin's recommendation was not carried out, and Stalin maneuvered himself into a position of complete control of the Soviet state. In 1928, Stalin imposed the beginnings of his command economy with centralized planning and rapidly collectivized Soviet agriculture. Stalin invested heavily in the steel industry and other heavy industries as a path to modernization, believing that world leadership in steel meant world economic leadership.

In 1929, Stalin completely eliminated free speech, forbidding even members of the Politburo, the ruling oligarchy in the Soviet government, to express political dissent. Stalin commenced with the literal elimination of everyone he believed was a threat to his regime, and his subsequent purges resulted in the deaths of more than 1.5 million party members prior to World War II, including virtually everyone who had been connected with the Bolshevik Revolution itself in 1917. Stalin constructed an immense bureaucratic authoritarian state with all authority and power flowing into his own hands, and he used that power to oppress the masses and eliminate any and all challenges to his authority (Baradat, 1989, 103).

In Stalin's authoritarian state, moreover, the Communist Party attempted not only to wipe out dissent, but the freedom to think differently in its entirety. Schoolbooks were rewritten to replace bourgeois values with the new proletarian values. Only art that was consistent with Marxist-Leninist values was allowed, and all professors who rejected Marxist theory were expelled from the country. Stalin created around himself a cult of personality, rewriting history books to make himself the hero of the Bolshevik Revolution and the provider of everything else that was positive in Soviet society. Stalin also declared that the interests of socialism and the Soviet state came first, and that the people would have to sacrifice and do without consumer goods in order to ensure the security of the Soviet state (Ingersoll, Matthews, and Davison, 2001, 171–172).

Stalin's theoretical contributions to communism were few, but it was he who first coined the term "Marxist-Leninism" to unify the two diverse streams of communist thought. Stalin also began the process of "canonizing" Marxist-Leninism and determined authoritatively exactly what was, and was not, correct Marxist-Leninism. In 1938, Stalin facilitated publication of the *History of the Communist Party of the Soviet Union: A Short Course*, and was himself identified as the author of the fourth chapter. In this work, Stalin emphasized the idea of "socialism in one country," as opposed to global Marxist revolution and the end of capitalism, a significant break with Marxist-Leninism (Ingersoll, Matthews, and Davison, 2001, 170). In 1946, however, in a speech that was labeled by U.S. Supreme Court Justice William O. Douglas as a "declaration of World War III," Stalin argued that communism and capitalism were on an inevitable collision course and that capitalism would eventually be destroyed, an apparent contradiction of his "socialism in one country" argument (Jones, 1996, 466).

Stalin also contended that there was only one path to communism—his path. Consequently, when Marshal Tito of Yugoslavia decided in 1948 to plot his own socialist course separate from Moscow, he was denounced by Stalin. It was only after Stalin's death that Soviet leadership under Nikita Khrushchev would proclaim that there could be different paths to socialism, thus validating the separate paths chosen by Tito and later by Mao Ze Dong in China. Khrushchev even went a step further, however, and argued that there could be peaceful coexistence between communism and capitalism, a direct contradiction with the arguments of Marx, Lenin, and Stalin (Ingersoll, Matthews, and Davidson, 2001, 176–178).

Problems with Communist Ideologies

The problems with communist ideology are legion, as are the criticisms of the ideology from the right; consequently, there is insufficient space here to cover the subject in any manner other than just to touch on the highlights, beginning with the criticisms of Hobbesian conservatives. Hobbesian conservatives argue that the abolition of private property violates the basic self-interest of human nature, and that people will work harder for themselves than they will for the collective. Consequently, Hobbesian conservatives argue that Marx's communist utopia, where there is an abundance of goods with fewer hours worked, and all persons are compelled to share with others based on need, rather than greed, is nothing more than delusional fantasy. Conservatives can point to the cases of Ananias and Sapphira in the "communist" society of first century Christianity, who, instead of selling all their property and giving all of the money to the community, kept back some of they money they made selling their property for themselves. Furthermore, the greedy couple attempted to deceive the Apostle Peter concerning the fact that they withheld some of the money they had made selling their property (Acts 5:1–2).

Hobbesian conservatives also point to William Bradford (1856, 1981, 132), who observed among the Pilgrims that their communal economic arrangement "was found to breed much confusion and discontent and retard much employment that would have been to their benefit and comfort." In other words, Bradford observed that communism among the Pilgrims provided disincentive to work and produced an unhappy society with "much confusion." Consequently, Bradford concludes that communism was not meant by God to be the ideal human living arrangement, since people appear to be unsuited to such a structure. Evidently, the collectivization of property in the Pilgrim community did not cause it to lose its "class character," as Marx and Engels predicted. Instead, Hobbesian conservatives argue that the "unhappy" and unproductive state of the Pilgrim society is the predictable result of selfish human nature.

The fact that no Marxist planned economy has ever risen to out-produce the economic juggernauts of the capitalist West is further proof to the conservative believers in the free market that the communist economic structure is basically flawed. Furthermore, there is little evidence to suggest that workers in the Soviet Union or People's Republic of China were any more likely to achieve self-actualization through their labor than they were under capitalist systems. Instead, the low productivity of the command economies in comparison to the capitalist West, and the "unhappy" and unproductive state of the Pilgrims recorded by Bradford, may suggest that the opposite is true.

THE FAILURE OF HISTORIC MATERIALISM

Critics of Marx argue that his idea that all of history is eventually moving toward an eventual communist order has not proven to be correct. First, it is unclear from a reading of history that the human experience is a linear progression toward anything. Instead, economic development is a history of fits and starts, with progress, such as that under the Greek and Roman empires, and regress, such as that in Europe during the Middle Ages after the destruction of the Roman Empire by barbarians. Furthermore, even if history is a record of human economic progress, and even if there are a few fits and starts along the way, it is not evident that global communist revolution will be its ultimate conclusion. Instead, no capitalist country has followed Marx's road map through advanced capitalist development to culminate in proletarian communist revolution. Instead, successful communist revolutions have all come in locations with little capitalist development and without even a well-developed proletarian class. The countries (other than Russia) with successful communist revolutions—China, Vietnam, Cambodia, Angola, and Cuba—were all agrarian societies dominated by agricultural peasant economies. Since becoming communist, none has surpassed the capitalist West in economic well-being.

Historic materialism has a second flaw in that it is certain that economics, though an important force, is not always the driving force behind human behavior. For example, the driving force behind al Qaeda, as well as the Christian Crusades of the eleventh and twelfth centuries, was as much religious as it was economic. The same could be said for the Iranian revolution of 1979 and the takeover of Afghanistan by the Taliban in the 1990s. Similarly, the Nazi movement in Germany in the 1930s was clearly as much about nationalism and patriotism as it was economics. The American Civil Rights movement of the 1960s may have been partially economic in character, but it was also clearly a reaction to racism and segregation, and a quest for equal rights and human dignity. The same perhaps could be said for the feminist movement of the 1970s and the gay rights movement of the present. Similarly, the Vietnam War protest movement of the 1960s was as much about moral revulsion to the human suffering in Southeast Asia as it was economically motivated. Even the re-election of George W. Bush in 2004 may have been as much about non-economic values as economic, as fundamentalist Protestants over-whelmingly supported George W. Bush, while secular Americans over-whelmingly supported John Kerry. Besides, the American election of 2004 essentially violates Marx's argument that society is always stratified into two classes, the bourgeoisie and the proletariat, who are directly at odds with each other. Working-class Americans in the southern and western agricultural states generally voted for the Republican Party, which in Marxist terms would be the party of the bourgeoisie.

Finally, the development of a global proletariat with common bonds across national lines appears as elusive as when Marx and Engels wrote their manifesto in 1848. While capitalism has indeed spread all over the earth as Marx and Engels predicted, the internationalization of the labor movement is in its infancy at best, and the working classes in different countries are as likely to view each other as competitors as they are com-rades. Nothing remotely approaching Marx's global proletarian organi-zation and revolution has ever come into existence, but wars of nationalism fragmented the Balkan peninsula in Europe throughout the early 1990s, even as nationalism in the various Soviet Republics contributed to the breakup of the USSR.

AUTHORITARIANISM

Instead of the bountiful freedom that Marx expected, the transition to communism created brutal and oppressive authoritarian states in China, Cuba, the Soviet Union, Cambodia, Vietnam, and North Korea. Millions died in Stalinist purges in the Soviet Union, the Great Leap Forward and the Great Cultural Revolution of the People's Republic of China, the "killing fields" of Pol Pot in Cambodia, and the purges of Castro's ene-mies in Cuba. Freedom, especially the freedom to dissent against the gov-ernment, was suppressed in all communist countries as they attempted to make their transitions toward true communism. In every case, the "dic-tatorship of the proletariat" in practice turned out to be nothing more than just another brutal dictatorship. Rather than "withering away," the commu-nist state structures became immense, invasive, oppressive, and corrupt.

In the end, there was virtually nothing that resembled Marx's communist utopia.

No Transitions to Communism

Marx did not provide a clear road map as to how the proletarian state would make its transition fully to communism. Perhaps because Marx was unclear, or perhaps because Marxist communism is in reality a delusional pipe dream, no Marxist proletarian state has ever successfully achieved the transition to communism, nor have any come close. Instead of the state withering away, the state has typically become all-powerful, oppressive, and in control of virtually everything, subject to the whims of an authoritarian dictator. Instead of a classless society, the proletarian dictatorship became stratified, with party elites often living in opulence while the masses continued to go without basic needs, just as they had under capitalism. In the Soviet Union, a popular joke was, "In capitalism, man exploits his fellow man, but in communism, it is the other way around" (Baradat, 1989).

Conflict with Capitalism

In every case, Marx appears to be correct in that communism has been in political and economic conflict with capitalism ever since the Bolshevik Revolution of 1917 ushered in the first communist state. In essence, the communist-vs.-capitalist Cold War dominated global politics from the end of World War II in 1945 to the time of the collapse of the USSR at the end of 1991, thus validating part of Marx's vision. Undoubtedly, the guiding force behind American foreign policy during that period was the containment of communism, and American capitalist antagonism was the impetus to foreign policy in the Soviet Union. That said, however, it is also true that the capitalist West traded with the communist bloc (with numerous interruptions) throughout the Cold War, and that despite the Vietnam War, the Berlin Wall, and the Iron Curtain, there were also numerous periods of rapprochement. These included a military alliance against a common foe in World War II, Khrushchev's "peaceful coexistence," Nixon's "détente," and the "glasnost" and "perestroika" of Mikhail Gorbachev that initiated the spiral to the demise of the communist system in the USSR. While democratic capitalism and communism have remained somewhat antagonistic to the present day, they have proved repeatedly since the Bolshevik Revolution that they are at times able to coexist and even work together when it is in their mutual best interests.

CONFLICT WITH RELIGION

Due to the fact that Marx considered religion the "opiate of the masses" that hindered the development of class consciousness and therefore helped the bourgeoisie stave off revolution, Marx called for the abolition of religion by the proletariat. As a result, the Soviet state in 1918 launched an attack on religion, divesting the Russian Orthodox Church of its land and abolishing religious schools. It was declared illegal for the clergy to provide religious instruction to anyone under the age of eighteen. The state took over the traditional church functions of recording births and deaths, and marriage came under the jurisdiction of the state. The clergy were condemned as members of the bourgeoisie and denied the right to vote, and their children were barred from schools beyond the elementary level. Priests were issued low-priority ration cards, meaning that they were among the poorest people in the Soviet Union (Baradat, 1989, 330). Religious dissent against the state was disallowed, and the authority for investigation and arrest for religious dissidence was given to the KGB (Baradat, 1989, 236). Soviet laws also prevented religious groups from providing many things that are normally considered standard religious activities, such as charity work, hospitals, child care, reading rooms, and religious services outside of church buildings. Furthermore, clergymen were forbidden from making political speeches, encouraging civil disobedience, encouraging separateness, compelling members to make donations, punishing disobedience, or worshiping in state institutions, prisons, or hospitals (Baradat, 1989, 333).

In addition to the formal laws; church members often found themselves harassed at their jobs and outside churches by Communist Party members. As a result, churches were closed all over the Soviet Union and the communist bloc during the Soviet era, and church membership, religiosity, and religious belief dwindled precipitously. It was estimated in the late 1980s that only approximately 15 percent of Soviet citizens could be considered religious believers (Baradat, 1989, 330). Similar patterns appear in the Soviets' former sphere of influence in Eastern Europe. For example, in the formerly communist East Germany in 1990, only 21 percent believed that there is a God, as opposed to 61 percent of Germans in the democratic capitalist West; and only 14 percent of East Germans believed in life after death, as opposed to 55 percent of their West German counterparts. Finally, 55 percent of East Germans reported no religious affiliation at all, as compared to 15 percent of West Germans (Hancock et al., 1993, 203).

The communist purge of religion, however, was not directed solely at Christianity, but at religion in general. Consequently, Muslims, who made up approximately 25 percent of the Soviet population in 1990, found themselves subject to state persecution as well, though the Soviets were generally more tolerant of Muslims than other religions so as to benefit Soviet foreign policies in the Middle East and prevent domestic unrest (Baradat, 1989, 310, 333). Soviet opposition to Islam was at least part of the impetus behind the Soviet invasion and occupation of Afghanistan in the 1980s as the Soviets attempted to prevent the takeover of the country by anti-communist Islamic extremists (Baradat, 1989, 331). Americans interpreted the invasion as another phase in the expansion of Soviet communism, but the Soviets viewed it as an attempt to prevent the development of an ideologically hostile government on their border.

Marx Lives

In spite of the failures of the Marxist-Leninist example in the Soviet Union and Eastern Europe, Marxist theory is not completely dead. Orthodox Marxists point out that Marx expected the entire world to have to go through the advanced stages of capitalism before global proletarian communist revolution would occur. Since this was not the case when the Bolsheviks took over Russia or when the communists of Mao Ze Dong toppled the government in China, it is still possible, they claim, that Marx's predictions will come true some time in the future when global capitalism has advanced through its final stages. To orthodox Marxists, these attempts to "give history a shove" and force communism prior to the time that the forces of historical dialectic could bring revolution as an inevitable course of events, merely prove that Marx was correct in arguing that the world must first go through the advanced capitalist stage before revolution may occur. For these Marxists, the theory remains alive, but there is little for the proletariat to do but watch and wait. Time will tell if the orthodox Marxists are correct, but their numbers have been few and their voices muted since the fall of the Soviet Union, and it does not appear that global communism will be on the horizon any time in the near future.

8

Dependency Theory

Over the last three decades of the twentieth century, there was perhaps no idea that stirred more lively debate in the scholarly study of economic development in lesser-developed countries (LDCs) than that which was spurred by dependency theory. The dependency perspective garnered a host of articulate adherents as well as detractors, and the debates over its merits and demerits occupied a substantial amount of space in professional political science and economic journals. Dependency theory is an important ideological perspective that mixes elements of liberation ideology with Marxist-Leninism to create a unique approach to the problem of development in LDCs. Dependency theory gained wide acceptance in Latin America and other developing areas in the late twentieth century, but also among left-leaning scholars in the United States and Europe. The dependency perspective itself is a leftist critique of, and alternative explanation for, the dominant liberal free-market modernization paradigm that provided the theoretical foundation for the post–World War II international political-economic order.

The basic argument of the dependency perspective is that a political-economic condition labeled as "dependency" produces underdevelopment in LDCs. In other words, dependency theorists hold that LDCs have been impoverished and remain so due to their past and present state of economic dependency. Dependency theorists argue that dependent economies in LDCs are qualitatively different from those in the developed world and that their state of dependency has negative consequences for their economic development. Furthermore, the state of dependency is caused by contact between the LDCs and advanced Western industrial democracies.

The dependency perspective is not monolithic, and the underdevelopment in LDCs that is the focus of dependency theory is itself is a multifaceted concept that encompasses different phenomena, depending on which segment of the dependency theory one espouses. The concept of underdevelopment in dependency literature typically refers to low GNP per capita, low rates of GNP per capita growth, high rates of income inequality, bureaucratic-authoritarian political regimes, and a failure of the political-economic system in meeting the basic human needs of the masses in LDCs.

The dependency perspective is constructed on the notion that powerful capitalist nations would use trade and the international world capitalist economic system to exploit other nations for their own gain. The result of this interaction, according to dependency theorists, is that the wealthy nations are enriched at the expense of the poorer nations, whose poverty is perpetuated through the processes involved in their contact with the supposedly exploitive wealthier nations.

Dependency Theory and Marxist-Leninism

Although dependency theory is clearly based in Marxist-Leninism, and the basic notion of dependency theory—that wealthy nations enrich themselves at the expense of poorer nations—is clearly present in the writings of both Marx and Lenin, there are enough important differences to merit the treatment of dependency theory as a separate ideological offshoot.

First, Marx and Lenin were concerned with explaining the causes of imperialism originating from alleged contradictions in capitalism and capitalism's need for expansion. Dependency theorists are instead primarily interested in the consequences of imperialist relations for LDCs. Although the arguments of Marx and Lenin as to the causes of imperialism are not of critical significance to dependency theory, they are important in substantiating the argument that it is the association with developed international capitalism that produced the dependent and underdeveloped economies in LDCs in the late twentieth century. Second, Marx and Lenin dealt with the formal colonial empires established and maintained by the great colonial powers of the 19th century. Dependency theorists are instead concerned with "neocolonialism," or the more informal systems of dominance maintained by the economic mechanisms of international capital, rather than by direct political control.

Dependency Origins

POLITICAL DOMINATION THROUGH ECONOMIC MEANS

Dependency theory is a reactionary ideology that arose in response to the international capitalist economic system that emerged after World

War II. In this system, new institutions were established, such as the United Nations, the World Bank, and the International Monetary Fund, partially to manage the world economy and partially to assist LDCs in economic development. Conditions that LDCs would have to meet in order to receive loans were established, and the international institutions made recommendations to LDCs as to what measures they should take to further their own economic development. In particular, the UN Economic Commission for Latin America (ECLA) advocated a strategy known as "import substitution," whereby LDCs would impose tariffs on imports in an effort to prop up their own fledgling industries, and then substitute their own domestic manufactured products for imports. The reaction in LDCs to the recommendations and stipulations of the international institutions was not overwhelmingly positive, and dependency theory was part of that reaction.

One of the first post-war scholars to apply ideas later termed dependency theory to the post-war political system was Albert Hirschman in his analysis of foreign trade as an extension of nation-state power. Hirschman provided a central argument of dependency theory: that commerce can be an alternative to war as a policy for dominating other nations. Furthermore, Hirschman (1945, 15) argued, "Even if war could be eliminated, foreign trade would lead to relationships of dependence and influence between nations." Hence, in Hirschman's perspective, trade becomes an instrument of domination rather than an item of mutual benefit as characterized by the classic liberal paradigm of Adam Smith. Hirschman (1945, 36–37) explains this dependent nature of trade between developed and less-developed nations through the following observations of Nazi trade policy:

> Germany's attempt to concentrate on exports of finished products, on the one hand, and on exports to agricultural countries, on the other, had obviously the result of giving her exports a quasi-monopolistic position so far as the productive system of her trading partners was concerned. In addition, to maintain this position, it was one of the great principles of German foreign economic policy to prevent the industrialization of her agricultural trading partners.... By offering a stable market for the agricultural surplus production of these countries, she tied landowners and peasants, the most powerful social groups in these countries, to her own interests.

UNEQUAL EXCHANGE

Two points are worth noting from this quotation. First, Hirschman describes what dependency theorists have since come to label as "unequal exchange," a trade relationship where dependent countries supply raw materials to the developed world and purchase finished manufactured products in return. Second, Hirschman argues that interests of the most powerful groups in the periphery (the LDCs) became coincidental with interests of international capital (the "core"). This, too, later became a central tenet of dependency theory. Finally, it should be noted that attempts by Germany to maximize its own national interest had an inadvertent detrimental effect on the development of the periphery nations, much as dependency theorists would later argue. Hirschman, however, did not imply that the results of his analysis of German trade policy were generalizable to other core-periphery relationships. That step was left to be taken by Raul Prebisch (1950, 1964) and Gunnar Myrdal (1957).

The dependency school of Prebisch and Myrdal developed out of Marxist thought as a direct reaction to the economic policies of the UN Economic Commission of Latin America (Love, 1990, pp. 1–2). By the early 1960s, it had become apparent to many, perhaps most notably one-time ECLA director Raul Prebisch, that the import substitution strategies advocated by the ECLA had not produced the desired economic growth in LDCs (Prebisch, 1961, p. 24). As a result, by the late 1960s, the United Nations Conference on Trade and Development (UNCTAD) was urging LDCs to liberalize their trade policies and accept greater foreign investment and penetration by developed industrial nations (Girvan, 1973, p. 8).

Unfortunately, the liberalization of trade policies, similar to the policy of import substitution, was subsequently perceived among many Latin Americans as also ineffective at stimulating growth. Furthermore, it had the added adverse effect of rendering Latin American states more vulnerable to the fluctuations in the external international capitalist system (Prebisch, 1961, p. 5).

According to Prebisch (1950, 1964), the basic problem in core-periphery relations was the long-term decline in terms of trade. Periphery nations were exporting primarily raw materials and importing primarily finished manufactured products from core nations, much as Hirschman had earlier observed in his study of trade between LDCs and Nazi Germany. Prebisch contended that the prices of manufactured goods tend to rise faster than those of raw materials, hence producing a long-term decline in terms of trade. Furthermore, Prebisch (1950, 1964) argued that the strength of organized labor in the core tended to make the price of raw materials exported by the core to the periphery rise at a faster rate than raw material imports from the periphery, thus exacerbating the terms of trade problem. Prebisch's declining terms of trade argument was later supported by a 1974 study from the International Bank for Reconstruction and Development, which concluded that terms of trade in LDCs had consistently declined in the 1950–1971 period.

In order to counteract the terms of trade problem, Prebisch asserted that LDCs were forced to constantly increase their volumes of exports, as compared to their import volumes, in order to achieve a positive balance of payments. Unfortunately, periphery states were unable to do so because of the inelasticity of demand for the raw materials which they produced (Prebisch, 1964). In other words, it is difficult for Honduras, for example, suddenly to make Americans eat more bananas. Consequently, Prebisch argued that the classic liberal free-market prescription would be unable to remedy the terms of trade problem for LDCs. In order to remedy this problem, Prebisch (1964) essentially prescribed that core states must subsidize periphery-manufactured imports through nonreciprocal tariff reduction, a position that developed capitalist nations rejected.

DEPENDENCY AND ECONOMIC INEQUALITY

The general idea of the dependency perspective, that the expansion of the capitalist economies of the industrialized West impedes the growth of lesser developed states, was also echoed by Gunnar Myrdal (1957). Myrdal argued that left unregulated, the international capitalist system tended to increase the movement of finance capital and skilled labor from developed to lesser-developed states. The higher the level of development by the core state, the greater the "spread" effect of the finance capital and skilled labor to the LDCs. Myrdal argued that this process produces uneven development between core and peripheral areas, which, left unchecked, will increase inequalities both between the core and periphery and within both the core and periphery. In other words, Myrdal expects the core countries to grow at a faster rate than LDCs, thereby creating an ever-larger income gap between core and periphery states. Simultaneously, within both core and periphery states, Myrdal expected the domestic income gap to continually increase.

Myrdal (1970, 297) later argued that international trade produces inequality, a standard argument of dependency theorists:

> International trade ... will generally tend to breed inequality, and will do so the more strongly when substantial inequalities are already established.... Unregulated market forces will not work toward reaching any equilibrium which could imply a trend toward an equalization of incomes. By circular causation with cumulative effects, a country superior in productivity and income will tend to become more superior, while a country

on an inferior level will tend to be held down at that level or even to dete-
riorate further—as long as matters are left to the free unfolding of the
market forces.

Both Myrdal and Prebisch place emphasis on the vested interests of
the core, and structures placed in the periphery by the core during the
colonial period, as major obstacles to subsequent development in LDCs.
Myrdal and Prebisch also both argued that cooperation and compromise
between core and periphery could be reached on developmental planning
issues, therefore possibly boosting development in the periphery. Dependency theorists later disputed this assumption following the publication
of Andre Gunder Frank's seminal 1967 work, *Capitalism and Underdevelopment in Latin America*. It was also following this publication that the
discipline of political science became flooded with dependency theory literature.

Radical Dependency Theory

Richard Bath and Dilmus James (1976, 10) label a group of scholars
who tend to hold to the positions of Andre Gunder Frank with little
important deviation as "radical dependency theorists." The radical dependency perspective of Frank and that of other radical dependency theorists,
such as James Cockroft (1974) and Dale Johnson (1973), is a direct rebut-
tal of classic liberal free-market modernization theorists, such as David
McClelland (1967) and Daniel Lerner (1958), who viewed underdevelopment as resulting from internal causes within LDCs. Reflecting the
Leninists' imperialism perspective, the radical dependency advocates pro-
pose that LDCs cannot follow the Western path to development because
of the history of exploitive colonialism in LDCs. More specifically, this
history of colonial experience drastically altered the infrastructures of
LDCs (Frank, 1967, 96).

In this perspective, the outcome of this historical process is an asym-
metrical structure of relations between the center and periphery states,
producing a widening gap between core states and periphery states in levels of development. Due to the differential returns from trade that results
from the trade of raw materials in the periphery in exchange for manufactured goods from the core, radical dependency theorists argue that the
international capitalist system has produced a system of exchange between
the core and periphery that is biased in favor of the core at the expense
of the periphery, thus exacerbating international inequalities. Underdevelopment, in this perspective, is caused by exploitation of LDCs (the

periphery) by industrialized nations (the core) through capitalist economic trade relationships. Radical dependency theorists argue that the only way for dependent states to break out of this "exploitive," dependent relationship is through socialist revolution.

ANDRE GUNDER FRANK

Perhaps the most important work from the radical dependency perspective is that of Andre Gunder Frank (1967). Frank's work was particularly important to the development of dependency literature since it led to a great volume of similar writings by like-minded scholars, and because it gave rise to lively debate between dependency theorists and other scholars who view the work of the dependency school less favorably (Mayer 1989, 93; Almond, 1987). In Frank's work, he enunciates positions that are central to those of virtually all radical dependency advocates, thereby providing a springboard on which the entire school of dependency was catapulted.

In a nutshell, Frank (1967, 197–211) proposed that capitalism simultaneously produces underdevelopment in some areas and development in others. This approach has been adopted by dependency advocates in general (Chilcote and Edelstein, 1974, 27–28), with a consensus that underdevelopment is produced in LDCs through contact with the West. Frank argues that the same historical and economic processes that create development in the Western "metropolis" simultaneously create underdevelopment in the "satellites." Dependency, according to Frank, is merely a stage in the development of the world capitalist system; however, Frank viewed this stage as one that will continue to retard, rather than promote, industrial development in the Third World. In the words of Frank, "They are rich, because we are poor" (1967, 97).

Frank (1967, 197–211) also viewed the structure of the international capitalist system as a system of metropolis-satellite relationships which linked the United States (metropolis) with dependent states (satellites), and linked the elites of dependent states with their own interior in dependent relationships, thus linking all areas of the world in a chain of dependency, class struggle, and unequal exchange. Additionally, the only method available for LDCs to break out of the dependent relationships was through socialist revolution (Frank, 1967, 200–211).

Frank is not alone in this prescription, but instead is joined by other radical dependency writers (for example, see Cockroft, 1974; Johnson, 1973; Petras, 1973; Chilcote and Edelstein, 1974), as well as some more moderate writers, such as Theotonio Dos Santos (1970), in viewing socialist revolution as a sound policy choice for LDCs who desire to shed dependency and underdevelopment. In addition, Frank (1967) draws a distinction between "*under*developed" and "*un*developed." Frank contends that the industrialized West was never *under*developed, a state which is only caused by contact between *un*developed states and developed states, since there were no developed states to exploit the undeveloped West during their earlier periods of development.

In Frank's view, which was widely supported by other radical dependency scholars (Chilcote and Edelstein, 1974, 27–28), the political, social, and economic structures and situations of LDCs are qualitatively different from those of Western industrialized states during their periods of development. Since modern LDCs are externally shaped by developed states, the developmental destinies of these LDCs are completely out of their own control, and instead are shaped by the core states (Chilcote and Edelstein, 1974; Frank, 1972, 318). Indeed, it is this external shaping of social, political, and economic structures which defines "dependency" in the views of the radical scholars. The radical view of the concept of dependency is well-captured by the following widely quoted dependency definition offered by Dos Santos (1970).

> By dependence we mean a situation in which the economy of certain countries is conditioned by the development and expansion of another economy to which the former is subjected. The relation of interdependence between two or more economies, and between these and world trade, assumes the form of dependence when some countries (the dominant ones) can expand and can be self-sustaining, while other countries (the dependent ones) can do this only as a reflection of that expansion, which can have either a positive or a negative effect on their immediate development.

According to Frank (1967), since the economic well-being of LDCs is shaped by the world capitalist system and their relationships with external industrialized states, the situation in the Third World is best described as the "development of underdevelopment." This process is divided into four stages, each defined by four different forms of monopoly exercised by the metropolis: commercial monopoly or mercantilism, prior to 1800; industrial monopoly, 1800–1900, monopoly of capital goods, 1900–1950; and technological monopoly, 1950 to present (Bath and James, 1976).

NATIONAL AND INTERNATIONAL BOURGEOISIE

Frank also argues that the bourgeoisie in dependent states is divided into two segments: one associated with the international sector, and another associated with the domestic sector. Frank posits that the international sector bourgeoisie are the most powerful and control the most dynamic industries because of access to international capital. The domestic sector bourgeoisie within LDCs are subordinate to the international sector, whose interests coincide with those of the international capitalists in the metropolis. The lower classes in LDCs are living in poverty and have no political power. As a result, power is concentrated in the hands of a few internationally oriented elites, therefore lending itself to authoritarian abuse. The masses and domestic bourgeoisie are too weak to establish democratic institutions. Furthermore, the interests of the international bourgeoisie are opposed to those of society as a whole within the LDCs; therefore, authoritarian rule is necessarily instituted by the international bourgeoisie in order to control society (Frank, 1967, 43–53). This central argument—that the bourgeoisie or elites in LDCs have similar interests to, and are controlled by, elites in the industrialized core—became another major area of consensus among dependency scholars (Bath and James, 1976, 11; Chilcote and Edelstein, 1974, 30–32, 53).

In summation, Frank's four most important hypotheses, as presented by Alvin So (1990), are presented below:

> Hypothesis #1. In contrast to the development of the world metropolis, which is no one's satellite, the development of national and other subordinate metropolises is limited by other satellite statuses. For instance, although Sao Paulo has begun to build up an industrial establishment, Frank does not believe Brazil can break out of the cycle of satellite development, which is characterized by non-autonomous and unsatisfactory industrial development.
> Hypothesis #2. The satellites experience their greatest economic development when their ties to the metropolis are weakest.
> Hypothesis #3. When the metropolis recovers from its crisis, and reestablishes the trade and investment ties that then fully reincorporate the satellites into the system, the previous industrialization of these regions is choked off.
> Hypothesis #4. The regions that are the most underdeveloped today are those that had the closest ties to the metropolises in the past. Archaic institutions in the satellites are historical products of the penetration of metropolis capitalism [So, 1990, 97–98].

In Frank's analysis, there is no room for development within the dependent satellites, which are merely economic colonies of the metropolis. In later works, Frank (1972, 318) takes his position that capitalist expansion produces underdevelopment even further, arguing that the earlier and more persistent the contacts between LDCs and capitalistic institutions, the more underdeveloped the lesser-developed states are likely to remain. Essentially, then, Frank's position is the direct opposite of that of classic liberal economic theorists.

Other scholars, including Chilcote and Edelstein (1974), Cockroft (1974), Johan Galtung (1971), Johnson (1973), and James Petras (1973), are in concurrence with Frank, taking the position that the interests of the core and the periphery are "definitely opposed" rather than complementary. Importantly, virtually all kinds of contact with the industrialized West, including foreign aid and foreign investment, are viewed as detrimental to LDCs (Chilcote and Edelstein, 1974, 27; Bath and James, 1976, 11).

Significant among these radical dependency scholars is the approach of Johan Galtung (1971). Like Frank, Galtung based his formulation on a center-periphery model of the international system. Galtung divides the global system into four hierarchical classes with the elites within the most developed states at the top, elites in LDCs underneath them, masses in developed states a notch lower, and the masses within the least developed states at the bottom. Galtung views dependency as a facet of imperialism, of which he offers the following definition (1971, 83):

> Imperialism is a relation between a Center and a Periphery nation so that (1) there is harmony of interest between the center in the Center nations and the center in the Periphery nation, (2) there is more disharmony of interest within the Periphery nation than within the Center nation, (3) there is disharmony of interest between the periphery in the Center nation and the periphery in the Periphery nation.

Galtung's first element of imperialism, the harmony of interests between core elites and periphery elites, is labeled by Paul Baran (1957) as clientelism. This clientelism tends to be viewed by dependency theorists as a major impediment to development in LDCs, since the interests of elites in both the core and periphery are viewed as contradictory to the needs of the lower class in the periphery.

Similar to Frank, in Galtung's writings, the processes at work which create development in the center and underdevelopment for the periphery are circular and cumulative. Additionally, Galtung concurs with Frank that only through the displacement of the center by the periphery can these processes be overcome. This assessment is essentially just another way of stating that dependency can be severed only through socialist revolution.

New Dependency Theory

Although dependency theorists generally tend to support the contentions of Frank, something of a paradigm shift has occurred within dependency literature after 1970, led by the work of Cardoso (1973), Cardoso and Faletto (1979), and Peter Evans (1976, 1979). Scholars who have produced this paradigm shift are labeled by Alvin So (1990) as "new dependency" scholars. The new dependency perspective surfaced primarily due to the inability of radical dependency theorists to explain how there had been increases in economic growth and economic development in LDCs in spite of increased contact with the supposedly exploitive core nations. Such an argument is central to that of Cardoso and Cardoso and Faletto, who coined the term "associated-dependent development" to refer to such phenomena.

ASSOCIATED-DEPENDENT DEVELOPMENT

Associated-dependent development, according to Cardoso, refers to a process of externally induced economic growth within LDCs which is achieved by curtailing or reducing domestic consumption and welfare. The policies which produce associated-dependent development are produced from liberal capitalist economic theories which stress capital formation. According to Cardoso, policymakers in LDCs attract foreign investment by providing low wages and other incentives to investors. The foreign investment then may provide robust, but uneven, growth.

Cardoso (1973, 149) argues that "to some extent, the interests of the foreign corporations become compatible with the internal prosperity of the dependent country. In this sense, they help promote development." Therefore, Cardoso and Faletto essentially vary from radical dependency scholars in arguing that a form of development for LDCs is possible in spite of their conditions of dependency. However, Cardoso and Faletto argue that such "associated-dependent development" tends to lead to bureaucratic authoritarianism because of a political alliance between elite interests in the core and elite interests in the periphery. According to Cardoso (quoted in Bonilla and Girling, 1973, 7–16), the type of development in dependent economies "creates a restricted, limited and upper class oriented type of market and society." In other words, associated-dependent development leads to great income inequality in LDCs. Cardoso (quoted in Bonilla and Girling, 1973) describes dependent development as "contradictory, exploitive, and generates inequalities." Cardoso (1973, 176) also argues that associated-dependent development may lead to an increase in the accumulation of wealth, but leads to "mass manipulation" and will not bring about development "favoring the majority and increasing the quality of life." Cardoso does not, however, explain what he means by "quality of life."

Cardoso and Faletto argue against a universal "theory of dependency" and state that different "situations of dependency" exist. The basic argument is that the exact nature of "dependency" depends on the nature of alliances between governmental elites, foreign capitalists, and other prominent economic and political groups internal to the societies. A similar argument is posed by Susan Bodenheimer (1976, 357), who concludes that dependent industrialization is integrated into and complementary to the needs of foreign economies and that clientele social classes in the periphery have a vested interest in the goals of the capitalists in the core.

Cardoso and Faletto (1979, xviii) state that their purpose is to show "how internal and external processes of political domination relate to one another" and how "external factors are interwoven with internal ones ... to determine the links between social groups." In other words, Cardoso and Faletto argue that the economic dependency of LDCs stems not only from the domination by external forces, but also from the much more complex interaction of economic forces, political structures, social movements, and historically conditioned alliances. Cardoso and Faletto take a historical approach to support their arguments, presenting examples of societies whose economies developed differently due to varying political alliances.

New Dependency Variances
From Radical Dependency

Cardoso and Faletto and other new dependency theorists differ from radical dependency theorists in a number of important ways. Cardoso and Faletto allow greater latitude to elites in LDCs in making development decisions than do their radical dependency counterparts, who essentially imply that all development decisions in LDCs are shaped by the core. Furthermore, Cardoso and Faletto (1979, 196) point out that LDCs have often been able to exert influence over core nations in procuring favorable treaties and credit lines, a situation that radical dependency theory does not allow.

Consistent with the arguments of Cadoso and Faletto, Peter Evans (1979) argues that decision-makers in LDCs have the freedom to make political choices about economic development within the constraints of dependent relationships. Such freedom of political choice for decision-makers in LDCs is absent in the arguments of radical dependency theorists. Similarly, Martin Staniland (1985) cites the decisions of governmental elites in Brazil as central to the issue of industrial development for the purpose of alleviating Brazilian economic sluggishness. Essentially, the argument of new dependency scholars is that increases in levels of development and industrialization in LDCs can occur, although that development is dependent on support from external forces and less efficient than indigenously-led development. In these analyses, the state and other prominent economic elites that benefit from development in the economic sectors under their control provide the means through which core states are able to develop at the expense of LDCs, while allowing some form of economic development within LDCs.

NEW DEPENDENCY, INEQUALITY, AND AUTHORITARIANISM

Cardoso, Cardoso and Faletto, and Guillermo O'Donnell (1973, 1979) argue that associated-dependent development results in uneven development and economic inequality within the LDCs; consequently, authoritarian regimes are installed in the LDCs in order to control the disturbances that result. Hence, these new dependency scholars imply that authoritarianism is necessary in LDCs in order to achieve the type of development which is produced in dependent economies.

Similarly, Ronaldo Munck (1985) argues that external dependency forces LDCs to accept a situation where their own development and the capital accumulation of core states are inextricably linked. The political ramifications of this situation are that state regimes in LDCs were forced to develop in order to reconcile these "opposing" goals. Consequently, populist regimes in LDCs are replaced with bureaucratic-authoritarian regimes.

Although the work of new dependency scholars is much less deterministic than those of the radical dependency approach, and they do provide examples of differing forms of dependency produced by diverse configurations of state and class alliances, these examples demonstrate that new dependency theory remains quite deterministic. Although Cardoso criticizes the deterministic nature of radical dependency scholarship, he and Faletto both use deterministic language themselves in their unbending arguments that dependency produces income inequality, authoritarianism, and depressed quality of life.

A second thread which binds them to the radical approach is the contention that external factors remain major determinants of economic underdevelopment in LDCs. Cardoso and Faletto argued that when there are economic or political crises in the core, LDCs tend to adopt policies targeting internal development. As an example, they cite the actions of Latin American states during World War II, when they essentially followed an import substitution strategy, imposing tariffs to boost the domestic sector and fund the establishment of state-owned steel and oil industries and electrical power plants (Cardoso and Faletto, 1979, 129).

MNCs in the New Dependency Paradigm

Cardoso and Faletto also place great stock in the role of multinational corporations (MNCs) as agents of dependency. Essentially, they argue that the rise of MNCs has placed greater economic restrictions on development in LDCs. In the words of Cardoso and Faletto:

> The linkages between the dependent economies and the internationalization of the market have solidified through the creation of industrial platforms for the export of products where MNCs seek a comparative advantage, the transformation of colonial enclaves into those of imperialist corporations, concentration of isolated production processes, and the control of local markets by MNC production [1979, 187].

Building on the work of Cardoso and Faletto, Munck (1985) argues that development in LDCs is directed by, and dependent on, foreign capital and interests. Similarly, Evans (1979) also views MNCs as having great importance in constraining the dependent states. Evans credits MNCs with transferring technical knowledge, finances, and liberal values to the state in Brazil; however, Evans allows the state a more independent role in economic development. In Evans' work, a "triple alliance" emerges, consisting of the state, MNCs, and local capitalists, all working together for the purpose of national development and profits. Similarly, Richard Sklar (1987) argues that a "managerial bourgeoisie" develops in LDCs, consisting of MNCs and domestic and international-oriented capitalists within LDCs. Like Evans, Sklar argues that the state and capitalists in LDCs are "socialized" by foreign capitalists to adopt liberal values. Although these new dependency scholars recognize that economic growth and industrialization are possible in dependent economies, they argue that the dependent growth leads to the strengthening of the state productive sector and creates increasingly repressive states. Once again, in the end, the new dependency approach retains its deterministic character.

NEW DEPENDENCY AND SOCIALIST REVOLUTION

Similar to radical dependency theorists, new dependency theorists tend to be supportive of the position that the chains of dependency can only be broken through a transition to socialism. Cardoso and Faletto (1979, 213), for example, argue that the only alternative to dependent development is the adoption of socialism.

SUMMARY OF NEW DEPENDENCY THEORY

In summation, dependency theory has evolved to encompass the possibility that some form of development may occur in dependent relationships; however, the development is inequitable and benefits only the elites. Furthermore, new dependency theorists argue that increases in industrialization and growth in LDCs do not lead to any basic changes in the structures of dominance and dependence between core and periphery states. This position is well articulated by Dos Santos (1976, 86):

> The new phase of big capital, relying on multinational corporations, leads to a new international division of labor which presupposes an increase in the industrialization of raw materials and of products of a low degree of technological development, and the export of these products to the dominant centers, particularly to the United States which, in its turn would specialize in the production of goods and services for export which have a high technological content, and the export of capital, thus raising the parasitism typical of the imperialist powers to its highest level.

In other words, Dos Santos argues that associated-dependent development will exacerbate unequal exchange and technological dependency with all of the negative long term effects still prevalent. Dos Santos refers to this continuance of structures of dominance and dependency as "neo-colonialism," a term which describes the set of mechanisms which reinforce the exploitive system supposedly established during the colonial period. According to Dos Santos, the three most important of these mechanisms are clientelism (when needs and goals of elites in LDCs coincide with those of international capital), aid, and multinational corporations.

One final comment is necessary concerning the possibility of economic development within LDCs in dependent relationships. Definitions of development among dependency scholars do not necessarily refer to growth and industrialization. Frank (1972, 28) argues that GNP growth is not what he means by development at all; rather, development is equated with income equity, which he argues dependency fails to produce.

Problems with Dependency Theory

The dependency perspective, not surprisingly, is not without its detractors. Criticisms leveled against the dependency framework include allegations that it is nothing more than leftist ideological political propaganda, is tautological, and is poorly conceptualized. Dependency is charged with being poorly defined, based on insufficient evidence, and inconclusive. Dependency theorists have also been charged with ignoring dependent relationships between socialist "metropoles" and "satellites," such as the former Soviet Union and Cuba. Furthermore, although dependency theory is essentially grounded in the Marxist paradigm, noted scholars have criticized dependency for its inconsistency with Marx. It must be noted, however, that the major critics of the dependency paradigm tend to be liberal rather than Marxist scholars. Furthermore, dependency theorists glaringly omit the possibility that physical quality of life may be unaffected by greater inequality. The following review expands on some of these more important disagreements with the dependency framework.

CONFUSION OF THE CAUSAL ORDER

Michael Brown (1974) argues that dependency theorists are unable to explain how, in the first place, some states became developed and others did not. Brown illuminates the fact that the vast majority of the underdeveloped world was already underdeveloped prior to contact between core and periphery and the colonial period which followed. Obviously, the core in Europe could not have caused underdevelopment in the Western Hemisphere prior to 1492, but at that time the peoples of the Western Hemisphere were obviously in many ways technologically behind, since they were paddling in canoes when Columbus sailed across the ocean. Columbus arrived in a world with no steel, no wheels, and boats that typically had no rudders or centerboards. Although there were many noteworthy achievements of the Native American societies, this relative lack of development prior to Columbus is a fact that dependency theorists conveniently ignore. This ability to ignore such relevant facts is a primary symptom of ideological thinking rather than reasoning based on analysis.

LEFTIST IDEOLOGICAL PROPAGANDA

Gabriel Almond (1987) argues that the dependency perspective should not be considered theory at all, but instead is merely an exercise in leftist pamphleteering or propaganda. In other words, Almond argues that dependency theory is merely ideology and not political analysis. Similarly, David Ray (1973) argues that the dependency perspective suffers from several logical flaws. For example, Ray points out that some dependency advocates, such as Frank, conceptualize dependency as a dichotomous variable. In this conception dependency becomes an all-or-none situation, a conceptualization which destroys the policy relevance of dependency analysis.

Concurring with Ray, Sanjaya Lall (1975) argues that dependency theorists have been unable to demonstrate either logically or empirically that dependent economies are qualitatively different in type from non-dependent economies and that the characteristics of dependency have an adverse effect on economic development. Lall argues that the failure to show that dependent economies are of a qualitatively different kind leaves open the possibility that development is a sequential stage phenomenon consistent with liberal modernization theory. Hence, dependency theory, according to Lall, cannot rule out the possibility that differences in development between the developed and underdeveloped world are merely a matter of degree, rather than of a qualitatively different type. Furthermore, Lall (1975, 800–807) observes that there are numerous characteristics shared by both developed and underdeveloped states, such as reliance on foreign investment, foreign technology, and foreign sources of media information. Lall, therefore, concludes that dependency is a matter of degree rather than type and that it ranges on a continuum from the most powerful, least dependent state to the least powerful, most dependent state. Furthermore, Lall argues that the problems of dependent growth, such as inequality, debt, and trade imbalances, are shared by both developed and underdeveloped states.

VAGARIES, OVERSIMPLIFICATIONS, AND OVERSTATEMENTS

Ray (1973) argues that dependency theorists work with a biased sample since they ignore dependent economies in the former communist bloc. This biased sample leads dependency theorists to come to the invalid conclusion that dependency is caused by capitalism when "simple disparity in power" is able to explain dependency both in the capitalist world and in the former communist bloc (Ray, 1973, 7). Concurring with Ray is Robert Packenham (1986), who also argues that the dependency framework ignores the core-periphery relationships between the former Soviet Union and its "satellites." As Packenham demonstrated through his Cuban case study, the dependency theory prescription of socialist revolution appears to be a poor way to sever the bonds of dependency. Finally, Ray argues that the dependency theory argument that direct foreign investment produces underdevelopment is too simplistic. Essentially, Ray argues that while investment in some types of industries (such as resource extraction) may distort development, investment in other industries, such as manufacturing or the service sector, may *not* have distorting effects on development.

In a similar vein, Phillip O'Brien (1975) argues that dependency theses are often overstated, over-generalized, vague, and full of unsubstantiated reasoning, such as the suggestion that multinational corporations can repatriate all of the profits from enterprises in LDCs. Alec Nove (1975) concurs with O'Brien, arguing that radical dependency theorists destroy their own case through broad overstatements and omission of solid evidence. Nove further chastises dependency theorists for ignoring the role of internal factors such as domestic politics, population demographics, and culture. Nove adds that the most serious flaw in dependency theory is the failure to distinguish between the concept of underdevelopment and foreign political and economic control or exploitation.

Furthermore, Bath and James contend that despite Johan Galtung's "structural approach," dependency (or imperialism, in his formulation) still suffers from a high degree of abstraction that renders it unreceptive to scientific methodology. Secondly, Bath and James argue that Galtung's formulation, like Frank's, remains quite deterministic in character, and fails to explain the apparent development during the 1960s in many LDCs, particularly the newly industrializing countries (NICs) of Asia (Bath and James, 1976, 11).

Misuse of Marxism

Taking a somewhat different approach, Gabriel Almond (1987) criticizes dependency theory for misuse of Marxism. Almond argues that Dependency theorists tend to adhere to Marxist paradigms of historic materialism, yet the historical evidence that should accompany such an argument is often slim or nonexistent. For their part, Marx and Engels (1955, 14) argued:

> The bourgeoisie, by the rapid improvement of all instruments of production, by the immensely facilitated means of communication, draws all nations, even the most barbarian into civilization.... It compels all nations ... to adopt the bourgeois mode of production; it compels them to ... become bourgeois themselves.

This statement suggests that Marx and Engels expected contact between core states and the periphery to produce development in the periphery, contrary to the views of Frank (1967). Similarly, Lenin argued that capitalist states will spread capitalism to the periphery in order to exploit the cheap labor. Lenin explained that capitalism, by nature, had to expand in order to siphon off surplus value; therefore, the core would develop markets in the periphery and acquire raw materials from the periphery. Essentially then, Lenin, Marx and Engels declared that capitalism contains the seeds of its own destruction and the core will destroy itself by spreading its capitalism to the periphery, which subsequently develops and surpasses the core. It is, perhaps, ironic that empirical testing of the dependency perspective cannot simultaneously support both the dependency position that periphery-core contact produces periphery underdevelopment, and the Marxist-Leninist position that periphery-core contact will develop the periphery at the expense of the core.

TAUTOLOGY

The dependency perspective is also criticized for often being very poorly operationalized (Lall, 1975; Nove, 1975; Obrien, 1975; Mayer, 1989). The general consensus is that the imprecision of operationalization makes it very difficult for scholars to measure the concept of dependency. Lall also contends that the arguments of Frank and other radical dependency theorists essentially follow the tautological circle, in stating that dependent countries are those which lack the capacity for autonomous growth because they are dependent.

DEPENDENCY THEORY IGNORES PROGRESS

In order to accept dependency theory, one must essentially ignore significant economic growth in LDCs throughout the world over extended time periods. Although all LDCs have not experienced robust growth, the average economic growth in LDCs from 1965 to 1990 was 3.85 percent (Farmer, 1999). From 1990 to 2000, the growth in LDCs averaged 3.79 percent (if the former communist bloc is excluded). Essentially, the associated-dependent development argument neglects the progress in LDCs over the last three decades in improving both GNP per capita and physical quality of life. Dependency theorists argue that dependency produces inequality. Implicit in this argument is the contention that the lower class suffers greater hardship due to dependency. While it remains unclear and unproven that dependency produces inequality to begin with, it is possible, if not probable, that what inequality does exist is likely to be produced by an increasing rate of growth of the wealth of the upper income class in LDCs vis-à-vis slower growth of the wealth of the lower class. In other words, when inequality increases, it does not necessarily mean that the lower class has experienced decreased physical quality of life; it may simply mean that the income gap between them and the wealthier class has increased because their collective wealth is growing at a faster rate than that of the lower classes. On the contrary, the physical quality of life of the lower class may even be improved as inequality increases if their standard of living has improved in an absolute sense, while simultaneously worsening in a relative sense to that of the wealthier classes. Furthermore, empirical analysis suggests that contact with the core increases the quality of life in LDCs, as indicated by increases in literacy, life expectancy and infant mortality rates that coincide with the introduction of more modern medical practices and humanitarian assistance. In fact, there appears to be a correlation between direct foreign aid from the core and improved physical quality of life in the periphery (Farmer, 1999).

DEPENDENCY THEORY IGNORES GEOGRAPHY

Geographers have observed for decades (if not centuries) that there is a correlation between some geographic phenomena and economic underdevelopment. For instance, with the possible exception of the Mayans in the Yucatan rain forest, there is no record of any advanced society developing in any tropical rain forest climate. Similarly, a good number of underdeveloped areas of the world are either desert climates or mountainous terrains. While there are exceptions, such as the Incan civilization of the Andes and the advanced Swiss society of the Alps, it is obvious that these geographical factors tend to hinder growth. Consequently, the underdevelopment of the Congo rain forest may have much more to do with the inhospitable nature of that climate to advanced human development than to core-periphery relationships. Furthermore, as Jared Diamond (1999) points out in his Pulitzer Prize–winning book *Guns, Germs, and Steel*, much of Western development in juxtaposition to LDCs correlates with the presence of large domesticated animals, specifically horses, swine, and cattle. Since there were no horses, domesticated swine, or cattle in the Western Hemisphere prior to Columbus, people were unable to take advantage of the power of these animals for their own development.

Diamond also illuminates the fact that Latin America is latitudinally oriented rather than longitudinally contiguous like the Eurasian landmass. The advantage of the longitudinally oriented landmass for the Europeans was that it made the sharing of ideas easier. For example, wheat will grow in similar latitudes of both China and Europe; hence, Marco Polo could bring pasta back to Europe from China, and the Italians could adopt it as a food staple.

The same idea-sharing was more difficult in Latin America, however, due to the latitudinal configuration that results in severe climate variations. For example, there are thousands of plants grown in the Amazon rain forest that cannot survive in the high mountains of the Andes. Similarly, the wooly llama of the Andes is not well-suited for the Amazon rain forest. The fact that Amazonians did not develop a significant wool export business from llamas living on the same continent has everything to do with their climate constraints and nothing to do with colonialism, core-periphery relationships, or international bourgeoisie. Instead of "you are rich because we are poor," perhaps a better explanation is, "We are poor because we were born in the Amazon and Congo rain forests, the Sahara and Kalahari Deserts, and the mountains of Africa and South America."

Finally, the very small geographic size of many LDCs makes them naturally susceptible to economic dependency, since it would violate all economic and geographical realities to suggest that a small geographic area would contain all of the raw materials necessary for constructing an advanced, industrial society. While it is true that many smaller countries—Japan and the UK, for example—have experienced tremendous economic development, it is also true that they are dependent on other societies for tremendous volumes of goods that are simply unavailable in their native geographic space. The Japanese and the British have proved that economic development is possible in their unique situations, but they have also proved that limited geographic area may introduce major challenges of its own. For example, the Japanese entry into World War II was at least partially related to their own deficiency in oil and other natural resources. Furthermore, the British and Japanese island ecosystems are in many ways unique, and therefore may be more conducive to development than the climates and terrestrial flora and fauna of other, less developed island societies, such as Madagascar or the Philippines. Does the tropical climate of the Philippines better explain their underdevelopment than colonialism and core-periphery exploitation? Dependency theory does not allow us to consider such a proposition and therefore closes off inquiry.

Dependency Theory and Ideological Conflict

Dependency theory obviously conflicts with the classic liberal ideology espoused by American and other Western free-market conservatives, hindering dialogue between the two by claiming that contact with the Western developed capitalist democracies is the cause of underdevelopment in LDCs. Under dependency theory, both foreign investment and even philanthropic efforts by developed capitalist democracies must be viewed as hostile, since any contact with the West, including humanitarian aid, is viewed as detrimental to development in the LDCs. As a consequence, measures that classic liberals believe to be helpful to LDCs may be rebuffed by the dependency theorists, producing political conflict and ill will.

Finally, dependency theory ignores political realities. For example, when Mexico was suffering from economic crisis in 1995, was the president of Mexico supposed to reject President Bill Clinton's offer of $24 billion in loans and allow the Mexican economic system to completely collapse? Similarly, at this writing, there is a significant humanitarian crisis in Niger, complete with famine, starvation, malnutrition, a lack of medical supplies, and widespread suffering. Are the political leaders of Niger to reject contact with developed democracies in this case and allow multitudes of people to die for the greater goal of ending the bonds of dependency? Any politician who answered affirmatively to these questions could most assuredly expect a very brief political career.

Concluding Remarks

In the end, dependency theory is exposed to be primarily ideology rather than scientific theory, and as such, suffers from all of the pitfalls of other ideologies. Although there certainly may be such a thing as dependent economies, dependency theory, like all ideology, creates tunnel vision for its adherents and eliminates all other possible conclusions. As any ideology could be expected to do, dependency theory also provides a simplistic analysis of a problem. In this case, the problem is economic underdevelopment in LDCs; the dependency theory verdict is that it is caused, in every case, by contact between LDCs and more advanced industrial economic powers. There can be no other explanations.

Dependency theory also provides simplistic solutions in the prescription for socialist revolution as a way for LDCs to break the bonds of dependency. Unfortunately for dependency theorists, the fall of the Soviet

Union and the collapse of the former communist bloc, along with the abandonment by the People's Republic of China of so many socialist principles, have largely discredited socialist revolution as a preferred path to development. Dependency theory could perhaps be discarded to the scrap heap of history, except that even the seemingly most discredited ideologies historically tend to find ways to reinvent themselves. As long as the problem of underdevelopment exists, it can be expected that some will seek a simplistic, ideological solution; hence, dependency theory may easily be reborn at some future date, complete with the same problems and pitfalls, only to be discredited again. Such, unfortunately, appears to be the historical pattern of human affairs and ideological thought.

9

Islamism

In 1979, Meg Greenfield wrote, "No part of the world is more hopelessly and systematically and stubbornly misunderstood by us than that complex of religion, culture and geography known as Islam" (*Newsweek*, March 26, 1979, 26). A quarter century later, the terrorist attacks of 9/11/01, along with numerous other terror attacks before and since, and the two wars launched by George W. Bush in Islamic countries, are evidence that little has changed since Greenfield's writing. Generally, the terror attacks of 9/11 appeared incomprehensible and irrational to Americans, and indeed they were, since it was not rational analysis that drove the terrorists, but ideology; and ideology is antithetical to rational analysis or critical thinking. Consequently, to fully understand what drove the terrorists to commit such irrational actions, it is necessary to understand their ideology.

Although the 9/11 terrorist attacks were bewildering to most Americans, they did not come as such a shock to those who have studied Islamist ideology. Samuel Huntington (1993), for instance, argued at the end of the Cold War that the world changed after the collapse of the USSR, and that the nature of conflict in the world would change to reflect that new order. Huntington argued that, since the U.S. stood alone as the world's only superpower, the struggles that threaten world peace would no longer focus on nationalism or capitalist-vs.-communist ideological conflict as they had for the previous 200 years, but instead would result from cultural confrontations. One of the major cultural factors that would cause this conflict, according to Huntington, is religion. Huntington correctly argued that America would be targeted by religious zealots from other cultural paradigms because these zealots would believe the U.S. had intervened in their area in violation of sacred norms.

Religious terrorists are different from other types of terrorists because they are not constrained by the same factors that inhibit other types

(Hoffman, 1995). Religious terrorists view their world as a battlefield between the forces of light and darkness. Winning is therefore not described in terms of political gains, but in terms of spiritual victories for God. Like non-violent traditional conservatives, religious terrorists subscribe to "ends politics," where seemingly immoral actions are justified by what they view as moral ends. In the spiritual battle between God's faithful and God's enemies, the infidels must be totally destroyed in the interest of heaven and for the salvation of all humankind. Hoffman argues that holy terrorists view their indiscriminate killing as a sacramental acts, and the purpose of their operations is solely to kill, rather than take territory or draw attention to themselves. Religious terrorists are not necessarily seeking a "wider audience," as are other terrorists, because their play is for God.

Speaking specifically of Islamic terrorism, Hoffman argues that the primary purpose of terrorism is to destroy the enemies of God. In doing so, religious terrorists, like conservative extremist, traditional conservative, or "loony left" ideologues, demonize their enemies. For example, like the Ayatollah Khomeini of Iran in the 1980s, Osama bin Laden of al Qaeda at the present time considers the United States to be not only a political enemy, but the "Great Satan." In turn, the demonization of the enemies makes murder and mayhem much easier because the enemies are no longer people, but are instead equated with enemies of the Most High and the ultimate source of evil. To the Islamists, their enemies are not just people with whom they disagree, but are devilish and demonic and in league with the forces of darkness. Consequently, it is not enough simply to defeat them; instead, they must be completely eradicated (Hoffman, 1995). Once the enemy has been sufficiently demonized, he becomes a scapegoat for all problems, and it becomes possible for the group to believe that all evil is the result of some sort of conspiracy involving their scapegoat and the evil entity. In the case of Islamic extremism, fanatic Muslims blame all of the world's problems on a conspiracy between the U.S. and Zionists in Israel (Berlet, 1995).

Indiscriminate killing is aided by apocalyptic thinking. All deterrents to violence are rendered meaningless by the promise of a new age that invites terrorists to fight as holy warriors in a period of fanatic zeal when the deity is about to bring creation to and end. In the Koran, Mohammed speaks of a final judgment against evil. The terrorists, therefore, view themselves merely as soldiers of God aiding him in his judgment (White, 2001, 53). The attacks of 9/11 were intended by the soldiers of God to humiliate and slaughter those who had defied the hegemony of God, and to please God by reasserting his primacy. What appeared to be senseless violence to the bewildered Americans made perfect sense to the terrorists, who viewed the mass killings as holy acts of worship, obedience, and redemption. Furthermore, since God is just, the innocents who were slain would receive their just reward in heaven from God, so the mass murder only accelerated their receipt of their just rewards (Benjamin and Simon, 2002, 40).

The Ideology of Islamism

Ideologically speaking, Islamism, or Islamic extremism, is essentially the Islamic form of extremist traditional conservatism in Islamic Societies. The central elements of traditional conservatism—the view that humans are depraved and society is in decay; a call to return to the better, vanished time; a premium on tradition; opposition to social change; a focus on moral absolutes; demonization of enemies; and "ends politics"—are all present, along with a preference for a blend between church and state and rule by the "good people," in this case identified as the Islamic clergy.

The better, vanished time that Islamists desire to return to is the golden age of Mohammed in the seventh century when Muslims conquered the Arabian Peninsula with God's help under Mohammed's leadership. The name "al Qaeda" itself means "the base," a specific reference to the group itself as the base from which a new global Islamic society will be constructed in conformity with the pure Islamic society of Mohammed in the seventh century. All things are justified in the pursuit of this righteous end, including indiscriminate killing (Gunaratna, 2002, 3).

Islam

In order to understand Islamism fully, it is necessary to have an understanding of Islam itself. Islam, like Christianity and Judaism that came before it, is monotheistic, and the one all-powerful, rational and ethical God in Islam is believed to be the God of Abraham of the Bible, worshipped by both Christians and Jews. The name for God in Islam, Allah, is formed by joining the definite article *al* (meaning "the") with *llah* (God). *Allah* literally means "the God," rather than "a" god, for Muslims believe there is only one, Allah. When the masculine plural ending *im* is dropped from the Hebrew word for God, *Elohim*, the two words sound much the same. "Islam" is properly a verbal noun meaning "surrendering one's self to God." The root s-l-m primarily means "peace" (cf.

"shalom"), but in a secondary sense, "surrender"; its full connotation is the peace that comes when one's life is surrendered to God. Surrender to God is consistent with both Christianity and Judaism (Smith, 1991, 221–222).

The Koran supports the Genesis story in its entirety, at least through God's promise to Abraham, and supports both Old and New Testament interpretations of Biblical prophets as true prophets of God. For example, in the Koran (Cattle VI: 83–90), it is stated that,

> Those who believe, and have not confounded their belief with evildoing—to them belongs the true security; they are rightly guided. That is Our argument, which We bestowed upon Abraham as against his people. We raise up in degrees whom We will; surely they Lord is All-wise, All-knowing. And We gave to him Isaac and Jacob—each one We guided, and Noah We guided before; and of his seed David and Solomon, Job and Joseph, Moses and Aaron—even so We recompense the good-doers—Zachariah and John, Jesus and Elias; each was of the righteous; Ishmael and Elisha, John and Lot—each one We preferred above all beings; and of their fathers, and of their seed, and of their brethren; and We elected them, and We guided them to a straight path. That is God's guidance; He guides by it whom He will of His servants; had they been idolaters, it would have failed them, the things they did. Those are they to whom We gave the Book, the Judgment, the Prophethood; so if these disbelieve in it, We have already entrusted it to a people who do not disbelieve in it. Those are they whom God has guided; so follow their guidance. Say: I ask of you no wage for it; it is but a reminder unto all beings.

In addition to its reverence for Biblical prophets—including Jesus of Nazareth, credited with virgin birth—the Koran itself does not necessarily declare that Muslims must be at odds with Christians or Jews, instead offering salvation for both if they are willing. For example, in The Table 5:70, it is stated, "We made a covenant of old with the Children of Israel and you have nothing of guidance until you observe the Torah and the Gospel." This verse essentially validates the Bible and entitles Jews and Christians to be included with Muslims as "People of the Book," meaning the Koran. Similarly, the Koran invites all people in all lands to join the people of the book. For example, in Jonah 10:47 it is stated that, "To every people we have sent a messenger.... Some We have mentioned to you, and some we have not mentioned to you."

Islamic Beginnings

From A.D. 610 to 613, in the town of Mecca in the Jabal Mountains of the Arabian Peninsula, Mohammed received the "revelation" of the

Koran and wrote down his "visions" on leaves. The visions came, and were written down, in no particular order. Consequently, there is no chronological ordering to the Koran. Instead, books are generally arranged from longest to shortest. Mecca, of course, is Islam's holiest location, since it is there that Mohammed received his visions. Mohammed was convinced that he was chosen to be a prophet and was told by an angel to proclaim what God had told him. Mohammed began preaching his revelation in 613. His first convert was his wife, further proof to Muslims of his authenticity, because no person knows a man's character more than his wife (Smith, 1991, 225–227).

Mohammed taught that although there had been many prophets before him, he was their culmination; hence, Muslims refer to him as the "Seal of the Prophets" and believe that no valid prophets have followed him. Mohammed never claimed deity, claiming only that he was a preacher of God's word (Smith, 1991, 223–224).

The first three years of Mohammed's ministry were a struggle for Mohammed; by the end of that time he had only about 40 converts. Between 616 and 622, however, Mohammed's teachings began attracting converts in ignorant, polytheistic and decadent 7th century Mecca, to the extent that, by 622, Mohammed's following was sufficient to alarm the Meccan nobility. Mohammed's monotheism violated pagan beliefs, and the Meccan nobility used Mohammed's "atheism" to inflame the masses against him, although their main fear was that he was a threat to their power. Mohammed was forced to flee Mecca to seek safe haven in Medina, where he continued his preaching. This moment, known as the *hejira* (migration), marks the beginning date of the Muslim era, Year One on the Islamic calendar (Smith, 1991, 228–231).

ISLAMIC JIHAD OR HOLY WAR

From the moment Mohammed arrived in Medina, he assumed a different role, becoming involved in governmental administration. Mohammed taught that his new religion could be spread by the sword if necessary, and Mohammed proceeded to engage in a holy war (*jihad*) in order to spread Islam. For example, in The Cow II: 187–188, it is stated that believers should

> fight in the way of God with those who fight with you, but aggress not: God loves not the aggressors. And slay them wherever you come upon them, and expel them from where they expelled you; persecution is more grievous than slaying. But fight them not by the Holy Mosque until they should fight you there; then, if they fight you, slay them—such is the rec-

ompense of unbelievers—but if they give over, surely God is All-forgiving, All-Compassionate.

Islamic extremists now use these verses to support their self-proclaimed holy war against infidels. It is noteworthy, however, that within these verses sanctioning war against the enemies of God, believers are also instructed to "aggress not: God loves not aggressors." Consequently, more moderate Muslims may condemn Islamic *jihad* and terrorism, depending on the importance they give to this verse and their interpretation of its application. In other words, Islam need not be a violent religion in spite of the Koranic sanction of *jihad*.

Believers are also instructed in the Koran that fighting would be "hateful" and "heinous" to them; however, they are also instructed that there are worse things than *jihad*, such as unbelief. For example, in The Cow II: 212–215, it is stated:

> Prescribed for you is fighting, though it be hateful to you. Yet it may happen that you will hate a thing which is better for you; and it may happen that you will love a thing which is worse for you; God knows and you know not. They will question thee concerning the holy month, and fighting in it. Say: 'Fighting in it is a heinous thing, but to bar from God's way, and disbelief in Him, and the Holy Mosque, and to expel its people from it—that is more heinous in God's sight; and persecution is more heinous than slaying.' They will not cease to fight with you, till they turn you from your religion, if they are able; and whosoever of you turns from his religion, and dies disbelieving—their works have failed in this world and the next; those are the inhabitants of the Fire; therein they shall dwell forever. But the believers, and those who emigrate and struggle in God's way—those have hope of God's compassion; and God is all-forgiving, All-compassionate.

These verses from The Cow II are especially useful to the jihadists in that they teach that the goal of the enemies of God is to turn the Muslims away from their religion so that when they die they go to an eternity of hell's fire. Against such an enemy, true believers would surely be compelled to fight even if the act itself is heinous. Unbelief would be a far more heinous thing. Furthermore, those who fight for Allah will be rewarded, and believers are obligated to fight against unbelievers and the "friends of Satan," according to Women IV: 73–78, where it is stated:

> O believers, take your precautions; then move forward in companies, or move forward all together. Some of you there are that are dilatory; then, if an affliction visits you, he says, 'God has blessed me, in that I was not a martyr with them.' But if a bounty from God visits you, he will surely

say, as if there had never been any affection between you and him, 'Would that I had been with them, to attain a mighty triumph!' So let them fight in the way of God who sell the present life for the world to come; and whosoever fights in the way of God and is slain, or conquers, We shall bring him a mighty wage. How is it with you, that you do not fight in the way of God, and for the men, women, and children who, being abased, say, 'Our Lord, bring us forth from this city whose people are evildoers, and appoint to us a protector from Thee, and appoint to us from Thee a helper'? The believers fight in the way of God, and the unbelievers fight in the idols' way. Fight you therefore against the friends of Satan; surely the guile of Satan is ever feeble.

For Islamic extremists, there is little more satanic than Israel, and the United States is easily identified as a "friend of Satan" since it is a friend of Israel. Furthermore, the martyrdom believers may experience through *jihad* against a "friend of Satan," such as the United States, is therefore sensible, since the martyrs are guaranteed a "mighty wage" in the world to come. In Islam, like Christianity, the "world to come" in the afterlife is believed to be infinitely better than the world of the here and now in the present life on earth. Elsewhere, in Muhammad XLVII, the afterlife is referred to as "Paradise," and those who die fighting for Allah will be admitted into the next life. Specifically, in Muhammad XLVII: 8–9, it is stated, "And those who are slain in the way of God, He will not send their works astray. He will guide them, and dispose their minds aright, and He will admit them to Paradise, that He has made known to them." Hence, to end one's own life as a martyr while killing the enemies of God makes sense if one believes that he will quickly be admitted to Paradise.

Concerning the prospects of peace between Muslims and unbelievers, it is stated that the believers are not to make friends with unbelievers, but are obligated to kill them wherever they are found; yet, if the infidels withdraw and offer peace, God does not allow them to be slain. In Women IV: 91–93, it is stated:

They wish that you should disbelieve as they disbelieve, and then you would be equal; therefore take not to yourselves friends of them, and slay them wherever you find them; take not to yourselves any one of them as a friend or helper except those that betake themselves to a people who are joined with you by a compact, or come to you with breasts constricted from fighting with you or fighting their people. Had God willed, He would have given them authority over you, and then certainly they would have fought you. If they withdraw from you, and do not fight you, and offer you peace, then God assigns not any way to you against them. You will find others desiring to be secure from you, and secure from their people, yet whenever they are returned to temptation, they are overthrown in it. If they withdraw not from you, and offer you peace, and restrain their hands, take them, and slay them wherever you come on them; against them We have given you clear authority.

Clearly, these Koranic verses provide room for interpretation and allow Muslims to make peace with non–Muslims if the "infidels" withdraw and offer peace; however, Islamic radicals prefer to focus on the command to "slay them wherever you come upon them," and they claim the full authority from God to do so.

In Islam, anything is possible if God is on the side of the believers; hence, believing that one can attack and defeat a much more powerful enemy, such as the United States, is well within reason. In The Spoils VIII: 66–68, for instance, it is stated that believers can win battles against larger odds because God is on their side. Taking prisoners, however, is not permitted until there is "wide slaughter." The entire passage reads:

> O Prophet, urge on the believers to fight. If there be twenty of you, patient men, they will overcome two hundred; if there be a hundred of you, they will overcome a thousand unbelievers, for they are a people who understand not. Now God has lightened it for you, knowing that there is weakness in you. If there be a hundred of you, patient men, they will overcome two hundred; if there be of you a thousand, they will overcome two thousand by the leave of God; God is with the patient. It is not for any Prophet to have prisoners until he makes wide slaughter in the land.

Given these verses, Osama bin Laden and his followers can believe that they can destroy the United States, a much more powerful entity, if they are patient and God is with them. For proof, the Islamists need look no further than the life of the prophet Mohammed himself. Mohammed's new religion, empowered by its adherents' belief in Allah, provided a powerful stimulus that mobilized Arab society almost overnight. By A.D. 630, Mohammed and the Medinese would defeat the more powerful Meccan army and control almost the entire Arabian Peninsula. Mohammed's victory is proof to Muslims that God was with him and sanctioned his holy war, thus allowing him to defeat a more powerful enemy. Mohammed captured the Arabian Peninsula by 629 and died in 632, but Arab armies carrying the banner of Islam formed, invaded, and conquered, converting wherever they went. By A.D. 700, Islam had reached far into North Africa, Transcaucasia, and most of Southwest Asia. By the year 1000, Islam had spread into Southern and Eastern Europe, and as far east as China (Ochsenwald and Fisher, 2004, 38–62).

SHARIA

To Islamic extremists, the Koran is not only a religious book, but also provides moral and civil codes for society. Islam forbids smoking, alcohol, social dancing and gambling; it acknowledges the virtues of monogamy, though it tolerates polygamy. Men can have up to four wives, but adulterers are sentenced to death by stoning. Amputations are prescribed for theft. Given that these laws are handed down by God through his prophet Mohammed, to deviate from them in any way is un–Islamic and makes one an apostate (i.e., one who abandons his faith) or an infidel, who must change his ways or face death. *Sharia* is essentially the Islamic law that is derived from the Koran and the Hadith, a collection of statements and deeds of Mohammed that was written some 250 years later. *Sharia* itself translates as "correct path," meaning the path to salvation. Obviously, it is therefore no stretch for Islamists to argue that deviations from *sharia* essentially remove Muslims from the correct path to salvation (Ochsenwald and Fisher, 2004, 85–86).

Ibn Taymiyya

The Koran, however, is not the only Islamic writing that is influential in Islam or influential to Islamic extremists. There are literally thousands of "Hadiths" (meaning "reports") testifying of God and Mohammed, and all Muslims do not necessarily accept all of the same Hadiths. The Hadiths touch on a myriad of topics including slavery, divorce, photographs, forgiveness, sexual activity, and *jihad* (Ochsenwald and Fisher, 2004, 77). From these thousands of writings, the Islamists in general and al Qaeda in particular place a premium on *jihad*, or holy war, and subscribe to the writings of ibn Taymiyya from 1269.

Taymiyya's primary goal was the restoration of what he viewed as pure Islam, and his method was *jihad*. Taymiyya taught that anyone who did not join with God's people should be attacked, whether they fought alongside the enemies of God or simply did business with them. Those who should be attacked included Muslim apostates or those who did not practice true Islam (Benjamin and Simon, 2002, 42). Taymiyya called for a restoration of the age of Mohammed, when the religious leader was also the leader of the state, and Islamic law was civil law. Taymiyya essentially argued that government should be subordinate to the clergy, and that the clergy should essentially share the responsibilities of government. Furthermore, any ruler who did not enforce *sharia* would be an apostate, and

Muslims were obligated to rebel against such a leader (Benjamin and Simon, 2002, 48). As a consequence, Islamic followers of Taymiyya oppose Islamic leaders, such as the former Shah of Iran, Hosni Mubarak of Egypt, Saddam Hussein of Iraq, and Bashar Assad of Syria, who Westernize their societies, institute laws other than Islamic *sharia*, allow Western-style music and dress, do not grow beards, and allow women to advance through education. Against such leaders, Taymiyya condoned assassination (Baer, 2002, 87). Taymiyya, however, considered the superior form of *jihad* to be combat against infidels.

Obviously, Taymiyya's call for the restoration of the age of Mohammed is a perfect example of a conservative ideological call for a return to a better, vanished time. His call for the overthrow of apostate rulers and his approval of assassination are clear preferences for "ends politics." Although murder is essentially an evil in all religions, including Islam, Taymiyya essentially condones the evil in the interest of preventing what he views as a greater evil, the falling away of society from true Islam.

Muhammad ibn Abd al-Wahhab

Similar to Taymiyya in ideology and influence is Muhammad ibn Abd al-Wahhab, the person essentially responsible for the rise of the Wahhabi sect of Sunni Islam in Saudi Arabia, the sect from which emerged Osama bin Laden and the 9/11 terrorists. Al-Wahhab was an eighteenth-century student of Islam who believed the Islam of his time had been corrupted (a clear traditional conservative ideological perspective) and reformulated Islam into what he viewed as "true Islam," drawing on the works of Taymiyya (Baer, 2002, 87). Al-Wahhab essentially desired to return Islam to its better, vanished time or "golden age" as it existed at the time of Mohammed. Consequently, al-Wahhab discarded customs that had developed between Mohammed's time and the eighteenth century. He condemned "innovation" in Islam as sinful, a clear example of traditional conservative ideological resistance to change. Al-Wahhab declared that those who committed sins of "innovation" should be executed. Al-Wahhab argued that delivering any legal ruling on the basis of anything other than the Koran or Hadith was apostasy, and condemned as heresies such beliefs and practices as the denial of predestination, profiting from trade, interpreting the Koran figuratively rather than literally, failing to attend public prayers on Fridays, and shaving one's beard (Benjamin and Simon, 2002, 52–53). Under the strict teachings of al-Wahhab, if his instructions are to be followed to the letter, more secular

Middle Eastern leaders Saddam Hussein, Bashar Assad, Hosni Mubarak, and the former Shah of Iran would merit execution if for no other reason than the fact that they shaved their beards.

Rashid Rida

Rashid Rida was a Cairo Islamic intellectual in the early twentieth century during the time of Western colonialism that followed World War I. Rida opposed the Islamic leaders at the time who substituted Western law for *sharia* and, in the words of Rida,

> thus abolish supposedly distasteful penalties such as cutting off the hands of thieves or stoning adulterers and prostitutes. They replace them with man-made laws and penalties. He who does that has undeniably become an infidel" [quoted in Sivan, 1990, 101].

Rida, like other traditional conservative Islamists, was obviously a moral absolutist whose source for his moral absolutes was the Koran. Rida used the word *jahiliyya*, a word from the Koran meaning "barbarity," to describe Muslims who submitted to "man-made" law rather than *sharia*. Rida condemned secular government as a violation of the Koran and, like other traditional conservative Islamists, favored a return to the better, vanished time of Islam by looking back to the age of Islamic caliphs as a model for the government of the present. Rida believed that only a return to true and pure Islam would bring Muslims political and economic power and end the rule of the colonialists (Benjamin and Simon, 2002, 56).

Muslim Brotherhood

Following in the traditions of Rida, in 1928, an Egyptian teacher from the Nile Delta named Hassan al-Banna formed a group to revive pure Islam and resist colonialism. Al-Banna and the Muslim Brotherhood, as his faction was known, argued that Muslims could not fulfill their rightful destiny in the absence of a true caliphate. Furthermore, al-Banna rejected Western culture and government, including the separation of church and state that accompanied Westernization. The Muslim Brotherhood's credo, again reflecting traditional conservative ideology, essentially called for the return to *sharia* and pure Islam, and for *jihad* as a means to those ends. In their credo, the Muslim brotherhood proclaimed, "God is our objective; the Koran is our constitution; the Prophet is our leader;

struggle is our way; and death for the sake of God is the highest of our aspirations" (quoted in Benjamin and Simon, 2002, 56). The Muslim Brotherhood began waging their *jihad* against the Egyptian government, with the result that al-Banna was killed by Egyptian governmental authorities in 1949. In spite of the death of al-Banna, the Muslim Brothers and their ideology spread throughout the Middle East over the next several decades: the Muslim Brothers have been involved in terrorism against both "apostate" Muslim governments and the "infidel" West ever since (Baer, 2002, 86–91).

Sayyid Qutb

Sayyid Qutb was a member of the Muslim Brotherhood imprisoned and eventually executed by the Egyptian government for his activities against the government in the 1960s. Qutb wrote a bestselling book in the Middle East titled *Signposts*, in which he argued that human political rule apart from God is illegitimate and that Muslims must answer to God alone. Qutb argued that human governments that claimed to be established by Islam, but were not subordinate to the clergy, were apostate governments and legitimate targets of *jihad*. Only by destroying these *jahiliyya* governments could a truly pure Islamic society emerge (Benjamin and Simon, 2002, 62).

Like other Islamic traditional conservatives, Qutb viewed current Islamic society as in decay and called for a return to the purity of the better, vanished time of Mohammed. In the words of Qutb, "Everything around us is *Jahiliyya* ... people's perceptions and beliefs, habits and customs, the sources of their culture, arts and literature, and their laws and legislations" (Armstrong, 2001, 240). Qutb further argued that Islam could not survive coterminous with *jahiliyya*. The idea that more traditional Islam could survive while simultaneously allowing other less traditional Muslims to worship Allah as they saw fit was simply impossible to Qutb. In the words of Qutb:

> Islam cannot accept any compromise with Jahiliyya.... Either Islam will remain, or Jahiliyya; Islam cannot accept or agree to a situation which is half Islam and half Jahiliyya. In this respect, Islam's stand is very clear. It says that truth is one and cannot be divided; if it is not the truth, then it must be falsehood. The mixing and coexistence of truth and falsehood is impossible. Command belongs to Allah or else to Jahiliyya. The Sharia of Allah will prevail, or else people's desires [quoted in Benjamin and Simon, 2002, 65].

Qutb further argued that Islam and Western values were fundamentally antagonistic, and that the true Muslims must remove themselves from the influence of infidels and *jahiliyya* and form a community of true Muslims based on the Koran. Once the community of true Muslims was strong enough, it could be used as a base from which *jihad* could be waged against infidels and *jahili* rulers. It is therefore from Qutb that al Qaeda essentially gets its name and purpose. Three decades after Qutb, Osama bin Laden would declare al Qaeda to be that pure Islamic base from which *jihad* could be waged against infidels (Benjamin and Simon, 2002, 65).

Anti–Semitism

Islamic extremism contains within it a serious degree of anti–Semitism due to the political history of Palestine since the late nineteenth century, the ideological influence of anti–Semitic Islamic extremists, and differing interpretations of Jews and Islamists concerning God's promise to Abraham in the Biblical book of Genesis. Qutb in particular subscribed to an intense anti–Semitism, arguing that Jews had conspired against Muslims since the time of Mohammed. Qutb went even further to contend that "anyone who leads this community away from its religion and its Koran can only be a Jewish agent" (quoted in Benjamin and Simon, 2002, 68). In other words, Qutb evidently believed that anyone who causes a Muslim to go astray is by definition a Jew, and the Jews are thus the incarnation of all that is un–Islamic. Qutb further warns that the Jews' "satanic usurious activity will deliver the proceeds of all human toil into the hands of the great usurious Jewish financial institutions. They will rob the believers and kill them" (quoted in Benjamin and Simon, 2002, 68).

This anti–Semitism is in spite of the fact that the Koran repeatedly refers to the Jews as "people of the book" who may be saved through belief in Islam. It is also repeatedly stated in the Koran that Mohammed did not come to "cancel out" or destroy the revelations from God delivered by the previous prophets of God, including the Jewish prophets Abraham, Moses, and Jesus, and it is even stated in the Koran that Jewish and Christian believers will have their "reward," meaning salvation. For example, in The Cow II: 62 from the Koran, it is stated:

> Surely those who believe, and those who are Jews, and the Christians, and the Sabians, whoever believes in Allah and the Last day and does

good, they shall have their reward from their Lord, and there is no fear for them, nor shall they grieve.

In The Food V: 69, this passage is repeated almost word for word, suggesting that there is little reason that Muslims must necessarily be at odds with Jews on the basis of religion. Conversely, however, there are numerous verses in the Koran that Islamists point to in order to justify anti–Semitism, essentially using the same religious text that praises the Jewish prophets to further their hatred. For example, in The Food V: 82, it is stated that,

> Certainly you will find the most violent of people in enmity for those who believe (to be) the Jews and those who are polytheists, and you will certainly find the nearest in friendship to those who believe (to be) those who say: We are Christians: this is because there are priests and monks among them and because they do not behave proudly.

Reinforcing this demonization of the Jews, in The Food V: 62, it is stated that, "And the Jews say: The hand of Allah is tied up! Their hands shall be shackled and they shall be cursed for what they say." There are numerous other verses that Islamists interpret as suggesting that the Jews are the enemies of Allah; consequently, their anti–Semitism is driven and justified by their religion, although other Muslims who interpret the Koran differently, or emphasize different passages, may beg to disagree.

HAMAS

One decidedly anti–Semitic Muslim group in the tradition of Qutb is the Palestinian Islamic resistance group known as Hamas. Hamas grew out of the Muslim Brotherhood in the 1980s for the purpose of unification of the entire Arab realm under Islam. In 1978, the group registered as a religious organization with the Israeli government, and its stated purpose was to be evangelical. When Yasser Arafat of the Palestinian Liberation Organization gravitated toward moderation in the 1980s, Hamas held to the position that the state of Israel and anyone who supports it are abominations to Islam. In its own literature, Hamas states that it is in a war with the Jewish people as well as with the state of Israel. The purpose of every operation is to kill Jews, thereby driving all Zionist settlers and their allies from Palestine. "Good" Muslims will kill anyone who accepts peace with the Jews or who speaks of an independent Palestine alongside, instead of replacing, the state of Israel. Hamas also enforces *sharia* or Islamic law among the Palestinians, including amputations, beatings, and the execution of sex offenders (White, 2001, 159–161).

Islamic Interpretation of "The Promise"

Among the most contentious areas of religious disagreement between Muslims and Jews is the dispute over the proper interpretation of God's promise to Abraham. Abraham is viewed as a man of God and the patriarch and father of the people by both Arabs and Jews, and both Jews and Muslims claim to worship the God of Abraham. Both Muslims and Jews essentially accept the Biblical Genesis story as holy scripture, but there is disagreement over which son of Abraham, Ishmael or Isaac, was to receive the benefit of God's blessings. In Genesis 15:1–6, for example, God promises Abraham a son from whom descendants would become "as numerous as the stars in the skies." This promise is followed a few verses later with the promise of Genesis 15:18, where it is stated, "On that day the Lord made a covenant with Abram and said, To your descendants I give this land, from the river of Egypt to the great river, the Euphrates." Geographically, God's promise to Abram is that his descendants will inhabit everything from the Nile in Egypt to the Euphrates River in present-day Iraq and the promise apparently includes all of the land between the two rivers. If taken literally, this promise would include not only the narrow 40-by-120-mile strip of the former Palestine where present-day Israel is located, but also all of Jordan, Syria, Lebanon, and the entire Arabian Peninsula, along with much of Iraq and Egypt.

Arab Muslims claim that they, not the Jews, were the recipients of God's promise to Abraham and the rightful heirs to all of the land promised to the descendants of Abraham by God. For proof, Arab Muslims point out that most of the land between the Nile and the Euphrates has been in Arab hands for hundreds if not thousands of years, and that the Jews have never possessed all of the land, or even a large fraction of it, even in the glory days of the Biblical kings David and Solomon. In fact, the Jews were expelled from the land almost completely by the Babylonians in the sixth century B.C., and again by the Romans in A.D. 70, suggesting that the land was not promised to them or God would not have allowed them to be expelled from it. Furthermore, it has been over 4,000 years since God's promise to Abraham, and since the Jews have never had most of the land, it suggests that either God has been very slow in fulfilling his promise, an unlikely proposition to devout Muslims, or else it was instead the Arab Muslims, who have inhabited nearly all of that land for centuries, who were the proper recipients of God's promise to Abraham.

For further proof, Muslims correctly point out that ancient societies of the Middle East, including the Jews, generally practiced primogeniture, meaning that the eldest son would receive the lion's share of the father's inheritance. It follows then that the eldest son of Abraham, Ishmael, traditionally recognized by both Jews and Arabs as the father of the Arab race, is the true heir to Abraham's inheritance, rather than Isaac, Abraham's second son, traditionally recognized by both Arabs and Jews as the father of the Jewish race.

Muslims also point to God's promises to Hagar, the mother of Ishmael, in the book of Genesis as further proof that Ishmael was the son of the promise. In Genesis 16:10, for example, God directly promised to Hagar, after she had slept with Abraham (Genesis 16: 4) and conceived his child, "I will so increase your descendants that they will be too numerous to count." The wording of God's promise to Hagar is almost a mirror image of God's promise to Abraham in Genesis 15:1–6, thus suggesting that God's promises to Abraham and Hagar are the same.

Religious Jews acknowledge that Hagar, like Abraham, received a promise from God, but they point to Genesis 17:15–22 where God promises that he will make of Ishmael a great nation, but then explicitly states that his covenant is with Isaac. Specifically, God is quoted as stating:

> And as for Ishmael, I have heard you: I will surely bless him; I will make him fruitful and will greatly increase his numbers. He will be the father of twelve rulers, and I will make him into a great nation. But my covenant I will establish with Isaac.

In other words, religious Jews argue that God made promises to both Abraham and Hagar, but the important child with whom God made his covenant, and to whom all of the land between the Nile and Euphrates belongs, is Isaac. Furthermore, the Jews point to Genesis 16: 11–12, which states that Hagar's son, to be named Ishmael, "will be a wild donkey of a man; his hand will be against everyone and everyone's hand against him, and he will live in hostility toward all his brothers." The Jewish religious interpretation of these verses is that God promised that the sons of Ishmael would be a populous, but hostile nation, and consequently the sons of Ishmael (the Arabs) and the sons of Isaac (the Jews) have lived in hostility toward one another ever since.

While Muslims generally accept Genesis as a valid holy book, and it is undeniable that Isaac is designated as the son of the covenant in the text, Muslims argue that the text has either been altered by the deceptive Jews or "confused in transmission" (Smith, 1991, 221–228). Proof to Muslims that the Jews have altered the text concerning Ishmael is found in Genesis 21:8–21, where Hagar and Ishmael are expelled from Abraham's camp due to the jealousy of Abraham's wife, Sarah. According to Genesis, fourteen years passed between the birth of Ishmael and Isaac, since

Genesis 16:16 states that Abraham was 86 years old when Ishmael was born, and Genesis 21:5 states that he was 100 years old when Isaac was born. Furthermore, Genesis 17:25 states that Ishmael was circumcised when he was thirteen years old, prior to Isaac's birth. Several years then passed between Ishmael's circumcision and the expulsion of Ishmael and Hagar, since Genesis 21:8 states that Isaac was weaned prior to Ishmael's expulsion. If that is the case, then Ishmael must have been approximately 15 to 17 years old when he and his mother were forced to leave Abraham's entourage, since he was 14 when Isaac was born and the child would not have been weaned for 1 to 3 years. Ishmael must have been essentially full adult size at the time, but the verses surrounding Hagar and Ishmael's expulsion appear to suggest that he is an infant or small child. For example, it is mentioned in Genesis 21:14 that Abraham handed bread, a skin of water, and "the boy" to Hagar, suggesting he was small enough for adults to carry in their arms, since he was handed from one person to the other. In the next verse (Genesis 21:15), Hagar then places "the boy" under a shrub, again suggesting he is little more than an infant. Most teenage boys obviously would not be placed "under a shrub." Furthermore, God commands Hagar in Genesis 21:18, "Arise, lift up the lad and hold him with your hand, for I will make him a great nation," again suggesting that a "lad" who can be held "with your hand" must be very young indeed, rather than the 15 to 17 years old that he had to be at the time. Finally, in Genesis 21:20, it is stated that "God was with the lad; and he grew and dwelt in the wilderness, and became an archer." Again, the reference that "the lad grew" is inconsistent with a description of a person who was already in his mid-teens at the time; it appears to be a reference to a much younger child. For Muslims, the answer is clear enough. Since there are inconsistencies in Genesis between the stated date of Ishmael's birth and the apparent references to him as a small child at a time that must have been 15 to 17 years later, the Jews must have made alterations to the original passages designating Ishmael as the son of the promise. Otherwise Jews, not Arabs, would have occupied the bulk of the land in the Middle East for the last 4000 years.

The Jewish and Islamic interpretations of "the promise" become extremely important for explaining the conflict in Palestine between Jews and Muslims. Since both Orthodox Jews and devout Muslims view the land of Palestine as rightfully theirs due to the promise from God in Genesis, neither are predisposed to compromise on the issue. Indeed, such a compromise would be viewed by Muslims and Orthodox Jews alike as blasphemy, since it would be ungodly to give away land that had been given to the people by God. As a consequence, Egyptian president Anwar

Sadat, who recognized Israel's right to exist, was assassinated by Muslim extremists, and Israeli prime minister Yitzak Rabin, who favored the return to the Arabs of some of the occupied territories, was assassinated by Jewish extremists (Ochsenwald and Fisher, 2004, 575–576).

Zionism and its Impact on Islamism

In the mid–19th century, the Zionist movement, a movement favoring the return of Jews to their "homeland" in Palestine, gained momentum in Europe and continued until World War II, due to prevalent anti–Semitism in Europe and the desire of Jews in the international community to help other Jewish persons escape persecution. As of the late nineteenth century, most of the world's Jews did not live in Palestine, but were instead scattered throughout both the Middle East and Europe, as they had been since the fall of Jerusalem to the Romans in A.D. 70. Between 1882 and 1900, Jewish migrations to Palestine increased greatly due to persecutions in Europe, but especially in Russia, and approximately 20,000 Jews, backed by international Jewish charities, migrated to Palestine. All across Europe, a political party known as Mizrahi ("spiritual center") arose. Mizrahi was a party of religious Jews who favored Zionism (Sachar, 1996).

Other adherents of Zionism, however, had little or nothing to do with religion. By the 1930s, a strong socialist faction developed within the Zionist movement that favored the establishment of a proletarian socialist state in Israel. Consequently, socialist Jews immigrated to Israel so as to embark on the great socialist experiment. A third segment of Zionism was not necessarily religious or socialist, but a heterogeneous stream of Jews who were merely fleeing persecution. Still, at the close of World War I, the population of Palestine was estimated to be 620,000 Muslims, 70,000 Christians, and 60,000 Jews. Most of the Christians were Arabic in ethnicity, most of the Jews spoke Arabic, and some of the ethnic Jews were adherents of Islam (Ochsenwald and Fisher, 2004, 447).

During World War I, the British assured the Arabs an independent state in Palestine, to be carved out of the remains of the Ottoman Empire that had controlled the area. In 1917, the British issued the Balfour Declaration, which offered new hope to the Zionist movement by guaranteeing "the establishment in Palestine of a National Home for the Jewish People." The two British promises, one to the Arabs and one to the Jews, each guaranteeing an independent state for each group, were obviously in conflict. After World War I, Britain was granted a mandate by the League of Nations to rule Palestine until it could be nurtured to independence.

The British tried to keep their promises to both the Arabs and Jews; between 1919 and 1922, they turned away several ships full of Jewish refugees from Europe due to Arab unrest. In 1922, however, the League of Nations instructed the British to facilitate Jewish immigration without prejudicing the rights and position of other sections or the population (Ochsenwald and Fisher, 2004, 447–459).

Massive immigration of Jews followed so that the Jewish population of Palestine by 1939 was 460,000, versus 950,000 Muslims and 120,000 Christians (Ochsenwald and Fisher, 2004, 450). Even without differences in ethnicity, religion, language, and income, one could perhaps expect political conflict to develop in a case where so many immigrants arrived in such a short span of time in a place so geographically small. With the demographic differences between the new immigrants and the natives compounding the problems, however, political conflict was perhaps unavoidable.

The scale of the immigration, plus the economic disparity between the Jews and Arabs, quickly created land pressures and economic conflict between the two groups. Jewish immigrants, aided by funding from the Jewish National Fund, purchased land from Arab absentee landlords at inflated prices. Arab landowners would happily sell their land, sometimes at two to three times the market rate. Jewish immigrants would move onto the land to work it in communal farms (Kibbutz), while Arab tenant farmers were displaced and subsequently unemployed. The Jews bought all of the best land, and left the Hill Country—land that could not be farmed by mechanized equipment—to the Arabs. By 1939, the Jewish farmers, heavily subsidized by the Jewish National Fund, exported ten million cases of citrus. Nevertheless, cost of development in Palestine between 1919 and 1939 was $400 million, while annual exports were only $4 million by 1939. Palestine never approached a self-supporting status, and only foreign gifts stabilized Jewish society at a standard of living above that of the Arab Palestinians. By 1939, 75 percent of Jews lived in towns or cities, most working in the service sector, while only 25 percent of Arabs in Palestine were urban. Jewish income by 1939 was 2.5 times that of the Arabs in Palestine. Immigration literally created new major Jewish cities. Tel Aviv, for example, was a small town of 2000 people in 1918, but had swelled to 150,000 by 1939. The Jews came from all over the world and spoke dozens of languages, so Hebrew was revived as their everyday spoken language in Palestine so as to forge commonality and national identity. Unfortunately, that language and identity were separate from those of the native Palestinians, thus contributing to political conflict (Ochsenwald and Fisher, 2004, 447–459).

INDEPENDENT ISRAEL

By 1942, the Holocaust was well underway in Europe, and Zionists reacted by drawing up a plan for a Jewish state in Palestine at the Biltmore Hotel in New York City. The Zionists were outraged by British policies in 1942 that would not allow Jews fleeing Nazi persecution to come to Palestine. Ships carrying Jewish immigrants had been turned back, and the passengers were interned on the island of Cyprus. In 1942, 769 Russian Jews died in the Black Sea when their overloaded ship, the *Struma*, was ordered back to Russia by the British. As a consequence of the Holocaust and the immigration tragedies that afflicted the Jews during the war, many religious Jews (though not the Orthodox) who had opposed Zionism prior to World War II softened their stance after the war. In general, it was believed that large numbers of European Jews surely would have left Europe and therefore survived the war, as opposed to suffering extermination at the hands of the Nazis, had Zionism been sanctioned by religious leaders. International Jewish groups pushed for the establishment of a Jewish state in Palestine, and in 1947, Britain announced an end to its Palestinian mandate, and the Palestine question was left to the U.N. (Jones, 2001, 242)

In November 1947, the U.N. General Assembly decided to partition Palestine into two States; one Arab (Lebanon) and one Jewish (Israel). The City of Jerusalem, desired by both Arabs and Jews, was to be governed under international supervision. While the Jewish Lobby was happy that they finally had their Jewish State, the Arab delegation in the U.N. stalked out in protest because there were more Arabs on the land in Israel than Jews, and the land set aside for the Jews contained the area's best roads, railroads, and farmland (Jones, 2001, 242).

On May 14, 1948, the British mandate came to an end, and the Jews declared the independent state of Israel. Fifteen minutes later, President Harry S. Truman extended recognition, and the USSR did the same three days later. Independence, however, proved to be an incitement to trouble, as Israel was almost immediately invaded by its Arab neighbors. The Israeli army was greatly outnumbered, but better equipped by the U.S. and Britain, and therefore quickly defeated the invaders in the first of what would eventually become five Arab-Israeli wars in the twentieth century. An armistice in February 1949 temporarily wound down the hostilities, but only because the Arab states had been defeated on the battlefield. International supervision of Jerusalem never materialized, and the city was divided between the states of Israel and Jordan. Arab states boycotted Israel and cut off its land access to the outside, and Egypt closed the Suez

Canal to Israeli shipping. The war also had a tremendous impact on the migration of people in the Middle East, as up to a million Palestinian refugees fled the Jewish state, most to neighboring Jordan, a poor country without oil that lacked the means to feed and absorb them. The Israelis destroyed the homes of the fleeing Arab refugees so as to discourage any thought of return. The homeless Palestinians, stripped of hope and means of support, began terrorist raids into Israel that have never ceased (Jones, 2001, 242).

Although it was threatened and its future was uncertain, the Jewish state had been established and had survived its first major challenge from its Arab Muslim neighbors, though the armistice between Israel and Jordan left the holy city of Jerusalem divided by a barbed-wire fence. The eastern part of the city, and most of the Old City containing the shrines holy to both Islam and Judaism, were left in Jordan, who refused to permit Jews access to the holy places. In spite of this contentious and uncertain status of the city, Israel announced the movement of its capital to Jerusalem, thus exacerbating the already tense political atmosphere (Sachar, 1996, 592).

In 1950, Israel officially sanctioned and attempted to boost Zionism when the Israeli Parliament passed the Law of Return. This law declared that every Jew in every country has the right to return to Israel, and that citizenship for any Jewish person would only be withheld in cases of "Acts against the Jewish Nation." Jews in other countries became formally recognized as part of the Jewish nation served by the state of Israel. (Ochsenwald and Fisher, 2004, 533–553).

Six-Day War

The Israelis and their Arab neighbors would fight five wars between 1949 and 1982, the most important of which was the Six-Day War in 1967. In 1964, Yasser Arafat and other Arab leaders established the Palestinian Liberation Organization (PLO), dedicated to liberating Palestine from Israel. Their purpose was to create a political organization to help form a multinational alliance against Israel and to unite Arab governments for a war against Israel. In furtherance of these goals, the PLO demanded withdrawal of the UN peace-keeping forces from the Egyptian-Israeli border. The UN withdrew in 1967, thus providing the PLO and their allies with an opportunity, and Egypt quickly took advantage of the situation to move its army into the Sinai and seize Sharm el-Sheikh, an Israeli port on the Gulf of Aqaba. Meanwhile, PLO terrorists from Syria and Jordan began a series of guerrilla raids on Israel, who in turn retaliated. Egypt, Syria, and Jordan mobilized their armies along Israel's borders, and the Israelis, sensing an impending invasion, attacked first on June 5, 1967. The Israeli Air Force, using American-made planes, destroyed virtually the entire Egyptian, Iraqi, Syrian, and Jordanian air forces while they were still on the ground. With total control of the air, the Israeli ground forces and tanks crossed the borders of their enemies, and within six days had taken Jerusalem and the West Bank of the Jordan River from Jordan, the Suez Canal, the Sinai Peninsula, and, the Gaza Strip from Egypt, and the Golan Heights from Syria. On June 11th, with the Arabs defeated, the Israelis accepted a UN cease-fire. The Israeli kill ratio in the war was 16 to 1 (Jones, 2001, 371–372).

The victory in the Six-Day War had a profound long-term effect on both Jewish and Muslim politics. The capture of the occupied territories was viewed by many religious Jews as a sign that the messianic age had begun. Just as God had created the heavens and the earth in six days, and on the seventh day he rested, in 1967, God had delivered Israel from the hands of its enemies in six days, and on the seventh day he rested. The religious symbolism could not be more obvious. Additionally, the capture of the Temple Mount in East Jerusalem was viewed as a sign that the war was part of God's plan to return Israel to the Jewish people. The top Orthodox Rabbi, Zvi Yehada Kook, declared that the state of Israel was "Heaven on Earth" and "every living Jew in Israel was Holy." Religious Jews viewed the occupied territories as gifts from God that could not be given back. Even discussion of such a return would be blasphemy (Sachar, 1996, 740–746).

The occupied territories created other political ramifications for the Jewish state as well. The territories were viewed as items to be kept, not only by the religious Jews, but also by security-minded secular Jews, who argued that retaining the territories would provide necessary security buffers against their enemies. In furtherance of this security goal, between 1967 and 2005, hundreds of thousands of new Jewish immigrants were settled in the West Bank (called Judea and Samaria by the Orthodox), creating a further logistical problem, since giving the land back to the Arabs would now require relinquishing the homes of all these settlers. The occupied territories also were home to large Arab populations, meaning Israel suddenly would have an area with more Arabs than Jews if the occupied territories were retained. Consequently, if Arab Muslims in the occupied territories were allowed to vote, Israel would be an Islamic state rather than Jewish, but to deny the Arabs the right to vote created an apartheid-type situation that is typically condemned by the international community (Sachar, 1996, 748).

A further problem is that the predominantly Arab areas of the occupied territories tend to have a much lower income per capita than Israel as a whole. For example, the GDP per capita of Israel as a whole is approximately $20,000 annually, while the average income of the Arab population in the Gaza strip, an area only 4 by 26 miles with a population of over one million, is only approximately $1000. This type of income disparity could perhaps be expected to lead to political problems even if religion and ethnicity were not factors (*Economist*, 2003).

ISLAMISTS AND THE SIX-DAY WAR

Religious Jews were not the only persons who viewed the Six-Day War as being religiously symbolic. Islamic fundamentalists viewed the loss of the Six-Day War as a sign from God as well. Since it is written in the Koran that Allah's faithful can defeat more powerful enemies if they are faithful to Allah, devout Muslims could only interpret the defeat as proof that Muslims had not been faithful to Islam; otherwise, Allah would not have allowed them to lose in battle to their enemies. Muslim extremists therefore called for an end to secularization and a return to a purer form of Islam (Sachar, 1996, 786).

Islamism and the Soviet/Afghan War

In 1979, the USSR invaded Afghanistan to protect a pro–Soviet government under Babrak Karmal that was under siege from Islamic extremists. Numerous militia groups, calling themselves holy warriors or "Mujahadeen," quickly formed to the resist the Soviets. The U.S. interpreted the Soviet invasion as Soviet expansionism and quickly joined the fray with arms and economic support for the resistance, under the long-standing policy of containment. Mujahadeen leaders made trips to the U.S. denouncing the Soviets as "foreign devils" and "infidels" and raising support for their cause. President Jimmy Carter and later Ronald Reagan and his advisors failed to notice that the Mujahadeen used the same terms to refer to Americans (Jones, 2001, 441–442).

The CIA sent millions of dollars to the Mujahadeen through Pakistan. The CIA trained and outfitted guerrilla units, taught them how to use weapons (including the hand-held Stinger missile), and in some cases even planned operations against the Soviet Union with them. In 1989, the USSR pulled out of Afghanistan; not only had the Soviets lost the war, but the Soviet Union itself totally collapsed within two years. The Mujahadeen gave credit to God for defeating their enemy and viewed the Soviet defeat and collapse as proof that God was on their side. After all, how else could the undermanned and under-equipped Islamic tribesmen defeat the Red Army? If, however, the Mujahadeen could bring down one of the world's great superpowers as warriors for God, then any other nation that faced God's holy warriors would be equally doomed to destruction. In their "thrill of victory," the Mujahadeen began searching for more infidels to destroy, and the primary targets of the Mujahadeen's holy war then shifted from the USSR to apostate Islamic governments in the Middle East, Israel, and the U.S. One of the Mujahadeen leaders who fervently believed in continuation of the holy war against the Muslim apostates and American and Israeli infidels was Osama bin Laden (Gunaratna, 2002, 18–22).

OSAMA BIN LADEN

Osama bin Laden, born in 1957, was one of 51 children of a rich Saudi Arabian construction magnate. Bin Laden was university-educated at Jeddah, where he was taught Islamic studies by Muhammad Qutb, the brother of Sayyid Qutb of *Signposts* fame and the Muslim Brotherhood; consequently, bin Laden developed a strict view of Islam at an early age and opposed the imposition of non–Islamic rule on Muslims (*The Sunday Times*, 2002). When the Soviets invaded Afghanistan in the 1980s, bin Laden was compelled to leave the lucrative family construction business in Saudi Arabia to join the Mujahadeen in Afghanistan in their effort to oust the Soviet infidels (*The Sunday Times*, 2002).

While in Afghanistan, bin Laden adopted the teachings of Sheik Abdullah Azzam, who had been expelled from Egypt in 1979 for Islamic activism (Bergen, 2001, 55–61). It was Azzam who conceptualized al Qaeda for the purpose of providing direction and purpose for the Mujahadeen. Azzam argued that the Soviet war was just the beginning, and it was time for Muslims to rise up and strike Satan all over the world, with the ultimate goal of converting the entire world into a pure Islamic society under a new caliphate. Azzam envisioned al Qaeda as an organization that would channel the ideology and direction of the Mujahadeen into fighting against infidels worldwide on the behalf of God and oppressed Muslims. Any time a Muslim country would be invaded by infidels, the Mujahadeen would arrive as a ready and able rapid action force to expel the invaders (Bergen, 2001, 55–61).

When the Soviets were preparing to withdraw from Afghanistan, the Pakistani Intelligence Service created its own Afghan guerrilla force and used it to take control of major areas of Afghanistan, thus "robbing" the

Mujahadeen of their victory in the eyes of Azzam. Azzam believed and taught that the United States was behind this Pakistani action. Bin Laden evidently agreed with Azzam's analysis and erroneously believed the U.S. to be in opposition to his Mujahadeen. In particular, bin Laden was angered by what he viewed as an ungrateful United States that had taken credit for defeating the Soviets in Afghanistan that should have gone to the Mujahadeen (Auster, 1998, 49).

Azzam was killed in a 1989 car bombing that may have been linked to bin Laden himself, but the ideological void left by Azzam's death was filled by Egyptian Dr. Ayman Muhammad Rabi' al Zawahiri, a member of a well-respected medical family in Egypt. Al Zawahiri, also a member of radical Islamic organizations in Egypt, had been engaged in covert terrorism for thirty years when he went to Afghanistan to aid the Mujahadeen in the 1980s. Al Zawahiri became bin Laden's personal physician and close associate. Al Zawahiri is a follower of the Salafi strand of Islam, a strict segment of Wahhabism. Salafis are known as "pious pioneers of Islam," and the Salafi Daway ("call of the Salafis") is Islam in its totality, applied to all humanity irrespective of ethnicity, culture, or national origin (Auster, 1998, 49).

The global outlook of Salafism allowed bin Laden to reach across the aisle to Shiite Muslims in a mutual effort to forge a new world based on the principles of strict worldwide adherence to the Koran. Bin Laden and his followers believe that Mohammed named the Salafis as the "best generation of Muslims," and that those who are Salafis are guaranteed success, victory, and salvation (Auster, 1998, 49).

Bin Laden returned to Saudi Arabia to resume work in the family construction business after the Afghan war and brought several of his Mujahadeen Afghans with him. In 1991, however, when Iraq under Saddam Hussein invaded Kuwait, bin Laden offered the services of his Mujahadeen to the Saudi government for the purpose of ousting the Iraqis from Kuwait. After all, if the Mujahadeen could destroy the Soviet Union (with the help of Allah), they certainly could oust the much less formidable Iraqi army from Kuwait (Gunaratna, 2002, 28–30).

The Saudi royal family essentially rejected bin Laden's offer of help and turned to the Americans instead, thus humiliating Allah's hero of the Afghan war. When the U.S. military showed up to help liberate Kuwait in the Persian Gulf War, bin Laden and other radical Muslims were appalled to see Muslims fighting and killing other Muslims under infidel American leadership. The Saudi royal family assured bin Laden that the Americans would depart from the holy land as soon as their mission was accomplished, but after the war, the Saudi government continued to allow

American troops to be stationed in Saudi Arabia and police the Persian Gulf region from Saudi soil. In reaction to what he viewed as an abomination against Islam, bin Laden began training and financing terrorist groups and calling for the overthrow of unsympathetic apostate governments, including the government of his own Saudi Arabia. The Saudi government, however, cracked down on dissidents, and bin Laden was forced to flee first to Afghanistan, then to the Sudan, where he began building his terrorist network (Gunaratna, 2002, 28–30).

Bin Laden waged war against what he viewed as apostate or *jahili* governments in the Middle East with a series of terrorist bombings in the 1990s. None of the governments targeted by bin Laden and al Qaeda, including Egypt and Saudi Arabia, were overthrown; consequently, bin Laden became convinced that their ability to survive his *jihadi* onslaught was due to U.S. support. This view necessitated a change in strategy away from the attacks on the apostate governments themselves and toward the U.S., the infidel nation that supported the *jahiliyya* governments. Bin Laden's hatred of America, therefore, was fueled not so much by American "decadence" or the infidel status of Americans, but because he viewed the United States as the power that propped up the rule by apostate or *jahiliyya* Muslim governments, and because of his belief that rule by *jahiliyya* governments was an abomination to God, detrimental to both Islam and Muslim people (quoted in Gunaratna, 2002, 45).

In August 1996, bin Laden officially declared war on the U.S. with a religious fatwa. In Islam, an attack on an enemy must be preceded by an Islamic decree, or *fatwa*, that can only be issued by an Islamic cleric. Many Muslims would not recognize the legitimacy of the 1996 *fatwa* since bin Laden is not a cleric; however, a group of forty Afghan clerics issued a *fatwa* calling for *jihad* against the United States on March 12, 1998, and another similar *fatwa* was issued by Pakistani clerics and signed by Sheikh Ahmed Azzam in April, 1998, thus legitimizing bin Laden's declaration of war on America after the fact (Bergen, 2001, 108–109).

In bin Laden's 1996 *fatwa*, he essentially provided three reasons for war with the U.S. First, bin Laden argued that the U.S. had been occupying the holy land (i.e., Saudi Arabia) for seven years and

> plundering its riches, dictating to its rulers, humiliating its people, terrorizing its neighbours, and turning its bases in the Peninsula into a spearhead through which to fight the neighboring peoples.... The best proof of this is the Americans' continuing aggression against Iraqi people using the Peninsula as a staging post, even though all its rulers are against their territories being used to that end, but they are helpless [quoted in Gunaratna, 2002, 44].

Second, bin Laden argued that the United States was planning to go to war with Iraq and annihilate Muslims there a second time. In the words of bin Laden:

> Second, despite the great devastation inflicted on the Iraqi people by the Crusader–Zionist alliance, and despite the huge number of those killed, which has exceeded one million.... despite all this, the Americans are once again trying to repeat the horrific massacres, as though they are not content with the protracted blockade imposed after the ferocious war or the fragmentation and devastation. So here they come to annihilate what is left of this people and to humiliate their Muslim neighbours [quoted in Gunaratna, 2002, 44].

Unfortunately, in the minds of many Muslims, George W. Bush has proven Osama bin Laden to be correct on this particular item; hence, it appears that the Iraqi terrorist insurgents have had little trouble in recruiting *jihadis* from throughout the Muslim world for the purpose of ousting the infidel American invaders from Iraq.

Finally, bin Laden argued that America's aims behind its wars against Muslims are both "religious and economic and the aim is also to serve the Jews' petty state and divert attention from its occupation of Jerusalem and murder of Muslims there" (quoted in Gunaratna, 2002, 44). Bin Laden goes on to argue that the proof of all he is saying is the Americans'

> ... eagerness to destroy Iraq, the strongest neighbouring Arab state, and their endeavour to fragment all the states of the region such as Iraq, Saudi Arabia, Egypt, and Sudan into paper statelets and through their disunion and weakness to guarantee Israel's survival and the continuation of the brutal Crusade occupation of the Peninsula [quoted in Gunaratna, 2002, 44].

Again, bin Laden made these statements in 1996, but George W. Bush's invasion of Iraq in 2003 clearly validated bin Laden's arguments in the minds of many Muslims. Bin Laden concluded his "declaration of war" *fatwa* by arguing that these "crimes and sins committed by the Americans are a clear declaration of war on God, his messenger, and Muslims," and by reminding Muslims that in such cases, *ulema* (Islamic scholars) throughout history "unanimously agreed that the *jihad* is an individual duty if the enemy destroys Muslim countries." Bin Laden then finally ends the *fatwa* with the statement that "[n]othing is more sacred than belief except repulsing an enemy who is attacking religion and life" (quoted in Gunaratna, 2002, 44).

Bin Laden followed his declaration of war on America by issuing two more religious *fatwas* in 1998 expanding his *jihad*. In these *fatwas*, bin Laden condemned the Saudi government for ignoring *sharia* and replacing it with man-made civil law, and condemned the Saudis for allowing the Americans to occupy the holy land. Bin Laden declared that the use of man-made law instead of *sharia* and support for infidels (Americans) against Muslims effectively strips the people who do so of their Islamic status, thus making it much easier to kill them under Islamic law. Bin Laden further declared that there is no more important duty for Muslims than expelling the Americans from the holy land (Gunaratna, 2002, 27). In a *fatwa* in February 1998, bin Laden went even further and called for the killing of any American anywhere in the world (Benjamin and Simon, 2002).

BIN LADEN'S USE OF SYMBOLISM

In any traditional conservative ideology, the use of symbols and symbolism take on enhanced importance. Close observers of Osama bin Laden will note that he is a master of using cultural and religious symbolism to enhance his legitimacy among his followers. For example, although bin Laden has frequently lived in large, luxurious houses and driven expensive luxury vehicles during his years leading *jihad*, his media interviews and taped conversations are always from caves, thus projecting an image of a common man who has piously foregone riches in the interest of Allah's service. On posters throughout the Middle East, bin Laden is depicted as a saint riding on a white horse, thus evoking images among viewers of the prophet Mohammed, who also fought on a white horse. Bin Laden, unlike the *jahili* leaders Saddam Hussein, Hosni Mubarak, and King Hussein, never wears a Western suit, and is usually seen wearing traditional Islamic clothing (although, in at least one video message, he wore Western-style military camouflage). In particular, bin Laden wears a headdress that relates to Jerusalem's al Aqsa mosque, one of Islam's holiest sites. At other times, bin Laden wears a plain white turban, signifying that he has near-clerical status. Bin Laden often carries a knife typical of the design of those for rulers on the Arabian Peninsula, and he wears a ring containing a black stone set in silver that symbolizes Mecca, the most holy place of Islam (Gunaratna, 2002, 41–42).

Status of Islamism since 9/11

The reaction of the masses in the Muslim world since the terrorist attacks of 9/11 has been decidedly sympathetic to the Islamists and opposed to the policies of the United States under the George W. Bush administration. Polls of Muslims in the Middle East in 2002 revealed that most Muslims did not believe the 9/11 attacks were carried out by Muslims. Instead, it was commonly believed that the attacks were most likely carried out by the CIA. The globally recognized head of al Qaeda, Osama bin Laden, thoroughly despised in the U.S. for his role in the 9/11 attacks (and others), remains quite popular in the Islamic world. For example, in the largely Muslim Nigerian city of Kano, seven out of ten boys born in 2002 were given the name "Osama" by their parents.

As the continued insurgency in Iraq demonstrates, the American-led war on terror has done little, if anything, to erode the prevalence of radical Islamic ideology. Instead, statistics from a RAND Corporation database show 5362 deaths from terrorism worldwide between March 2004 and March 2005, a figure that is almost double the total for the same twelve-month period before the 2003 invasion (*Amarillo Globe News*, July 10, 2005), a figure that does not include the deaths in Iraq. Although the number of Islamists captured and killed in the Iraqi campaign possibly exceeds this number, the characterization of the War on Terror as a "long hard slog" appears, unfortunately, to be accurate.

While America's invasion of Iraq has served to unite diverse groups of radical Muslims, including radical Shiites under Moqtada al Sadr and radical Sunnis under Abu Musab al–Zarqawi against the American invasion of Iraq (Phillips, 2005, 165, 219), some subsequent developments are more heartening. For example, Sunnis voted in greater numbers than expected in an October 2005 referendum successfully adopting Iraq's new constitution. On the other hand, the Iraqi branch of al Qaeda claimed responsibility for bombing three hotels in Amman, Jordan, the following month. With similar fits and starts, the culture clash between the West and the Islamists may be expected to continue indefinitely.

Bibliography

Aaron, Henry, and William B. Schwartz. *The Painful Prescription: Rationing Hospital Care*. Boston, Beacon Press, 1984.

Adelson, Joseph, and Robert O'Neil. "Growth of Political Ideas in Adolescence: The Sense of Community." In Roberta S. Sigel, ed., *Learning About Politics: A Reader in Political Socialization*. New York: Random House, 1970.

Aiken, Henry D. *The Age of Ideology: The Nineteenth Century Philosophers*. New York: Mentor, 1956.

Alexander, Charles C. *The Ku Klux Klan in the Southwest*. Lexington, KY: University of Kentucky Press, 1965.

Almond, Gabriel. "The Development of Political Development." In Myron Weiner and Samuel Huntington, eds., *Understanding Political Development*. New York: HarperCollins, 1987.

Amarillo Globe News. July 10, 2005.

American Civil Liberties Union. "ACLU Submits Statement Before House Anti-Gay Marriage Hearing." Washington, D.C.: *ACLU*, May 22, 1996.

_____. "ACLU Says that Clinton Panders to Bigotry With Announcement That He Will Sign Ban on Same-Sex Marriage." Washington, D.C.: *ACLU*, May 22, 1996.

_____. "ACLU Criticizes Allies for Jumping Ship on Gay Marriage." Washington, D.C.: *ACLU*, July 11, 1996.

_____. "Testimony Regarding S. 1740-Defense of Marriage Act." Washington, D.C.: *ACLU*, July 11, 1996.

_____. "ACLU Condemns House Passage of Anti-Gay Marriage Bill, Says Measure is Unconstitutional and Bad Public Policy." Washington, D.C.: *ACLU*, July 12, 1996.

_____. "ACLU Background Briefing: Congress Considers Anti-Gay Marriage Bill and Employment Non-Discrimination Act." Washington, D.C.: *ACLU*, August 6, 1996.

_____. "ACLU Blasts Senate Passage of Anti-Gay Marriage Ban." Washington, D.C.: *ACLU*, September 10, 1996.

_____. "Statewide Anti-Gay Marriage Law." Washington, D.C.: *ACLU*, January 6, 1998.

Anderson, Ronald, and John F. Newman. "Societal and Individual Determinants of Medical Care Utilization in the United States." In S.J. Williams, ed., *Issues in Health Services*. New York: Wiley, 1990.

Andrews, Pat. *Voices of Diversity*. Guilford, CT: Dushkin, 1993.

Armstrong, Karen. "Was it Inevitable—Islam Through History." In James F. Hoge, Jr., and Gidon Rose, eds., *How did this happen? Terrorism and the New War*. New York: Public Affairs, 2001.

Attarian, John. "The Entitlement Time Bomb." *The World and I*. November, 1996.

Auster, Bruce B. "The Recruiter for

Hate." *U.S. News and World Report.* August 31, 1998.

Bacon, Kenneth H. "AARP Now Championing Health Care for All, Scrambles to Prove it's More than a Paper Tiger." *Wall Street Journal.* December 27, 1989.

Baer, Robert. *See No Evil.* New York: Three Rivers Press, 2002.

_____. *Sleeping With the Devil.* New York: Crown, 2003.

Balagushkin, E.G. "The Building of Communism and the Evolution of Family and Marital Relations." *Soviet Sociology.* Volume 1: Winter, 1962/63.

Bane, M.J., and D. Ellwood. *Welfare Realities: From Rhetoric to Reform.* Cambridge, MA: Harvard University Press, 1994.

Baradat, Leon P. *Soviet Political Society.* Second Edition. Englewood Cliffs, NJ: Prentice-Hall, 1989.

Baran, Paul. *The Political Economy of Growth.* New York: Monthly Review Press, 1957.

Bardach, Eugene, and Robert Kagan. *Going by the Book: The Problem of Regulatory Unreasonableness.* Philadelphia: Temple University Press, 1982.

Bath, Richard C., and Dilmus D. James. "Dependency Analysis of Latin America: Some Criticisms, Some Suggestions." *Latin American Research Review.* 11 (3) 3–53.

Bayer, Ronald, and Daniel Callahan. "Medicare Reform: Social and Ethical Perspectives." *Journal of Health Politics, Policy, and Law.* 10 (3) 1985.

Beck, Allen. "Survey of State Prison Inmates." Washington, D.C.: U.S. Department of Justice, Bureau of Justice Statistics, March, 1995.

Begala, Paul. *It's Still the Economy, Stupid.* New York: Simon and Schuster, 2002.

Bell, Daniel. *The End of Ideology: On the Exhaustion of Political Ideas in the Fifties.* New York: Free Press, 1960.

Bell, P.M.H. *The Origins of the Second World War in Europe.* London and New York: Longman, 1986.

Bellah, Robert, Richard Madsen, William Sullivan, Ann Swidler, and Steven M. Tipton. *Habits of the Heart: Individualism and Commitment in American Political Life.* Berkley, CA: University of California Press, 1985.

Benjamin, Daniel, and Steven Simon. *The Age of Sacred Terror.* New York: Random House, 2002.

Bennett, Ralph Kinney. "Tour Risk Under the Clinton Health Plan." *Reader's Digest.* March, 1994.

Bergen, Peter L. *Inside the Secret World of Osama bin Laden.* London, Weidenfeld and Nicolson, 2001.

Berlet, Chip. "Dances with Devils." *Political Research Associates.* www.public eye.org., 1998.

Billig, Michael. *Fascists: A Social Psychological View.* New York: Academic Press, 1979.

Blumstein, Alfred. "Prisons." In James Q. Wilson and Joan Petersilia, eds., *Crime.* San Francisco: Institute for Contemporary Studies, 1995.

Bodenheimer, Susanne. "The Ideology of Developmentalism: American Political Science's Paradigm Surrogate for Latin American Studies." *Berkeley Journal of Sociology.* 15 (1) 1976, 95–137.

Bonilla, Robert, Andre Gunder Frank and Robert Girling, eds. *Structures of Dependency.* Stanford, CA: Institute of Political Studies, 1973.

Bosso, Christopher J. "Environmental Groups and the New Political Landscape." In Kraft and Vig, eds., *Environmental Policy.* 4th ed. Washington, D.C.: Congressional Quarterly Press, 2000.

Boston Globe. March 21, 2001.

Bradford, William. *Of Plymouth Plantation 1620–1647.* 1856. New York: Random House, 1981.

Breckenridge, Adam C. "The History of the Constitution of the United States." In Bruce Stinebricker, ed., *Annual Editions: American Government 02/03.* Guilford, CT: Dushkin/McGraw-Hill, 2002.

Brinkley, Alan. *American History: A Survey.* 11th ed. Boston, MA: McGraw-Hill, 2003.

Brown, Lawrence D. "The Managerial Imperative and Organizational Innovation in Health Services." In Eli K. Ginzberg, ed., *The U.S. Health Care System: A Look to the 1990s.* Totowa, NJ: Rowman and Allenheld, 1985.

Brown, Michael B. *The Economics of Imperialism.* London: Penguin, 1974.

Broyles, J. Allen. *The John Birch Society: Anatomy of a Protest.* Boston: Beacon Press, 1964.

Bryce, James. *The American Commonwealth.* 1888.

Buckley, William F. *God and Man at Yale: The Superstitions of Academic Freedom.* Washington, D.C.: Regnery Gateway, 1951.

Buckley, William F., and Brent Bozell. *McCarthy and His Enemies: The Record and Its Meaning.* Chicago: Regnery, 1954.

Burner, David. *Herbert Hoover: A Public Life.* New York: Knopf, 1979.

Butz, Arthur R. *The Hoax of the Twentieth Century: The Case Against the Presumed Extermination of European Jewry.* Chicago: Theses and Dissertations Press, 2003.

Callahan, Daniel. *Setting Limits: Medical Goals in an Aging Society.* New York: Simon and Schuster, 1987.

Calvert, Robert A., Arnoldo De Leon, and Gregg Cantrell. *The History of Texas.* Third Edition. Wheeling, IL: Harlan Davidson, 2002.

Campbell, Angus, Philip E. Converse, Warren E. Miller, and Donald E. Stokes. *The American Voter.* New York: Wiley, 1960.

Cannon, Lou. *President Reagan: The Role of a Lifetime.* New York: Simon and Schuster, 1991.

Cardoso, Fernando Henrique. "Associated Dependent Development: Theoretical and Practical Implications." In Alfred Stepan, ed., *Authoritarian Brazil: Origin, Policy, and Future.* New Haven, CT: Yale University Press, 1973.

Cardoso, Fernando, and Enzo Feletto. *Dependency and Development in Latin America.* Berkeley: University of California Press, 1979.

Carson, Gerald H. "Who Put the Borax in Dr. Wiley's Butter?" In Kenneth G. Alfers, C. Larry Pool, and William Mugleston, eds. *Perspectives On America, Volume 2: Readings in United States History Since 1877.* New York: Forbes Custom Publishing, 1997.

Carter, Stephen L. *Reflections of an Affirmative Action Baby.* New York: Basic Books, 1991.

Cassels, Alan. *Fascist Italy.* Wheeling, IL: Harlan Davidson, 1968.

Center for Budget and Policy Priorities. "Number of Americans Without Health Insurance Rose in 2002." October 8, 2003.

_____. "Poverty Increases and Median Income Declines for Second Consecutive Year." September 29, 2003.

Chalmers, David M. *Hooded Americanism: The History of the Ku Klux Klan.* New York: Doubleday, 1965.

Chamberlin, William Henry. *America's Second Crusade.* Chicago: Ralph Myles Publishing, 1962.

Charles, Robert B. "From Democracy to Regulocracy?" In George McKenna and Stanley Feingold, eds. *Taking Sides: Clashing Views on Political Issues.* 9th ed. Guilford, CT: Dushkin, 1995.

Chilcote, Ronald H., and Joel C. Edelstein. "Alternative Perspectives of Development and Underdevelopment in Latin America." In Chilcote and Edelstein, eds., *Latin America: The Struggle With Dependency and Beyond.* New York: Wiley, 1974.

Chodorov, Frank. *Income Tax: The Root of All Evil.* New York: Devin-Adair, 1954.

Cleage, Albert B., Jr. *Black Christian Nationalism.* New York: Morrow, 1972.

Clear, Todd, and George F. Cole. *American Corrections.* 2nd ed. Pacific Grove, CA: Brooks/Cole, 1990.

Cockroft, James D. "Mexico." In Chilcote and Edelstein, eds., *Latin Amer-*

ica: The Struggle With Dependency and Beyond. New York: Wiley, 1974.

Cohen, Jeffrey. *Politics and Economic Policy in the United States.* 2nd ed. Boston, MA: Houghton Mifflin, 2000.

Cole, Wayne S. *America First: The Battle Against Intervention 1940–1941.* Madison, WI: Octogon Books, 1971.

Conason, Joe, and Gene Lyons. *The Hunting of the President: The Ten Year Campaign to Destroy Bill and Hillary Clinton.* New York: Bedford/St. Martin's 2000.

Cone, James H. *Black Theology and Black Power.* New York: Seabury Press, 1969.

_____. *Liberation.* Philadelphia: Lippincott, 1970.

Congressional Budget Office. "Budget and Economic Outlook: Fiscal Years 2002–2011." January 1, 2001.

Congressional Quarterly Weekly Report. "Administration of Justice Escapes Deep Spending Cuts in New Reagan Budget Plan." February 13, 1983.

Corn, David. *The Lies of George W. Bush.* New York: Crown, 2003.

Cram, Ralph Adams. *The End of Democracy.* Boston: Marshall Jones, 1937.

Crispino, Ralph J. "The EPA Dilemma." In Theodore and Theodore, eds., *Major Environmental Issues Facing the 21st Century.* Upper Saddle River, NJ: Prentice-Hall, 1996.

Croce, Benedetto. *Historical Materialism and the Economics of Karl Marx.* Kila, MT: Kessinger, 2004.

Csikszentmihalyi, Mihaly, and Reed Larson. *Being Adolescent: Conflict and Growth in Teenage Years.* New York: Basic Books, 1984.

Dahl, Robert. *Democracy and Its Critics.* New Haven: Yale University Press, 1989.

Daly, Mary. "The Women's Movement: An Exodus Community." *Religious Education.* Volume 67: September/October, 1972.

_____. *Beyond God the Father: Toward a Philosophy of Women's Liberation.* Boston: Beacon Press, 1985.

D'Emilio, John. *Sexual Politics, Sexual Communities: The Making of a Homosexual Minority in the United States, 1940–1970.* Chicago: University of Chicago Press, 1983.

Denton, Sally. *American Massacre: The Tragedy at Mountain Meadows, September 1857.* New York: Random House, 2004.

Denver Post. March 15, 2001.

De Toqueville, Alexis. *Democracy in America.* 1835. New York: HarperCollins, 2001.

Diamond, Jared. *Guns, Germs and Steel: The Fates of Human Societies.* New York: W.W. Norton, 1999.

DiIulio, John. "The Federal Role in Crime Control." In James Q. Wilson and Joan Petersilia, eds., *Crime.* San Francisco: Institute for Contemporary Studies, 1995.

Dobelstein, Andrew. *Moral Authority, Ideology, and the Future of American Social Welfare.* Boulder, CO: Westview Press, 1999.

Dolbeare, Kenneth, and Patricia Dolbeare. *American Ideologies: The Competing Political Beliefs of the 1970s.* 3rd ed. Chicago: Rand McNally, 1976.

Dos Santos, Theotonio. "The Structure of Dependence." *American Economic Review.* 60 (1), May 1970, 231–236.

_____. "The Crisis of Contemporary Capitalism." *Latin American Perspective.* 3: Spring 1976, 84–99.

Dunn, Charles W., and J. David Woodard. *American Conservatism from Burke to Bush: An Introduction.* Lanham, MD.: Madison Books, 1991.

Eatwell, Roger. "The Nature of the Right, 2: The Right as a Variety of Styles of Thought." In Roger Eatwell and Noel O'Sullivan, eds., *The Nature of the Right.* Boston, MA: Twayne, 1989.

Ebenstein, William, and Alan O. Ebenstein. *Introduction to Political Thinkers.* Fort Worth, TX: Harcourt Brace, 1992.

Economist. "Inequality: For Richer, For Poorer." November 5, 1994, 19–21.

_____. "Honor Laws." June 21, 2003.

_____. November 1, 2003.

_____. "New Fuel for the Culture Wars." March 5, 2004.

_____. "Forever Young." March 27, 2004.

_____. "A Matter of Trust." April 3, 2004.

_____. April 10, 2004.

_____. "Lexington: A House Divided." May 8, 2004.

_____. June 26, 2004.

Edwards, Lee. *Goldwater: The Man Who Made a Revolution.* Washington: Regnery, 1995.

Egan, Timothy. "Triumph Leaves No Targets for Conservative Talk Shows." *New York Times.* January 1, 1995.

Ellerbe, Helen. *The Dark Side of Christian History.* Orlando, FL: Morningstar and Lark, 1995.

Emery, Edwin. *The Press and America: An Interpretive History of the Mass Media.* 9th ed. Englewood Cliffs, NJ: Pearson, 1999.

Emswiler, Sharon Neufer. "How the New Woman Feels in the Old Worship Service." In Sharon Neufer Emswiler and Thomas Neufer Emswiler, eds., *Women and Worship: A Guide to Non-Sexist Hymns, Prayers, and Liturgies.* New York: Harper and Row, 1974.

Engels, Friedrich. "Socialism: Utopian and Scientific." In Lewis S. Feuer, ed., *Marx and Engels: Basic Writings on Politics and Philosophy.* New York: Doubleday, 1959.

Epstein, Cynthia Fuchs. *Women's Place: Options and Limits in Professional Careers.* Berkeley: University of California Press, 1971.

Etzioni, Amitai. "Has the ACLU Lost Its Mind?" *Washington Monthly.* October 1994, 9–11.

Evans, Peter. "Continuities and Contradictions in the Evolution of Brazilian Dependence." *Latin American Perspectives.* 3: Spring 1976, 30–54.

_____. *Dependent Development: The Alliance of Multinational, State, and Local Capital in Brazil.* Princeton, NJ: Princeton University Press, 1979.

Farmer, Brian R. *American Domestic Policy: Substance and Process.* Lanham, MD: University Press of America, 2003.

_____. *The Question of Dependency and Economic Development: A Quantitative Analysis.* Lanham, MD: Lexington Books, 1999.

Ferry, Barbara. "New Mexico Congressman Linked to 'Wise Use' Movement." *States News Service.* June 5, 1997.

Fingerhut, Lois, and Joel C. Kleinman. "International and Interstate Comparisons of Homicide Among Young Males." *Journal of the American Medical Association.* 263 (24) June, 1990.

Flynn, John T. The *Decline of the American Republic and How to Rebuild It.* New York: Devin-Adair, 1955.

Fowler, Robert Booth, and Jeffrey R. Orenstein. *An Introduction to Political Theory.* New York: HarperCollins, 1993.

Frank, Andre Gunder. *Capitalism and Underdevelopment in Latin America.* New York: Monthly Review Press, 1967.

_____. *Latin America: Underdevelopment or Revolution.* New York: Monthly Review Press, 1972.

_____. *Lumpenbourgeoisie: Lumpendevelopment, Dependence, Class and Politics in Latin America.* New York: Monthly Review Press, 1974.

Franken, Al. *Lies and the Lying Liars Who Tell Them: A Fair and Balanced Look at the Right.* New York: E.P. Dutton, 2003.

_____. *Rush Limbaugh is a Big Fat Idiot: And Other Observations.* New York: Dell, 1999.

Franklin, Daniel. "Act Now—There's Still Time to Stop the Revolution." *The Washington Monthly.* September, 1995.

Freeden, Michael. *Ideology: A Very Short Introduction.* Oxford and New York: Oxford University Press, 2003.

Freidel, Frank. *The New Deal and the American People.* Englewood Cliffs, NJ: Prentice-Hall, 1964.

Fremstad, Shawn. "Recent Welfare Reform Research Findings: Implications for TANF Reauthorization and State TANF Policies." *Center on Budget and Policy Priorities.* January 30, 2004.

Fremstad, Shawn, and Sharon Parrott. "Superwaiver Provision in House TANF Reauthorization Bill Could Significantly Weaken Public Housing, Food Stamps, and Other Low-Income Programs." *Center on Budget and Policy Priorities.* March 23, 2004.

Friedman, Milton. *Capitalism and Freedom.* Chicago: University of Chicago Press, 1962.

Friedman, Milton, and Anna J. Schwartz. *The Great Contraction, 1929–1933.* Boston: Houghton Mifflin, 1966.

Frost, Brian. "Prosecution and Sentencing." In James Q. Wilson and Joan Petersilia, eds., *Crime.* San Francisco: Institute for Contemporary Studies, 1995.

Frost, Brian, and Kathleen Brosi. "A Theoretical and Empirical Analysis of the Prosecutor." *Journal of Legal Studies.* 6, 1977.

Galston, William. "Civic Education in a Liberal State." In Nancy L. Rosenblum, ed., *Liberalism and the Moral Life.* Cambridge: Harvard University Press, 1989.

_____. "Liberalism and Public Morality." In Alfonso J. Damico, ed., *Liberals on Liberalism.* Totowa, NJ: Rowman and Littlefield, 1986.

Galtung, Johan. "Feudal Systems, Structural Violence and the Structural Theory of Revolutions." *IPRA: Studies in Peace Research,* Volume 1. Netherlands: Van Gorcum, 1970.

_____. "A Structural Theory of Imperialism." *Journal of Peace Research.* 8, 1971, 81–119.

Garraty, John A. The *American Nation: A History of the United States Since 1865.* 7th ed. New York: HarperCollins, 1991.

Gilliard, Darrell K. *Prisoners in 2002.* Washington, D.C.: Bureau of Justice Statistics. May, 2003.

Girvan, Norman. "The Development of Dependency Economics in the Caribbean and Latin America: Review and Comparison." *Social and Economic Studies.* 22 (1) March, 1973, 434–461.

Glamour, June, 2000.

Goldenberg, Naomi. *Changing of the Gods: Feminism and the End of Traditional Religions.* Boston: Beacon Press, 1979.

Goodman, John C. *The Regulation of Medical Care: Is the Price Too High?* Washington, D.C.: Cato Institute, 1980.

Goodman, Walter. *The Committee: The Extraordinary Career of the House Committee on UnAmerican Affairs.* Baltimore, MD: Farrar, Straus, and Giroux, 1969.

Goodwin, Doris Kearns. *No Ordinary Time: Franklin and Eleanor Roosevelt: The Home Front During World War II.* New York: Touchstone, 1995.

Gordon, Robert Aaron. *Economic Instability and Growth: the American Record.* New York: Harper and Row, 1974.

Gould, Lewis L. *Progressives and Prohibitionists: Texas Democrats in the Wilson Era.* Austin: University of Texas Press, 1973.

_____. *Grand Old Party: A History of Republicans.* New York: Random House, 2003.

Grant, Madison. *The Passing of the Great Race, or, the Racial Basis of European History:* Manchester, NH: Ayer, 1970.

Greenstein, Robert. "What the Trustees' Report Indicates About the Financial Status of Social Security." *Center on Budget and Policy Priorities.* March 31, 2004.

Greenstein, Robert, and Edwin Park. "Health Savings Accounts in Final Medicare Conference Agreement Pose Threats Both to Long-Term Fiscal Policy and to the Employer-Based Health Insurance System." *Center on Budget and Policy Priorities.* December 1, 2003.

Greenstein, Robert, and Peter Orszag. "Misleading Claims About New Social Security and Medicare Projections." *Center on Budget and Policy Priorities.* April 2, 2004.

Grier, William, and Price Cobbs. *Black Rage.* New York: Bantam, 1968.

Griffith, Robert. *The Politics of Fear: Joseph McCarthy and the Senate.* Boston: University of Massachusetts Press, 1987.

Grunhut, M. *Penal Reform.* London: Oxford University Press, 1948.

Gunaratna, Rohan. *Inside Al Qaeda: Global Network of Terror.* New York: Columbia University Press, 2002.

Haas, Ben. *KKK: The Hooded Face of Vengeance.* Evanston, IL: Regency, 1963.

Hamby, Alonso. *Beyond the New Deal.* New York: St. Martin's Press, 1973.

Hamilton, Charles. *Black Preacher in America.* New York: Morrow, 1972.

Hancock, M. Donald, David P. Conradt, G. Guy Peters, William Safran, and Raphael Zariski. *Politics in Western Europe.* Chatham, NJ: Chatham House, 1993.

Hardball with Chris Matthews. August 11, 1998.

Harwood, Richard. *Did Six Million Really Die? The Truth at Last.* Uckfield, East Sussex, U.K.: Historical Review Press, 1974.

Hasenfeld, Y., and J. Rafferty. "The Determinants of Public Attitudes Toward the Welfare State." *Social Forces.* 67, 1989.

Hayek, Friedrich a. *The Road to Serfdom.* Chicago: University of Chicago Press, 1944.

Heclo, Hugh. "Poverty in Politics." In S. Danziger, G.D. Sandefur, and D. Weinberg, eds., *Confronting Poverty: Prescriptions for Change.* Cambridge, MA: Harvard University Press, 1994.

Heilbroner, Robert L. *The Worldly Philosophers.* New York: Simon and Schuster, 1953.

Henly, Julia R., and Sandra K. Danziger. "Confronting Welfare Stereotypes: Characteristics of General Assistance Recipients and Postassistance Employment." *Social Work Research.* December 20, 1996.

Herrnstein, Richard J., and Charles Murray. *The Bell Curve: Intelligence and Class Structure in American Life.* New York: Touchstone, 1996.

Hersh. Seymour M. "Target Qaddafi." *New York Times Magazine.* February 22, 1987.

Hess, Karl. *Community Technology.* New York: Harper and Row, 1979.

Hiro, Dilip. *Iraq: In the Eye of the Storm.* New York: Nation Books, 2002.

Hirschman, Albert. *Development Projects Observed.* 1945. Washington, D.C.: Brookings Institution, 2004.

Hoffman, Bruce. "Holy Terror: The Implications of Terrorism Motivated by a Religious Imperative." *Studies in Conflict and Terrorism.* 18: 271–284, 1995.

Hoffman, Peter, and Barbara Stone-Meierhoefer. "Post-Release Arrest Experiences of Federal Prisoners: A Six Year Follow-Up." *Journal of Criminal Justice.* 7, 1979.

Hoover, Herbert. *Addresses from the American Road.* 1941. New York: American Libraries Press, 1972.

Hoover, Kenneth. *Ideology and Political Life.* Second Edition. Belmont, CA: Wadsworth, 1994.

Huntington, Samuel. "Conservatism as an Ideology." *American Political Science Review.* 51: 1957, 454–473.

_____. "The Clash of Civilizations?" *Foreign Affairs.* 72: 22–49.

Hyman, Herbert H. *Political Socialization.* Glencoe: Free Press, 1959.

Ingersoll, David E., Richard K. Matthews, and Andrew Davison. *The Philosophic Roots of Modern Ideology.* Upper Saddle River, NJ: Prentice-Hall, 2001.

Interpol. *International Crime Statistics.* March, 2001.

Ivins, Molly, and Lou Dubose. *Shrub: The Short but Happy Political Life of George W. Bush.* New York: Vintage, 2002.

James, Clayton. *The Years of MacArthur 1941–1945.* Boston: Houghton Mifflin, 1975.

Janda, Kenneth, Jeffrey M. Berry, and Jerry Goldman. *The Challenge of Democracy: Government in America.* 3rd ed. Boston, Houghton Mifflin, 1992.

Johnson, Dale. *The Sociology of Change and Reaction in Latin America.* Indianapolis, Bobbs, Merrill, 1973.

Johnstone, Ronald L. *Religion in Society: A Sociology of Religion.* 4th ed. Englewood Cliffs, NJ: Prentice-Hall, 1992.

Jones, Howard. *Quest for Security: A History of U.S. Foreign Relations.* New York: McGraw-Hill, 1996.

_____. *Crucible of Power: A History of American Foreign Relations from 1897.* Wilmington, DE: SR Books, 2001.

Justice Assistance News. Washington, D.C.: U.S. Department of Justice, November 2, 1981.

Karger, Jacob, and David Stoesz. *American Social Welfare Policy.* New York: Longman, 1998.

Katz, M. *The Undeserving Poor.* New York: Pantheon, 1989.

Kellstedt, Lyman A., and Corwin E. Smidt. "Doctrinal Beliefs and Political Behavior: Views of the Bible." In David C. Leege and Lyman A. Kellstedt, eds., *Rediscovering the Religious Factor in American Politics.* Armonk, NY: M.E. Sharpe, 1993.

Kellstedt, Lyman A., and John C. Green. "Knowing God's Many People: Denominational Preference and Political Behavior." In David C. Leege and Lyman A. Kellstedt, eds., *Rediscovering the Religious Factor in American Politics.* Armonk, NY: M.E. Sharpe, 1993.

Kemper, Vicki, and Viveca Novak. *Common Cause Magazine.* January–March, 1992.

Keohane, Robert, and Joseph S. Nye. *Power and Interdependence.* Cambridge, MA: HarperCollins, 1989.

Keynes, John Maynard. *The Collected Writings of John Maynard Keynes.* London: Macmillan, 1980.

Khrushchev, Nikita S. "Special Report to the Twentieth Congress of the CPSU." In Frederick L. Bender, ed., *The Be-*

trayal of Marx. New York: Harper and Row, 1975.

Kinsey, Alfred. *Sexual Behavior in the Human Male.* 1948. Bloomington, IN: Indiana University Press, 1998.

Kirk, Russell. "Libertarians: Chirping Sectaries." *The Heritage Lectures: Proclaiming a Patrimony.* Washington, D.C.: The Heritage Foundation, 1982.

Kneese, Allen V., and Charles L. Schultze. *Pollution, Prices, and Public Policy.* Washington, D.C.: Brookings Institution, 1975.

Koh, Harold Hongju. "Rights to Remember." *The Economist.* November 1, 2003.

Kohlberg, Alfred. "China Via Stilwell Road." *The China Monthly.* October, 1948.

Koon, Richard L. *Welfare Reform: Helping the Least Fortunate Become Less Dependent.* New York: Garland, 1997.

Kosterlitz, Julie. "Itching for a Fight?" *National Journal.* January 15, 1994.

Kraft, Michael E., and Norman J. Vig. "Environmental Policy from the 1970s to 2000: An Overview." In Kraft and Vig, eds., *Environmental Policy.* 4th ed. Washington, D.C.: Congressional Quarterly Press, 2000.

Kristol, Irving. *Two Cheers for Capitalism.* New York: New American Library, 1983.

LaHaye, Tim. *The Battle for the Mind.* Old Tappan, NJ: Revell, 1980.

Lall, Sanjaya. "Is Dependence a Useful Concept in Analyzing Underdevelopment?" *World Development.* 3, 1975, 799–810.

Lane, Robert E. *Political Life.* Glencoe, New York: Free Press, 1959.

Lasswell, Harold. *Politics: Who Gets What, When, How.* New York: Meridian Books, 1958.

Lav, I.J., E. Lazere, R. Greenstein, and S. Gold. "The States and the Poor: How Budget Decisions Affected Low Income People in 1992." Washington, D.C.: Center on Budget and Policy Priorities.

Lenin, V.I. "Imperialism: the Highest

Stage of Capitalism." In V.I. Lenin, *Selected Works in Three Volumes*. Moscow: Foreign Languages Publishing, 1960.

Lerner, Daniel. *The Passing of Traditional Society*. Glencoe, IL: Free Press, 1958.

Levy, Leonard. "The Framers and Original Intent." In George M. McKenna and Stanley Feingold, eds., *Taking Sides: Clashing Views on Controversial Political Issues*. 8th ed. Guilford, CT: Dushkin, 1993.

Lindblom, Charles. *Politics and Markets: The World's Political-Economic Systems*. New York: Basic Books, 1977.

Lindorff, David. *This Can't Be Happening!: Resisting the Disintegration of American Democracy*. Monroe, ME: Common Courage Press, 2004.

Lindsay, James. "Apathy and Interest: The American Public Rediscovers Foreign Policy After September 11th." In James M. Lindsay, ed., *American Politics After September 11th*. Cincinnati, OH: Atomic Dog, 2003.

Lindsay, James. "Chronology of America's War on Terrorism." In James M. Lindsay, ed., *American Politics After September 11th*. Cincinnati, OH: Atomic Dog, 2003.

Lippman, Walter. *The Good Society*. 1937. Piscataway, NJ: Transaction, 2004.

Lipset, Seymour Martin. *Political Man*. Garden City, NY: Doubleday, 1967.

_____. *The First New Nation*. Garden City, NY: Doubleday, 1967.

Lipset, Seymour Martin, and Earl Raab. *The Politics of Unreason: Right-Wing Extremism in America, 1790–1970*. New York: Harper and Row, 1970.

Loconte, Joe. "I'll Stand Bayou." *Policy Review*. May/June, 1998.

Love, Joseph. "Origins of Dependency Analysis." *Journal of Latin American Studies*. 22(1), February 1990, 142–168.

Lynch, James. "Crime in International Perspective." In James Q. Wilson and Joan Petersilia, eds., *Crime*. San Francisco: Institute for Contemporary Studies, 1995.

Lynd, Staughton. *The Intellectual Origins of American Radicalism*. Cambridge, MA: Harvard University Press, 1982.

MacArthur, Douglas. *Reminiscences*. 1964. New York: Perseus, 1985.

Machan, Tibor. *The Libertarian Alternative*. Chicago: Nelson Hall, 1974.

Manchester, William. *The Last Lion: Winston Spencer Churchill*. Boston: Little, Brown, 1983.

Manning, D.J. *Liberalism*. New York: St. Martin's, 1976.

Martinson, Robert. "What Works? Questions and Answers about Prison Reform." *Public Interest*. 35: Spring, 1974.

Marx, Karl. *Capital: A Critique of Political Economy*. New York: Penguin, 1992.

_____. "Critique of the Gotha Program." In Lewis S. Feuer, ed., *Marx and Engels: Basic Writings on Politics and Philosophy*. Garden City, NY: Doubleday Anchor, 1959.

_____. *Grundrisse*. New York: Random House, 1974.

_____. "Grundrisse." In Robert Tucker, ed., *The Marx-Engels Reader*, 2nd ed. New York: W.W. Norton, 1978.

Marx, Karl, and Friedrich Engels. "Manifesto of the Communist Party." In S. Beer, ed., *The Communist Manifesto*. New York: Appleton-Century-Crofts, 1955.

_____. "The Communist Manifesto." In William Ebenstein and Alan O. Ebenstein, eds., *Introduction to Political Thinkers*. Fort Worth, TX: Harcourt Brace, 1992.

Maxwell, William, and Ernest Crain. *Texas Politics Today*. 7th ed. Belmont, CA: West Publishing, 1995.

_____. *Texas Politics Today*. 10th ed. Belmont, CA: Wadsworth, 2002.

_____. *Texas Politics Today*. 11th ed. Belmont, CA: Wadsworth, 2003.

Mayer, George H. *The Republican Party 1854–1966*. New York: Oxford University Press, 1967.

_____. "The Republican Party, 1932–1952." In Arthur M. Schlesinger, Jr., ed., *History of U.S. Political Parties*. Volume 4, 1973.

Mayer, Lawrence C. *Redefining Comparative Politics*. Newbury Park, CA: Sage, 1989.

McClelland, David. *The Achieving Society*. New York: Free Press, 1967.

McKinlay, John B., and Sonja M. McKinlay. "The Questionable Contribution of Medical Measures to the Decline of Mortality in the United States in the Twentieth Century." In Stephen J. Williams, ed., *Issues in Health Services*. New York: Wiley, 1980.

McQueen, Michel. "Voters, Sick of Current Health-Care System, Want Federal Government to Prescribe Remedy." *Wall Street Journal*. June 28, 1991.

Mencken, H.L. *A Carnival of Buncombe*. New York: John Hopkins University Press, 1996.

Mezey, Jennifer. Sharon Parrott, Mark Greenberg, and Shawn Fremstad. "Reversing Direction on Welfare Reform: President's Budget Cuts Child Care for More than 300,000 Children." *Center on Budget and Policy Priorities*. February 10, 2004.

Micklethwait, John, and Adrian Wooldridge. *The Right Nation: Conservative Power in America*. New York: Penguin Press, 2004.

Miles, Michael. *The Odyssey of the American Right*. New York, Oxford: Oxford University Press, 1980.

Miller, Mark Crispin. *The Bush Dyslexicon: Observations on a National Disorder*. New York: Norton, 2000.

Miner, Brad. *The Concise Conservative Encyclopedia*. New York: Simon and Schuster, 1996.

Moore, John. "Going to Extremes, Losing the Center." *National Journal*. June 18, 1994.

Moore, Michael. *Stupid White Men*. New York: HarperCollins, 2001.

_____. *Dude, Where's My Country?* New York: Warner Books, 2004.

Morgenstern, George, *Pearl Harbor: The Story of the Secret War*. 1947. New York: Institute for Historical Review, 1987.

Mosse, George. *The Crisis of German Ideology: Intellectual Origins of the Third Reich*. New York: Grosset and Dunlap, 1964.

Msnbc.msn.com/id/6409042/.

Muccigrosso, Robert. *Basic History of Conservatism*. Melbourne, FL: Krieger, 2001.

Muller, Jerry Z. *The Other God that Failed: Hans Freyer and the Deradicalization of German Conservatism*. Princeton, NJ: Princeton University Press, 1987.

Muller, Jerry Z. *Conservatism: An Anthology of Social and Political Thought from David Hume to the Present*. Princeton, NJ: Princeton University Press, 1997.

Munck, Ronaldo. *Politics and Dependence in the Third World*. London, Zed Press, 1985.

Murray, Charles. *Losing Ground*. New York: Basic Books, 1986.

Murrin, John R. *Liberty, Equality, Power*. Fort Worth: Harcourt Brace, 1996.

Mussolini, Benito. "The Doctrine of Fascism." In John Somerville and Ronald E. Santoni, eds., *Social and Political Philosophy*. Garden City, NY: Doubleday, 1963).

Myrdal, Gunnar. *Challenge of World Poverty*. New York: Knopf, 1957, 1970.

Naess, Arne. *Ecology, Community, and Lifestyle: Outline for an Ecosophy*. Cambridge: Cambridge University Press, 1984.

Nagle, Robert. *American Conservatism: An Illustrated History*. New York: Allied Books, 1988.

Nakane, Chie. *Japanese Society*. Berkeley, CA: University of California Press, 1986.

Nash, Gary B., Julie Roy Jeffrey, John R. Howe, Peter J. Frederick, Allen F. Davis, and Allan M. Winkler. *The American People: Creating a Nation and a Society*. New York: Harper and Row, 1987.

_____. *The American People: Creating a Nation and a Society*. 4th ed. New York: Longman, 1998.

National Women's Political Caucus. May 26, 1987.

Natural Resource Defense Council. "Rewriting the Rules: The Bush Administration's Assault on the Environment." April 22, 2002.

Newsweek, March 26, 1979, 26.

New York Post. March 17, 1990.

New York Times. August 6, 1941.

_____. August 6, 1953.

_____. "Clinton Plan Alive Upon Arrival." October 3, 1993.

_____. February 4, 2002.

_____. February 24, 2002.

_____. February 28, 2002.

Nietzsche, Friedrich. *Thus Spake Zarathustra.* 1883–85. New York: Penguin, 1969.

Nock, Albert J. *The Theory of Education in the United States.* New York: Arno Press, 1931.

_____, *Our Enemy the State.* 1936. New York: Arno Press, 1972.

Northwest Arkansas Times. "Human Dignity Resolution Fails." 11/4/98.

Nove, Alec. "On Reading Andre Gunder Frank." In Ivar Oxaal., Tony Barnett, and David Booth, eds., *Beyond the Sociology of Development: Economy and Society in Latin America and Africa.* London: Routledge, 1975.

Nozick, Robert. *Anarchy, State, and Utopia.* New York: Basic Books, 1974.

NYPost.com/millenium/mill. 2003.

Observer. September 29, 1987.

O'Brien, Philip. "A Critique of Latin American Theories of Dependency." In Ivar Oxaal, Tony Barnett, and David Booth, eds., *Beyond the Sociology of Development: Economy and Society in Latin America and Africa.* London: Routledge, 1975.

Ochsenwald, William, and Sydney Nettleton Fisher. *The Middle East: A History.* 6th ed. New York: McGraw-Hill, 2004.

O'Donnell, Guillermo. *Modernization and Bureaucratic-Authoritarianism: Studies in South American Politics.* Berkeley: Institute of International Studies, University of California, 1979.

Ollman, Bertell. *Alienation: Marx's Conception of Man in Capitalist Society.* 2nd ed. New York: Cambridge University Press, 1976.

O'Sullivan, John, and Edward F. Keuchel. *American Economic History: From Abundance to Constraint.* New York: Markus Wiener, 1989.

Ozawa, Martha, and Stuart A. Kirk. "Welfare Reform." *Social Work Research.* 20(6), 194–195.

Packer, H. *The Limits of Criminal Sanction.* Palo Alto, CA: Stanford University Press, 1968.

Packenham, Robert A. "Capitalist Dependency and Socialist Dependency." *Journal of InterAmerican Studies and World Affairs.* Volume 28, Number 1, Spring 1986, 59–91.

Paine, Thomas. *Common Sense.* 1776. Dover, DE: Dover, 1997.

Palumbo, Dennis J. *Public Policy in America: Government in Action.* 2nd ed. Fort Worth: Harcourt Brace, 1994.

Paniccia, Domonic. "The Environmental Movement." In Theodore and Theodore, eds., *Major Environmental Issues Facing the 21st Century.* Upper Saddle River, NJ: Prentice-Hall, 1996.

Park, Edwin, and Robert Greenstein. "The AARP Ads and the New Medicare Prescription Drug Law." *Center on Budget and Policy Priorities.* December 11, 2003.

Park, Edwin, Melanie Nathanson, Robert Greenstein, and John Springer. "The Troubling Medicare Legislation." *Center on Budget and Policy Priorities.* December 8, 2003.

Pach, Chester J., and Elmo Richardson. *The Presidency of Dwight D. Eisenhower.* Lawrence: University Press of Kansas, 1991.

People For the American Way Foundation. "Anti-Gay Politics and the Religious Right." Washington, D.C.: People for the American Way, 2000.

Perdue, Theda, and Michael Green. *The Cherokee Removal: A Brief History with Documents.* 2nd ed. Boston: Bedford/ St. Martin's, 2005.

Perlstein, Rick. *Before the Storm: Barry Goldwater and the Unmaking of the*

American Consensus. New York: Hill and Wang, 2001.

Petersilia, Joan, Susan Turner, James Kahan, and Joyce Peterson. *Granting Felons Probation: Public Risks and Alternatives.* Santa Monica, CA: Rand Corporation, 1985.

Petras, James. *Latin America: From Dependence to Revolution.* New York: Wiley, 1973.

Phillips, David L. *Losing Iraq: Inside the Postwar Reconstruction Fiasco.* Boulder, CO: Westview Press, 2005.

Poliakov, Leon. *The Aryan Myth.* New York: New American Library, 1974.

Pollack, Andrew. "Medical Technology Arms Race Adds Billions to the Nation's Bill." *New York Times.* April 29, 1991.

Prebisch, Raul. *The Economic Development of Latin America and Its Principal Problems.* New York: United Nations, 1950.

_____. "Economic Development or Monetary Stability: The False Dilemma." *Economic Bulletin for Latin America.* Volume 6, Number 1, March 1961, 7–38.

_____. *Towards a New Trade Policy for Development.* New York: United Nations, 1964.

Prewitt, Kenneth, Sidney Verba, and Robert H. Salisbury. *An Introduction to American Government.* 6th ed. New York: HarperCollins, 1991.

Quinton, Anthony. *The Politics of Imperfection: The Religious and Secular Traditions of Conservative Thought in England from Hooker to Oakeshott.* London: Routledge, 1978.

Rand, Ayn. *The Virtue of Selfishness.* New York: New American Library, 1961.

_____. *Conservatism: an Obituary.* 1962.

_____. *Capitalism: The Unknown Ideal.* New York: Signet Books, 1966.

Rankin, Robert, and David Hess. "Reinventing Welfare." *Wisconsin State Journal.* June 15, 1994.

Ray, David. "The Dependency Model of Latin American Underdevelopment: Three Basic Fallacies." *Journal of InterAmerican Studies and World Affairs.* Volume XV, Number 1, February 1973, 4–20.

Reagan, Michael. *Curing the Crisis: Options for America's Health Care.* Boulder, CO: Westview Press, 1992.

Regan, Tom. *The Case for Animal Rights.* Berkeley: University of California Press, 1983.

Reinhardt, Uwe. "Book Review of Rosemary Stevens' *In Sickness and in Wealth.*" *New York Times.* August 20, 1989.

Rhodes, Steven. *Valuing Life: Public Policy Dilemmas.* Boulder, CO: Westview Press, 1980.

Rice, Condoleeza. "Promoting the National Interest." *Foreign Affairs.* January-February, 2000.

Roark, James L., Michael P. Johnson, Patricia Cline Cohen, Sarah Stage, Alan Lawson, and Susan M. Hartmann. *The American Promise: A History of the United States. Volume I: To 1877.* 3rd ed. Boston, New York: Bedford/St. Martin's, 2005.

Rokeach, Milton. *The Open and Closed Mind: Investigations into the Nature of Belief Systems and Personality Systems.* New York: Basic Books, 1972.

Rosengren, William R. *Sociology of Medicine: Diversity, Conflict and Change.* New York: Harper and Row, 1980.

Rosenman, Samuel I., ed. The *Public Papers and Addresses of Franklin D. Roosevelt.* New York: Random House, 1938.

Rosenthal, Elisabeth. "Health Problems of Inner City Poor Reach Crisis Point." *New York Times.* December 24, 1994.

Rossiter, Clinton. *Conservatism in America.* 2nd ed. Cambridge, MA: Harvard University Press, 1982.

Rothbard, Murray. *America's Great Depression.* New York: New York University Press, 1975.

Sachar, Howard M. *A History of Israel: From the Rise of Zionism to Our Time.* New York: Random House, 1996.

Sale, K. *The Green Revolution.* New York: Hill and Wang, 1993.

Sanders, Bernard. "What's Really Going on with the Economy." *USA Today Magazine*. March, 1997.

Sargent, Lyman Tower. *Contemporary Political Ideologies: A Comparative Analysis*. 9th ed. Belmont, CA: Wadsworth, 1993.

Schaeffer, Eric. "Clearing the Air: Why I Quit Bush's EPA." *Washington Monthly*. July/August, 2002.

Schram, Stuart R., ed. *The Political Thought of Mao Tse-tung*. New York: Praeger, 1969.

Schudson, Michael. "America's Ignorant Voters." *The Wilson Quarterly*. Spring, 2000, 16–22.

Schultz, Andrew. "PETA Calls Fishing 'Cruelty' While Supporting 'Terrorism.'" *The Hendersonville Tribune*. September 9, 2002.

Schumacher, E.F. *Small is Beautiful*. New York: Harper and Row, 1973.

Schumaker, Paul, Dwight C. Kiel, and Thomas Heilke. *Great Ideas/Grand Schemes*. New York: McGraw-Hill, 1996.

_____. *Ideological Voices: An Anthology in Modern Political Ideas*. New York: McGraw-Hill, 1997.

Schwartz, William B. "Do Advancing Medical Technologies Drive Up the Cost of Health Care?" *Priorities*, Fall 1992.

Serafini, Marilyn Werber. "Welfare Reform, Act 2." *National Journal*. June, 2000.

Shabecroff, Philip. *A Fierce Green Fire*. New York: Hill and Wang, 1993.

Shapiro, Isaac, and Joel Friedman. "Tax Returns: A Comprehensive Assessment of the Bush Administration's Record on Cutting Taxes." *Center on Budget and Policy Priorities*. April 23, 2004.

Siegel, Larry J. *Criminology*. 3rd ed. St. Paul, MN: West Publishing, 1989.

Sinclair, Upton. *The Jungle*. 1906. New York: Sharp Press, 2003.

Singer, J.L., and D. G. Singer. *Television, Imagination and Aggression: A Study of Preschoolers*. Hillsdale, NJ: Erlbaum, 1981.

Singer, Peter. *Animal Liberation*. New York: Avon Books, 1973.

Sivan, Emmanuel. *Radical Islam: Medieval Theology and Modern Politics*. New Haven: Yale University Press, 1990.

Skidmore, Max. *Ideologies: Politics in Action*. 2nd ed. Fort Worth, TX: Harcourt Brace, 1993.

Sklar, Richard. "Postimperialism: A Class Analysis of Multinational Corporate Expansion." In David G. Becker, Jeff Frieden, Sayre P. Schatz, and Richard L. Sklar, eds., *Postimperialism: International Capitalism and Development in the Late Twentieth Century*. Boulder, CO: Lynne Rienner, 1987.

Skocpol, Theda. *Protecting Soldiers and Mothers*. Cambridge, MA: Harvard University Press, 1992.

_____. "The Legacies of New Deal Liberalism." In Douglas MacLean and Claudia Mills, eds., *Liberalism Reconsidered*. Totowa, NJ: Rowman and Allenheld, 1983.

Sloan, John Henry. "Handgun Regulations, Crime, Assaults, and Homicide." *The New England Journal of Medicine*. November 10, 1998.

Sloan, William David, James G. Stovall and James Startt. *The Media in America: A History*. Upper Saddle River, NJ: Gorsuch Scarisbrick, 1993.

Smith, Adam. *Wealth of Nations*. 1776. Amherst, NY: Prometheus Books, 1991.

Smith, B.D., and J.J. Vetter. *Theoretical Approaches to Personality*. Englewood Cliffs, NJ: Prentice-Hall, 1982.

Smith, Huston. *The World's Religions*. New York: HarperCollins, 1991.

So, Alvin Y. *Social Change and Development*. Newbury Park, CA: Sage, 1990.

Somerville, John, and Ronald Santoni. *Social and Political Philosophy: Readings from Plato to Gandhi*. New York: Anchor, 1963.

Sorel, G. *Reflexions on Violence*. Glencoe, IL: Free Press, 1969.

Specter, Michael. "Unhealthy Care for

the Poor." *Washington Post National Weekly Edition.* July 15–21, 1991.

Spencer, Herbert. "The Survival of the Fittest." In *Social Statics.* New York: D. Appleton, 1851.

Squire, Peverill, James M. Lindsay, Cary R. Covington, and Eric R.A.N. Smith. *Dynamics of Democracy.* 3rd ed. Cincinnati, OH: Atomic Dog, 2001.

Stainiland, Martin. *What is Political Economy?: A Study of Social Theory and Underdevelopment.* New Haven, CT: Yale University Press, 1985.

Stanfield, Rochelle. "The New Federalism." *National Journal.* January 28, 1995.

Steinbruner, John. *The Cybernetic Theory of Decision.* Princeton, NJ: Princeton University Press, 1974.

Stillman, Richard J. *Preface to Public Administration: A Search for Themes and Direction.* New York: St. Martin's Press, 1991.

Stockman, David. *The Triumph of Politics.* New York: Random House, 1987.

Storey, John W. *Texas Baptist Leadership and Social Christianity, 1900–1980.* College Station, TX: Texas A&M University Press, 1986.

Strossen, Nadine. "Regulating Racist Speech on Campus: A Modest Proposal?" In George McKenna and Stanley Feingold, eds., *Taking Sides: Clashing Views on Controversial Political Issues.* 9th ed. Guilford, CT: Dushkin, 1995.

Sunday Times. London, January, 2002.

Suskind, Ron. *The Price of Loyalty: George W. Bush, the White House, and the Education of Paul O'Neill.* New York: Simon and Schuster, 2004.

Swoboda, Frank. "Major Firms, Unions Join National Health Insurance Bid." *Washington Post.* March 14, 1990.

Taft, Robert A. "The Future of the Republican Party." *The Nation.* December 13, 1941.

Talk. September, 1999.

Territo, Leonard, James Halstead, and Max Bromley. *Crime and Justice in America.* St. Paul, MN: West Publishing, 1989.

Thompson, Frank J. *Health Policy and the Bureaucracy: Politics and Implementation.* Cambridge, MA: MIT Press, 1981.

Thompson, James J. Jr. *Tried as by Fire: Southern Baptists and the Religious Controversies of the 1920s.* Macon, GA: Mercer University Press, 1982.

Time. October 22, 2001.

Tinder, Glen. *The Political Meaning of Christianity.* Baton Rouge, LA: Louisiana State University Press, 1989.

Toner, Robin. "Gold Rush Fever Grips Capital as Health Care Struggle Begins." *New York Times.* March 13, 1994.

Tsai, Mark. "Now It Can Be Told." *The China Monthly.* September, 1948.

Tsou, Tang. *America's Failure in China.* Chicago: University of Chicago Press, 1967.

Tucille, Jerome. *Radical Libertarianism: A Right Wing Alternative.* New York: Macmillan, 1970.

Tweedie, Jack. "When Welfare Ends." *State Legislatures.* October/November, 1998.

United Nations. *Human Development Report 2003.* New York and Oxford: Oxford University Press, 2003.

United States Census Bureau. "The Official Statistics." U.S. Government Printing Office. Washington, D.C.: September 9, 1998.

United States Department of Energy. "OEPA Environmental Law Summary: Clean Air Act." *Office of Environmental Policy and Assistance.* Washington, D.C.: January 25, 1996.

United Stated Department of Health, Education, and Welfare. *Health in America 1776–1976.* Washington, D.C.: Government Printing Office, 1976.

United States Department of Justice. "Crime and Victims Statistics." Washington, D.C.: Bureau of Justice Statistics, 2003.

United States General Accounting Office. "Waste Water Dischargers are Not Complying with EPA Pollution Control Permits." Washington, D.C.: *General Accounting Office,* 1983.

_____. "Water Pollution: Many Violators Have Not Received Appropriate Federal Attention." Washington, D.C.: *General Accounting Office*, 1996.

United States Office of Management and Budget. "Budget of the United States Government." Washington, D.C.: Government Printing Office, 1976.

_____. "Budget of the United States Government." Washington, D.C.: Government Printing Office, 1986.

_____. "Budget of the United States Government." Washington, D.C.: Government Printing Office, 1999.

USA Today. November 3, 2000.

Vachss, A.H., and Y. Bakal. *The Life-Style Violent Juvenile.* Lexington, MA: Lexington Press, 1979.

Vaisse, Justin. "French Reactions to the 2000 U.S. Presidential Election." Brookings Institution. Washington, D.C., 2001.

Vold, George B., and Thomas J. Bernard. *Theoretical Criminology.* 3rd ed. New York: Oxford University Press, 1986.

Von Hoffman, Nicholas. *Citizen Cohn.* New York: Bantam Dell, 1988.

Wall Street Journal. October 13, 1993.

Waltz, Kenneth. *Theory of International Politics.* New York: Random House, 1978.

Waltzman, Nancy. "Socialized Medicine Now-Without the Wait." *The Washington Monthly.* 23, October 10, 1991.

Washington Post. February 28, 1994.

_____. March 14, 2001.

_____. January 20, 2002.

Wechsler, William F. "Follow the Money." *Foreign Affairs.* July-August, 2001.

Weisberg, Jacob. *In Defense of Government: The Fall and Rise of Public Trust.* New York: Scribner, 1996.

Welch, Michael R., David C. Leege, Kenneth D. Wald, and Lyman A. Kellstedt. "Are the Sheep Hearing the Shepherds? Cue Perceptions, Congregational Responses, and Political Communication Processes." In David C. Leege and Lyman A. Kellstedt, eds., *Rediscovering the Religious Factor in American Politics.* Armonk, NY: M.E. Sharpe, 1993.

Wells, Donald. *Environmental Policy.* Upper Saddle River, NJ: Prentice-Hall, 1996.

Westerfield, Bradford H. *Foreign Policy and Party Politics.* New Haven, CT: Yale University Press, 1955.

Wheeler, James O. and Peter O. Muller. *Economic Geography.* New York: Wiley, 1986.

Wheless, Joseph. *Is it God's Word?* Kila, MT: Kessinger, 1997.

White, Jonathan. *Terrorism: An Introduction.* Belmont, CA: Wadsworth, 2001.

White, Morton. *The Age of Analysis: The Twentieth Century Philosophers.* New York: Mentor, 1956.

White, William S. *The Taft Story.* New York: Harper and Row, 1954.

Wiles, P.J.D. *The Political Economy of Communism.* Cambridge, MA: Harvard University Press, 1962.

Wilson, James Q. *Thinking About Crime: A Policy Guide.* 2nd ed. New York: Basic Books, 1983.

_____. "Crime and Public Policy." In James Q. Wilson and Joan Petersilia, eds., *Crime.* San Francisco: Institute for Contemporary Studies, 1995.

Wilson, James Q., and John DiIulio. *American Government.* 6th ed. Lexington, MA: D.C. Heath, 1995.

Wolfskill, George. *Revolt of the Conservatives.* Cambridge, MA: Greenwood, 1974.

Woods, Roger. "The Radical Right: The Conservative Revolutionaries in Germany." In Roger Eatwell and Noel O'Sullivan, eds., *The Nature of the Right.* Boston, MA: Twayne, 1989.

Woodward, Bob. *Bush at War.* New York: Simon and Schuster, 2002.

World Bank. *World Development Indicators.* Washington, D.C.: World Bank, 1998.

www.epa.gov/globalwarming/climate/index.html

www.lib.virginia.edu/small/exhibits/sixties/leary.html

Zastrow, Charles. *Social Work and Social Welfare.* 6th ed. Pacific Grove, CA: Brooks/Cole, 1996.

Index

217